CATHOLIC HIGHER EDUCATION AND CATHOLIC SOCIAL THOUGHT

EDITED BY
BERNARD G. PRUSAK AND
JENNIFER REED-BOULEY

FOREWORD BY
CARDINAL MICHAEL CZERNY, SJ

Paulist Press
New York / Mahwah, NJ

Cover illustration *Jesus Walking on Water* by Brian Whelan
Cover design by Joe Gallagher
Book design by Lynn Else

Library of Congress Cataloging-in-Publication Data
Names: Prusak, Bernard G, editor. | Reed-Bouley, Jennifer, editor.
Title: Catholic higher education and Catholic social thought / edited by Bernard G Prusak and Jennifer Reed-Bouley ; foreword by Cardinal Michael Czerny, SJ.
Description: New York / Mahwah, NJ : Paulist Press, [2023] | Summary: "Responding to the signs of the time, this book brings the lens of Catholic social thought (CST) to the enterprise of Catholic higher education in the United States. This book throws light on what Catholic colleges and universities might and must do in order both to preserve their mission and renew it for the future"—Provided by publisher.
Identifiers: LCCN 2022029952 (print) | LCCN 2022029953 (ebook) | ISBN 9780809155408 (paperback) | ISBN 9781587689352 (ebook)
Subjects: LCSH: Catholic universities and colleges. | Christian sociology—Catholic authors.
Classification: LCC LC487 .C24155 2023 (print) | LCC LC487 (ebook) | DDC 378/.0712—dc23/eng/20220707
LC record available at https://lccn.loc.gov/2022029952
LC ebook record available at https://lccn.loc.gov/2022029953

ISBN 978-0-8091-5540-8 (paperback)
ISBN 978-1-58768-935-2 (e-book)

Published by Paulist Press
997 Macarthur Boulevard
Mahwah, New Jersey 07430
www.paulistpress.com

Printed and bound in the
United States of America

To our daughters
Helena and Anna Prusak
Maya and Rosa Reed-Bouley

CONTENTS

Contents

FOREWORD

Cardinal Michael Czerny, SJ

Prefect of the Dicastery for Promoting Integral Human Development

THIS VOLUME IS A CELEBRATION of Catholic social thought and a detailed illustration of its application in American postsecondary education. I wholly agree with the editors' hope stated in the introduction that "CST might help to anchor Catholic colleges and universities as they seek to weather the times, or as they rebuild in the pandemic's wake. In particular, CST might help to anchor Catholic colleges and universities in their missions as distinctively Catholic institutions." This does not apply only to CST as subject matter and the curriculum as context. Our editors join with the Association of Catholic Colleges and Universities in declaring that "CST should be incorporated into 'all aspects of institutional life,' including employment policies, environmental practices, and finances." True to this stance, the introduction provides an excellent extended "case study" of childcare during COVID-19 to urge that CST should supply the "lenses that the institution employs in conducting its business."

The volume is of its time and place, including a look at the trends in recent decades. CST can be deployed constructively to guide policies, but it can also serve as a destructive cudgel to vilify "the other side" in campus battles. Stepping back from such controversies, readers interested in the state of American Catholic higher education will increase their appreciation of how these institutions "are in fact living out CST"—or not living it out—"through what they do day-in, day-out:

for example, through the particular population of students they serve, or through the local community they support."

Concrete business decisions are not "just business," as in the cliché that "business is business"—meaning that nothing else matters, no other criteria apply. On the contrary, as the introduction's childcare analysis shows, the teachings and traditions of Catholic social thought provide plenty of material to expand the frame of questions and interpretations. There are more measures of "success" than simply the bottom line. Take the principle of participation, for instance, which the editors describe as "the name for the claim right people have, based on their dignity as children of God, not to be excluded from the means of developing themselves, or, as it is often put, fulfilling themselves as human beings." This extends to full participation in the economy. Accordingly, following a path laid out by CST, we arrive at an imperative to seek social justice, lest the rights of individuals to full participation be voided in practice by exceedingly large and implacable forces: "On this account, the duty to work for social justice is a duty to engage in social action with the aim of righting injustices that, solely by ourselves, we are 'helpless' to overcome. If there is to be effective change, it must be at the systemic level of institutions."

I agree with this conclusion. At the same time, having followed the banner of social faith and justice into various fraught situations over the years, I would extend CST's reach to the level of the societies in which Catholic higher education operates.

In 1990, following the assassinations of Ignacio Ellacuría, SJ, the rector (or president) of San Salvador's Universidad Centro Americana (UCA), five fellow Jesuits, and two women coworkers, I found myself director of the UCA's Human Rights Institute and, in the second year, vice rector for Proyección Social (Social Outreach). I also inherited the martyred rector's course called Pensar la realidad latinoamericana (Think about the Latin American Reality).

The students were Jesuit seminarians, and each one had to choose a topic, a situation, or a problem somewhere in Central America and show that he was learning how to *think* it. Such was Ellacuría's vision for the UCA: philosophy was essential, not primarily in its being universal, but because it flowed out of Latin American reality and aimed at its liberation. The young students, members of the same religious order and community as their six elder martyred companions, were well aware that this commitment to live their Christian faith, Jesuit vocation, and pastoral or educational ministry in a transforming dialogue with the surrounding reality could cost them the ultimate price. I now realize that the course anticipated the first of four key precepts provided by Pope Francis in *Evangelii Gaudium*: "Realities are greater than ideas" (233), which is indeed a subversive, even dangerous, axiom.

In 2002, after eleven years as Social Justice Secretary at the Jesuit Curia (headquarters) in Rome, I founded and directed the African Jesuit AIDS Network, dedicated to helping Jesuits and their institutions throughout sub-Saharan Africa to respond to the raging pandemic. This led to my occasionally offering a course on HIV/AIDS at Hekima University College in Nairobi, the seminary for Jesuit and other students.

Besides the usual lectures, the course invited people with HIV and caregivers to share their experiences. Here we have the classical inductive method of CST proposed by *Gaudium et Spes*: to see, hear, and scrutinize; to interpret and judge; to act and respond (cf. 44). Given the prejudices, falsehoods, and ideologies that accompanied HIV/AIDS (and still do!), it was important, as Pope Francis would write years later, to take hold of "those questions which are troubling us today and which we can no longer sweep under the carpet. Our goal is not to amass information or to satisfy curiosity, but rather to become painfully aware, to dare to turn what is happening"—here we can cite HIV/AIDS, social injustice, grinding poverty, environmental degradation, COVID-19, and all else that undermines human dignity—"into our own personal suffering and thus to discover what each of us can do about it" (*Laudato Si'* 19). The course tried to put the tools and insights of CST into the hands of future priests, for them to pass on to the people of God to apply in their daily lives in society.

So CST is about how the Catholic college or university is run—as applied in this volume to institutions in the United States—and how everyone involved "reads" the surrounding reality and responds, where "surrounding reality" includes every corner of our globalized world. If Catholic higher education institutions succeed in both applying and teaching CST, both within the cauldron of local challenges and on the wider world scene, then it seems to me that the very logic running through this good book would lead to making CST a mandatory and indeed defining course in Catholic higher education institutions throughout the United States. For the graduate we want is a well-educated believer (of whatever faith, in dialogue with all) and a well-educated citizen (responsible, within whatever *polis*, interconnected with all the others). For this purpose, I can think of no better, no livelier guide to CST than *Laudato Si'* and *Fratelli Tutti*, especially the latter.[1] These impressively contemporary encyclical letters of Pope Francis are more accessible than the necessarily voluminous *Compendium*, and they provide rich further developments of the social thinking of his two predecessors, whom he frequently quotes with the greatest appreciation and respect.

We look forward to the continued development of Catholic social thought. It is never complete in the topics it touches or in the applications that are needed. The editors assert, for instance, that "CST might be a drag, so to speak, on some issues, for example those of race and diversity, where the tradition is underdeveloped or even in need of significant correction." Good! I cannot think of anything more satisfying than for all members of the Body of Christ—lay and religious, leading and participating, educational and pastoral, specialized and broad based—to walk together on a synodal path of discovering the meaning of Jesus's words in the world of today and tomorrow.

Vatican City, September 2021

Note

1. See in this connection Michael Czerny and Christian Barone, *Fraternità–segno dei tempi: Il magistero sociale di Papa Francesco* (Vatican City: Libreria Editrice Vaticana, 2021); *Siblings All, Signs of the Times: The Social Teaching of Pope Francis*, trans. Julian Paparella (Maryknoll, NY: Orbis, 2022). It provides a synthesis of the magisterium of Pope Francis, in continuity with the pronouncements of the Second Vatican Council, urging universal brother- and sisterhood as a "sign of the times" for our age—a rejuvenated vision for contemporary humanity, including all the religions, walking together and joining forces to build a more just and united world.

ACKNOWLEDGMENTS

This volume has its origins in the Catholic Social Thought Learning and Research Initiative (CSTLRI), a collaboration of faculty and administrators from a dozen or so Catholic colleges and universities across the United States, through which the editors first came to know one another in 2015. CSTLRI colleagues contributed to and guest edited the precursor of this volume, a collection of articles published in the *Journal of Catholic Higher Education* 37, no. 1 (2018). We thank the journal's editors, Edward P. Mahoney and Paula Moore, for opening its pages to the CSTLRI's work. We thank our CSTLRI colleagues for their camaraderie, intellectual companionship, and personal dedication to the mission and potential of Catholic higher education. Special thanks to Kathleen Maas Weigert, Jay Brandenberger, and Bill Purcell, who got the CSTLRI up and running.

The impetus to produce this volume also came out of a year-long faculty-staff development program at King's College (PA) on Catholic higher education and Catholic social thought. One lesson of organizing that program was that it was quite difficult, at that time (2018–2019), to find articles that lent themselves well to the program's purposes: to stimulate, structure, and support substantive discussion of contemporary challenges and opportunities in Catholic higher education in light of Catholic social thought. This volume is intended to serve that need. Thanks to King's colleagues Margarita Rose and Tom Looney, CSC, for helping to organize that faculty-staff development program, which is one kind of venue we imagine for this volume. Other venues include board retreats and seminars for senior-level administrators.

CSTLRI colleagues, among others, also played key roles in the development of the chapters in this volume. Prepandemic, we had imagined that the chapters' authors might present work-in-progress at campuses where CSTLRI colleagues work. The pandemic scrambled that plan, but colleagues stepped up to host presentations via Zoom during the winter and spring of 2021. Thanks to Erin Brigham for hosting two events through the Lane Center at the University of San Francisco; to Thomas Landy for hosting three events through Collegium; and to Michael Murphy for hosting four events through the Hank Center at Loyola University Chicago. Thanks also to Harry Dammer for hosting an event through the University of Scranton; to Katherine Feely, SND, for hosting an event through John Carroll University; and to Kathryn Getek Soltis for hosting an event through Villanova University. Further thanks to colleagues for support in hosting events at College of Saint Mary and at King's College. Finally, we are grateful to the colleagues who served as respondents in these events: namely, Ursula Aldana (University of San Francisco), Jane Bleasdale (University of San Francisco), Jennifer Boyle (Loyola University Chicago), Kathleen Sprows Cummings (University of Notre Dame), Daniela Domínguez (University of San Francisco), Karen Eifler (Collegium and University of Portland), Edward Fierros (Villanova University), Travis Foster (Villanova University), Kyra Gause (College of Saint Mary), Bonnie Gunzenhauser (John Carroll University), Thomas Landy (Collegium and College of the Holy Cross [MA]), Norah Martin (University of Portland), Rhonda McGee (University of San Francisco), Alan Miciak (John Carroll University), Daniel Rhodes (Loyola University Chicago), Margarita Rose (King's College), Michael Schuck (Loyola University Chicago), Maryanne Stevens, RSM (College of Saint Mary), and Kathleen Maas Weigert (Loyola University Chicago). The chapters' authors benefited from the respondents' conversation, constructive criticism, and questions.

Thanks are also due to Paulist Press, especially to Senior Academic Editor Donna Crilly, who was immediately supportive of this project. Stephanie Russell, Vice President for Mission Integration at the Association of Jesuit Colleges and Universities, and Dennis Holtschneider, CM, President of the Association of Catholic Colleges and Universities, were early supporters to whom we are grateful. And the editors would be remiss not to thank the chapters' authors, not only for their contributions, but also for their patience as we worked together through this project's stages. We are likewise grateful to Cardinal Michael Czerny, SJ, for the foreword to this volume, and to Sara Binaghi, for her assistance.

On more personal notes, Bernard Prusak is grateful to King's College for sabbatical leave in spring 2020, when he and Jennifer pitched this project. I also thank colleagues at King's who helped with the winter–spring 2021 lecture series: Josh Ulanoski, Carol Simonovich Scholl, and Wendy Hinton did excellent work, as they always do. I thank my friend and King's colleague Margarita Rose for her CST companionship, as well as her dedication to the Catholic character of our institution. My father, Bernard P. Prusak, is a model of service to the Church and academy; my mother-in-law, Mary Doherty, has embodied CST in her Ignatian-inflected "way of proceeding." Margaret Kowalsky is my most truth-telling critic and supporter. Sometimes she hears too much from me about Catholic higher education in light of the Catholic social and intellectual traditions, but it's my fortune both that she has a lot to say in turn and that her love is patient and kind. Helena and Anna, may the work of this volume make some difference for you. Jennifer Reed-Bouley is grateful to Kimberly Allen and Maryanne Stevens at College of Saint Mary for their enthusiastic support for this project, including a semester-long research sabbatical in fall 2021. Thanks to Pam Humphrey, Emily Kahm, and Andrea Stapleton, generous colleagues who shouldered extra administrative work during my sabbatical leave so that I could focus on this project. I thank Kristin Mattson for her friendship and many years of collaboration on faculty and staff development initiatives, which also helped me to envision how this volume might be used. My deepest thanks go to my family: the Reeds, Bouleys, and especially Ken, Maya, and Rosa Reed-Bouley, with all my love.

Finally, we thank Brian Whelan and his agent, Wendy Roseberry, for permission to use his *Jesus Walking on Water* as the cover illustration. Of course, that Gospel story, which is found in Mark, Matthew, and John, is different from the story of Jesus rebuking and quelling a violent storm, in Mark, Matthew, and Luke, to which we refer in the introduction. The story of Jesus walking on water seems fitting to our project for several reasons. First, Jesus enjoins the disciples to take heart or courage and not to be afraid. Second, in Matthew's telling, Jesus exhorts Peter's faith. Third, in Mark's telling, after Jesus has gotten into the boat with the disciples, there is the beautiful and mysterious verse, commenting on the disciples' astonishment, "they did not understand about the loaves" that Jesus had multiplied earlier that day (6:52). May this volume contribute to a greater understanding of the plenitude of Catholic social thought and embolden readers to apply it to the work of Catholic higher education.

INTRODUCTION

A System Adrift? Catholic Social Thought as an Anchor for Catholic Higher Education

Bernard G. Prusak and Jennifer Reed-Bouley

ANYONE WHO HAS WORKED FOR a few years as faculty or administration at a Catholic college or university likely is familiar with how Catholic social thought (CST) often figures in the life of the institution: namely, as a cudgel for faculty to wield against the administration, or vice versa. Respect for human dignity, concern for the common good, the preferential option for the poor and vulnerable, and even more obscure principles like subsidiarity crop up in faculty-administration disputes over such matters as health insurance coverage, adjunct pay and benefits, hiring decisions, diversity on campus, and more recently childcare, return-to-work protocols, and vaccination mandates during the coronavirus pandemic. There is sometimes a whiff of opportunism to these arguments. In those cases, the combatants wield the principles of CST not out of deep commitment, but because they are the principles that the college or university is supposed to observe as a Catholic institution—and shame on you, it is implied, for not embodying your commitments.

Unfortunately, there can be a measure of truth to that accusation. As Joseph McCartin, one of the contributors to this volume, has written elsewhere, "Catholic campuses are increasingly entangled in a larger economy that promotes yawning inequalities."[1] He points to the so-called gigification of teaching positions, as tenure lines devolve into contingent, semester-to-semester appointments; the subcontracting of auxiliary services, such as feeding students, to for-profit corporations with checkered records in labor law and extravagant executive pay; and the vigorous opposition to unionization by more than a few institutions, which is ironic against the background of Pope Leo XIII's 1891 encyclical *Rerum Novarum*, affirming the right to form "working men's associations…for helping each individual member to better his condition to the utmost in body, soul, and property."[2] Others have drawn critical attention to investment and licensing practices, which may entangle Catholic colleges and universities in exploitative supply chains and earth-degrading industries.[3]

While that picture is not pretty, it also is not the whole story. For example, McCartin points to Georgetown University's Just Employment Policy, mandating that all campus workers be paid a living wage,[4] and he notes that several institutions, including Georgetown, Fordham University, and Saint Louis University, did not oppose but even welcomed the formation of adjunct faculty unions.[5] Consider further the University of Dayton's board-driven decision to divest from fossil fuels, anticipating by a year Pope Francis's landmark 2015 encyclical "on care for our common home," *Laudato Si'*.[6] Finally, experiments like Arrupe College, a Jesuit community college associated with Loyola University Chicago, put flesh on the commitment to serve the marginalized.[7] Catholic social thought is by no means alien to the operations of all Catholic colleges and universities. Instead, it might well be the case that, in some instances, institutions do not appreciate sufficiently how they are in fact living out CST through what they do day-in, day-out: for example, through the particular population of students they serve, or through the local community they support.

Even before the coronavirus pandemic, however, scandals in the Church and the growth of religious nonaffiliation in the culture had made being Catholic greatly challenging for Catholic colleges and universities.[8] The pandemic only exacerbated the already fragile economics of higher education, mounting a threat to the very viability of many institutions, just as the numbers of traditional college-age students had begun to decline significantly across the United States.[9] What's more, the work of educating students in Catholic colleges and universities has become complicated by a narrow public understanding of Catholicism as identical with, for example, conservative positions on gender identity and sexual orientation, even while other voices engage the tradition to address the climate crisis, immigration, racial injustice, and wealth inequality. It is a vast understatement that these are trying times for American Catholic higher education.[10]

The title of this introduction alludes to Peter Steinfels's 2003 book, *A People Adrift: The Crisis of the Roman Catholic Church in America*,[11] which itself alludes to the story, in the Synoptic Gospels, of Jesus rebuking and quelling a violent storm that threatened to capsize the boat that he and his disciples had boarded to cross the Sea of Galilee.[12] Jesus has fallen asleep. Terrified of drowning, the disciples wake him for help. It is not unthinkable or even unlikely that a number of Catholic colleges and universities will go under, so to speak, in the aftermath of the pandemic.[13] The crisis that Steinfels depicted in 2003 has new, untold dimensions.

At the same time, it would be naive to believe that CST is the means of salvation. This volume accordingly makes a more modest proposal: namely, that CST might help to anchor Catholic colleges and universities as they seek to weather the times, or as they rebuild in the pandemic's wake. In particular, CST might help to anchor Catholic colleges and universities in their missions as distinctively Catholic institutions.[14] To be clear, CST is not the only such "anchor," and we do not believe it should be.[15] But we have sought to shape this volume to show the relevance of CST to multiple dimensions of Catholic higher education. We also acknowledge that it is possible that CST might be a drag, so to speak, on some issues, for example those of race and diversity, where the tradition is underdeveloped or even in need of significant correction. In such cases, the intellectual resources and practices of Catholic higher education can contribute to developing CST.

Responding to the signs of the times, this volume thus brings the lens of CST to the enterprise of Catholic higher education in the United States. Though the aftermath of the pandemic will not allow us to remake our social world from scratch, it does present an opportunity to examine whether the "old normal" was sustainable, desirable, or, for Catholic institutions, adequately faithful to Christ. We have produced this volume as a resource for college and university administrators, faculty, staff, and boards of trustees. We envision the chapters that follow being used in board retreats, or in workshops for faculty and staff development, or for self-reflection among senior administration. There is a logic to the order of the chapters, and they often refer to one another, but they need not be read and discussed in order, and they were written to stand independently. Each chapter concludes with questions for consideration and discussion formulated by the editors. Our objective is to stimulate, structure, and support discussion of contemporary challenges and opportunities in Catholic higher education in light of CST. The Association of Catholic Colleges and Universities (ACCU) proposes in its 2012 vision statement on "Catholic Higher Education and Catholic Social Teaching" that CST should be incorporated into "all aspects of institutional life," including employment policies, environmental practices, and finances.[16] Toward the goal of making the ACCU's vision a reality, the chapters in this volume consider the opportunities and challenges CST presents for Catholic institutions to differentiate themselves from other colleges and universities while preserving and advancing their missions and responding to current challenges in the Church and world.

We use the *T* in CST to stand for thought, but it also may stand for teaching or tradition. CST is a living, dynamic tradition that advances a vision of justice—of right relations in social life on our common home, "mother" and "sister" earth[17]—expressed and developed through magisterial teaching, scholarship, and the lived experience of faithful Catholics and other people of good will. CST includes key principles such as respect for human dignity, concern for the common good, the preferential option for the poor and vulnerable, care for creation, solidarity, and subsidiarity, but those principles, while oft-cited and best understood as diverse "expressions of the requisites of justice,"[18] do not exhaust CST, which draws upon Scriptures, the natural law tradition, the lives of holy women and men, Catholicism's rich symbols and sacramental imagination, and a complex theological anthropology.[19]

It is a basic premise of our project that what makes a college or university "Catholic" includes not only the curriculum and the faculty,[20] but also the lenses that the institution employs in conducting its business. Those lenses make a difference in whether a Catholic college or university in fact represents "a Christian presence" in the world of higher education, as Pope John Paul II enjoined Catholic institutions to do.[21] Concrete business and operational decisions form part of an institution's so-called hidden curriculum, communicating to students and all other stakeholders what the institution truly values. A college or university, with its brick-and-mortar campus, might appear to be a massive, alien object indifferent and impervious to the wishes and projects of its current generation of students and faculty and staff, much as the natural world is set over and against its present flora and fauna. After all, as anyone who has served on a core curriculum committee knows well, change normally comes quite slowly in higher education; otherwise liberal faculty can be remarkably conservative in some respects. Nonetheless, we are convinced that, as the historian and former college president Francis Oakley has claimed, "institutional life is a fragile social construct," "a frail tissue of human purpose, intentionality, aspiration, and hope."[22] From this perspective, the nature of an institution is never a given. It is always being shaped and reshaped by the ways in which its leaders—whether trustees, administrators, or faculty—define, proclaim, and embody the institution's purpose and values.

The days in which it could be taken for granted that a college or university was Catholic because its leaders were vowed religious are coming to an end, if they are not over already. As Vatican II urged, the laity's apostolate must now be "broadened and intensified" if the institutions that they lead are to go on being Catholic in meaningful ways.[23] But this new reality brings new challenges: for example, for the selection, education, and formation of boards of trustees, who increasingly come from "the very top of the income ladder."[24] While we await a comprehensive study of boards of trustees of Catholic colleges and universities, recent research suggests that the education of boards in the mission and identity of Catholic colleges and universities tends to be thin, and the readiness of boards to bring Catholic mission and identity to bear on matters of policy cannot be taken for granted.[25] The situation is hardly better for lay administrators and faculty, whose formation for leadership roles is seldom given nearly the attention accorded to vowed religious.[26] As Steinfels remarked, the upshot is that lay leaders arrive "with new questions but increasingly without old knowledge" that vowed religious brought to the task.[27]

Let us conclude this introduction, then, with a fuller account of CST—more precisely, what seeking to live it out might look like for a given institution in our challenging times. Consider, as a case study, the issue of childcare, which, as we noted, arose with urgency in the context of the coronavirus pandemic. Working parents scrambled as their children's schools opened only online or adopted a "hybrid" model combining some days of in-person instruction with some days of online instruction. Childcare is expensive and, frankly, frightening when the threat of infection is high. Who wants to send his child off to daycare when it has been judged too risky for schools to open? And who wants to open her home to a caregiver who might prove to be a carrier of the virus? In any event, some parents could afford neither.

Historically and to this day, childcare responsibilities have disproportionately fallen on women. During the last one hundred years in the United States, women made great gains in combining family and work, or in other words children and careers. The economist Claudia Goldin warns, however, that "the increased burden from school closings...could erase years of gains by young women."[28] Once more in her words, "The COVID economy...magnified gender differences at work and at home." Because "couple equity is expensive for the family unit"—it limits couples' career choices, or raises the costs of childcare, or poses opportunity costs for family life (e.g., no piano lessons if no parent can take the child to the lessons)—Goldin expects that men will go back to work full-time and "revert to BCE [before coronavirus era] childcare levels," while "women's careers by and large probably will be set back."[29] The data so far suggest just that. According to the Pew Research Center, from February 2020 to February 2021, 2.4 million women quit the workforce, as opposed to 1.8 million men.[30] For colleges and universities, the effects will be seen in the composition of the professoriate and the future of academic leadership.[31] What's more, it should be noted that the typical obstacles faced by students who are mothers became even more daunting during the pandemic. Providing for their children through paid employment was already a lot. During the pandemic, they often had to provide some education, too, lest their children fall behind.

Magisterial teaching is shot through with gender essentialism and sexism about the proper place of women,[32] but there are countervailing principles that cut against the (nonstarter) position that mothers simply should stay home, which often is neither desirable, nor feasible in our economy. First and thankfully, the equal dignity of all persons, whether male, female, or gender nonconforming, is a given in Catholic thought, though the Church is quite divided about how to respond to the LGBTQ+ movement.[33] Second, the principle of participation figures prominently in accounts of CST.[34] Consider, as a way to put flesh on this principle, participation in a classroom. Class participation is both a duty and a right, and it seems plausible to argue that the right to participate is grounded in the duty to do so, which might be unpacked as a duty to contribute to the common good that is the class.[35] Imagine, though, that the teacher refuses to call on you, or that, on account of systemic prejudice against you because of your gender, race, or ethnicity, your contributions are brushed aside and discounted. You are the victim of what philosophers call epistemic injustice: you have been wronged in your capacity as a knowing subject.[36] In that context, it makes sense to construe your right to participate as a claim right that you hold over and against others, who owe you better.[37] Otherwise, you are not accorded the respect that you are due as a person, and you are blocked from developing yourself as a student and as an educated member of our society.

In CST, the principle of participation is the name for the claim right people have, based on their dignity as children of God, not to be excluded from the means of developing themselves, or, as it is often put, fulfilling themselves as human beings.[38] In the U.S. context, we might compare the April 2020 ruling by the U.S. Court of Appeals for the Sixth Circuit that public school children have a constitutional right, protected by the Fourteenth Amendment, to an education that plausibly enables them to become literate.[39] In CST, the focus falls on participation in the economy, and a key document is Pope John Paul II's 1991 encyclical *Centesimus Annus*, published one hundred years after *Rerum Novarum*. Pope John Paul observes that

> many people, perhaps the majority today, do not have the means which would enable them to take their place in an effective and humanly dignified way within a productive system in which work is truly central [to human fulfillment, as it has become in contemporary economies]. They have no possibility of acquiring the basic knowledge which would enable them to express their creativity and develop their potential. They have no way of entering the network of knowledge and intercommunication which would enable them to see their qualities appreciated and utilized. Thus, if not actually exploited, they are to a great extent marginalized; economic development takes place over their heads, so to speak, when it does not actually reduce the already narrow scope of their old subsistence economies.[40]

Such an economy of exclusion, as it is termed, facilitates and is an expression of what Pope Francis calls a "throwaway culture," which regards the "masses of people…excluded and marginalized: without work, without possibilities, without any means of escape" as mere "leftovers" of a bygone age, whose well-being is a matter of general indifference.[41]

According to CST, however, "work is more than a way to make a living; it is a form of continuing participation in God's creation,"[42] and as such access to work that enables one both to make a living and to realize oneself, like access to a basic education, is a right of each and every human being whom the Creator has called into being. In brief, work is a pro-life issue.[43] Yet several qualifications are in order. To begin with, the right to work is not, of course, "absolute." Like other rights, it is held in a network of duties to respect not only other people's rights and duties, but the integrity of the natural world. Work must be both just and sustainable. Further and yet more to the point, a right to work is inert—it does nothing for no one—both if work is not available and if the obligation to provide it falls on no one or no body in particular. A right to work is dependent on social structures and institutional frameworks.[44] A society must organize itself to make work available, and people with social and other forms of capital must see themselves as obligated to provide it. In other words, if there is a right to work, as CST holds there is, satisfying it is a matter of social justice properly speaking: it demands social action, which is to say the collaboration and sometimes creation of groups, bodies, and institutions that take it on themselves to bring about systemic change.[45]

Two quotations from Pope Pius XI illustrate this point. In his 1931 encyclical *Quadragesimo Anno*, issued forty years after *Rerum Novarum*, Pius remarks,

> Every effort must…be made that fathers of families receive a wage large enough to meet ordinary family needs adequately. But if this cannot always be done under existing circumstances, social justice demands that changes be introduced as soon as possible whereby such a wage will be assured to every adult workingman.[46]

Beyond the blatant sexism, what warrants attention is the implicit distinction Pius draws between so-called commutative justice, which has to do with right relations between individuals, like an employer and an employee, and social justice, which demands systemic change *so that* individual relations can be right. Pius uses the same example in his 1937 encyclical *Divini Redemptoris*:

> It happens all too frequently...under the salary system that individual employers are helpless to ensure justice unless, with a view to its practice, they organize institutions the object of which is to prevent competition incompatible with fair treatment for the workers. Where this is true, it is the duty of contractors and employers to support and promote such necessary organizations as normal instruments enabling them to fulfill their obligations of justice.[47]

On this account, the duty to work for social justice is a duty to engage in social action with the aim of righting injustices that, solely by ourselves, we are "helpless" to overcome. If there is to be effective change, it must be at the systemic level of institutions.[48] New norms and sets of rules, likely requiring new social structures with new positions and roles, must be developed to reorganize social interactions.

In that light, let us return to the issue of childcare in the context of the pandemic. Were Catholic colleges and universities duty-bound to accommodate employees with school-age children at home, for example by permitting faculty in need to teach online? Given the principle of participation, as well as Catholicism's commitment to the goodness of procreation and family life, which follows from the basic faith commitment to the goodness of creation, it might appear that such a course of action was indeed mandatory. But let us imagine that, at a particular college or university, resources were quite tight. Moreover, the great majority of students, and the great majority of tuition-paying parents of students, wanted instruction to be in person rather than principally online. Finally, competition for students among comparable colleges and universities is fierce. Would it have been unjust for the administration to reject faculty demands for accommodation? It might have been unwise to do so without first exploring creative alternatives. Further, perhaps it was feasible to grant a limited number of requests for the cases of greatest need. If so, an institution that takes its Catholic identity to heart should have granted those requests. But the availability of high-quality, affordable childcare is not a problem that any one college or university can solve. The availability of childcare is a social problem, the solution of which requires social action.

Note that, on this account, CST is no mere cudgel for faculty to wield against the administration, or vice versa. Instead, CST is a means to clarify and elaborate the moral stakes of the issue at hand—here, the issue of childcare, where what is at stake is participation in meaningful work and the fulfillment and financial security that it brings. The broader point is that the various principles of CST do not yield simple answers or dictate solutions. More critically, they raise, frame, and provide substantive terms to discuss and deal with morally fraught questions. To that end, CST foregrounds the social context (more fully: the socio-politico-economic context) in which Catholic colleges and universities operate. It demands both that we reckon with the constraints imposed by that context and that we see institutions as potential agents of social change—and sometimes perhaps as obstacles, especially if they or their leaders benefit from the current order. Socio-politico-economic constraints are not, however, an excuse for inaction. They do not provide cover for quiescence. As Pius XI wrote in *Divini Redemptoris*, where it is true that there are obstacles to justice, it is a *duty* to seek creative ways to overcome those obstacles.

By way of example, College of Saint Mary (CSM), a women's university in Omaha, Nebraska, elected to allocate some of its CARES Act funding (for expenses incurred because of the pandemic) to establishing in August 2020 an on-campus "Kids Club" after local school districts decided to teach fully online or in a hybrid plan. Fifteen CSM undergraduates, under the guidance of a full-time director, provided supervised tutoring, computer help for online classes, and activities for kindergarten through sixth-grade children during the days that they were not physically in school. CSM offered the program every weekday from 8:00 a.m. until 4:00 p.m., and about forty children participated. Because about 10 percent of CSM students are single mothers, for whom safe childcare is difficult to secure and may be prohibitively expensive, the program was essential to the university's mission to empower women to complete their education. It also allowed faculty and staff with children to continue to provide in-person instruction and support to students rather than leave the workforce to attend to their own children's education.

This volume's chapters extend and deepen these reflections with respect to other challenges and opportunities now before U.S. Catholic colleges and universities. Although, to reiterate, the chapters stand independently of one another and can be read in any order, we have organized them into four rough and to some extent overlapping groupings. The chapters by Laura Nichols, Tia Noelle Pratt and Maureen O'Connell, and Michelle Gonzalez Maldonado concern the students at Catholic colleges and universities: more precisely, the students these institutions are serving, should be serving in light of their missions, have not historically served well or even disserved, and ought to serve better. Nichols's chapter focuses on first-generation and low-income students and the "decoupling" of mission and admission practices; Pratt and O'Connell's chapter examines and exposes systemic racism *within* Catholic higher education, past and present; and Maldonado's chapter draws attention to the relative exclusion and marginalization of Latinx students from Catholic colleges and universities, despite the fact that Latino/as now account for around 40 percent of U.S. Catholics. Each of these chapters is also much richer than these brief characterizations suggest.

The second rough grouping of chapters concerns curriculum. Anna Moreland and Mark Shiffman's chapter reimagines a core curriculum guided by CST principles and dedicated to student formation. Reflecting on Pope Francis's *Laudato Si'*, Vincent Miller's chapter focuses on the kind of education that students need in order to be prepared, as much as possible, for "the volatility of climate disruption" and the increased likelihood of "profound discontinuities and disruptions" such as we experienced with the COVID-19 pandemic. Arguably, in such a world, the liberal arts are more relevant than ever.

A concern with institutions' so-called hidden curriculum—what we teach by what we do, as opposed to what we say in the classroom or in official pronouncements or on solemn occasions—unites the chapters in our third rough grouping: Joseph McCartin's examination of labor policies and practices and Matt Mazewski's study of extreme inequalities in wealth (and thus resources for students). Both McCartin's and Mazewski's chapters grapple with how to counter the real and perceived economic constraints that have led, in McCartin's terms, to a "growing divergence between praxis and teaching" at many Catholic institutions. Mazewski, for example, proposes pooling some endowment funds and creatively investing them in ways consonant with CST.

Our last rough grouping is accordingly concerned with leadership, or in other words the challenge of realizing the vision of CST in the very nonideal circumstances of the early twenty-first century. Jennifer Reed-Bouley and Catherine Punsalan-Manlimos's chapter interrogates the perduring obstacles to women's full participation in Catholic higher education. James L. Heft's chapter reflects on the formation, knowledge, and skills that presidents and board members will need for Catholic colleges and universities to be "in" the world but not entirely "of" it—not "countercultural" through and through, but also not assimilated to "the dominant culture," whether economically, politically, intellectually, or religiously.

Paul Kollman's chapter on global Catholic education serves as a coda of sorts to the other chapters. Kollman calls attention to the particularities of the U.S. context of higher education and cautions that "many CST-inspired proposals for Catholic higher education in the United States do not translate…to international contexts." At the same time, he invites readers to reflect on ways that U.S. Catholic colleges and universities can both contribute to global Catholic higher education and be enriched by developing ties with institutions, scholars, and students beyond the United States, especially in the Majority World or so-called Global South. Kollman's chapter thus echoes Cardinal Michael Czerny's reflections, in his preface to this volume, on his teaching experiences in El Salvador and in Kenya. It seems clear that Cardinal Czerny learned as much from those experiences as he taught.

As we noted above, at the end of each chapter, and of this introduction as well, we present a handful of questions for consideration and discussion. We formulated these questions with group discussion in mind. Our hope for this volume is that it will contribute to fostering a richer discourse on our campuses and thereby help to strengthen our institutions in these turbulent times. *Deo volente*.

Questions for Consideration and Discussion

1. Prusak and Reed-Bouley suggest that some institutions may be living out CST already in ways that they either do not recognize or currently lack the language to articulate. Is that the case for your

institution? If so, does CST suggest a richer story about your institution? How would you begin to tell it?

2. Prusak and Reed-Bouley remark that "though the aftermath of the pandemic will not allow us to remake our social world from scratch, it does present an opportunity to examine whether the 'old normal' was sustainable, desirable, or, for Catholic institutions, adequately faithful to Christ." Are there ways in which the "old normal" at your institution was unsustainable, undesirable, or inadequately faithful to Christ? What do you want to change postpandemic, and how can that change be realized?
3. According to Prusak and Reed-Bouley, "Concrete business and operational decisions form part of an institution's so-called hidden curriculum, communicating to students and all other stakeholders what the institution truly values." What is your institution's hidden curriculum? What values do your institution's business and operational decisions communicate? Are these values you want to affirm, or reconsider?
4. Prusak and Reed-Bouley focus on the issue of childcare during the coronavirus pandemic as a means of giving a fuller account of what seeking to live out CST might look like for an institution. What are other issues that might helpfully be framed and discussed with the resources of CST? The question of whether to mandate vaccination against COVID-19 might be an example, but propose and examine examples of your own, beyond the confines of the pandemic.

Notes

1. Joseph A. McCartin, "Confronting the Labor Problem in Catholic Higher Education: Applying Catholic Social Teaching in an Age of Increasing Inequality," *Journal of Catholic Higher Education* 37, no. 1 (2018): 71–88, at 83. See also Gerald J. Beyer, *Just Universities: Catholic Social Teaching Confronts Corporatized Higher Education* (New York: Fordham University Press, 2021), 4, on the "structures of sin" that beset Catholic higher education.

2. Pope Leo XIII, *Rerum Novarum* (May 15, 1891), 57, available at https://www.vatican.va, as are all Vatican documents cited in this book. Pope Leo's encyclical is often cited as the origin of modern CST. As Michael Schuck notes, however, that "standard identification" both simplifies the historical record and "reinforce[s] the pope's position as broker" of what counts as CST. See Michael J. Schuck, "Early Modern Roman Catholic Social

Thought, 1740–1890," in *Modern Catholic Social Teaching: Commentaries and Interpretations*, ed. Kenneth R. Himes, OFM (Washington, DC: Georgetown University Press, 2005), 99–124, at 100.

3. See Bill Purcell and Margarita Rose, "Engaging Mission: Applying the Catholic Social Tradition to Investing and Licensing," *Journal of Catholic Higher Education* 37, no. 1 (2018): 53–69. See also McCartin, "Confronting the Labor Problem," 82–83.

4. Compare *Rerum Novarum* 43–45, though Pope Leo does not use the term *living wage*, which has a complex history. See, for a helpful discussion, Patricia Ann Lamoureux, "Is a Living Wage a Just Wage?" *America*, February 19, 2001, https://www.americamagazine.org.

5. The collective bargaining agreements can be found online. St. Mary's College of California is a further, non-Jesuit example.

6. See Brian Roewe, "How the University of Dayton Divested from Fossil Fuels—and What Happened to Its Bottom Line," *National Catholic Reporter*, July 14, 2020, https://www.ncronline.org.

7. See Ashley A. Smith, "Growing Numbers of Religious Universities Offer Two-Year Degrees," *Inside Higher Ed*, August 23, 2017, https://www.insidehighered.com, discussing Arrupe College and Dougherty Family College, associated with the University of St. Thomas (MN).

8. For an overview of the changing U.S. Catholic landscape, see Patricia O'Connell Killen and Mark Silk, eds., *The Future of Catholicism in America* (New York: Columbia University Press, 2019). For a detailed account of the growth of nonaffiliation among Catholics, see Carol Ann MacGregor and Ashlyn Haycock, "Lapsed Catholics and Other Religious Non-affiliates," in *Empty Churches: Non-affiliation in America*, ed. James L. Heft, SM, and Jan E. Stets (Oxford: Oxford University Press, 2021), 79–105.

9. See Jill Barshay, "College Students Predicted to Fall by More Than 15% after the Year 2025," *The Hechinger Report*, September 10, 2018, https://hechingerreport.org.

10. The times are likewise trying for Catholic primary and secondary schools. See Giulia McDonnell Nieto del Rio, "A Growing Number of Catholic Schools Are Shutting Down Forever," *New York Times*, September 5, 2020, https://www.nytimes.com.

11. Peter Steinfels, *A People Adrift: The Crisis of the Roman Catholic Church in America* (New York: Simon & Schuster, 2003).

12. See Mark 4:35–41, Matt 8:23–27, and Luke 8:22–25.

13. Holy Family College (formerly Silver Lake College) in Wisconsin closed in August 2020. Notre Dame de Namur University in California decided, in March 2020, not to enroll new undergraduate students for fall 2020 and, in January 2021, "to transform into a primarily graduate and online university."

14. Although our metaphor is different, we agree with Beyer that CST "can provide a bulwark against the further erosion of important aspects of the mission" of Catholic higher education. See Beyer, *Just Universities*, 7.

15. For example, Don J. Briel, Kenneth E. Goodpaster, and Michael J. Naughton propose that two "intellectual principles" distinguish Catholic higher education, namely, the principle of the unity of knowledge and the principle of the complementarity of faith and reason. See their *What We Hold in Trust: Rediscovering the Purpose of Catholic Higher Education* (Washington, DC: Catholic University of America Press, 2021), 18–19.

16. Association of Catholic Colleges and Universities, "Catholic Higher Education and Catholic Social Teaching: A Vision Statement" (Washington, DC: ACCU, 2012), 4.

17. See Pope Francis, *Laudato Si'* (May 24, 2015), 1–2.

18. Gerard V. Bradley and E. Christian Brugger, "Introduction: Contingency, Continuity, Development, and Change in Modern Catholic Social Teaching," in *Catholic Social Teaching: A Volume of Scholarly Essays*, ed. Gerard V. Bradley and E. Christian Brugger (Cambridge: Cambridge University Press, 2019), 1–8, at 3. As Robert G. Kennedy nicely observes in the same volume, "One of the characteristics of the Church's magisterium regarding social issues is that it is shaped and elicited by challenges of the day. That is to say, it is topical and not at all a systematic, comprehensive reflection on principles." See Kennedy, "International Finance and Catholic Social Teaching," in Bradley and Brugger, *Catholic Social Teaching: A Volume of Scholarly Essays*, 387–413, at 388.

19. See, by way of introduction, such diverse texts as Himes, *Modern Catholic Social Teaching*; Bradley and Brugger, *Catholic Social Teaching: A Volume of Scholarly Essays*; William O'Neill, SJ, *Catholic Social Teaching: A User's Guide* (Maryknoll, NY: Orbis, 2021); and Kathleen Maas Weigert and Alexia K. Kelley, eds., *Living the Catholic Social Tradition: Cases and Commentary* (Lanham, MD: Rowman & Littlefield, 2005). Todd David Whitmore's contribution to that volume, "Catholic Social Teaching: Starting with the Common Good" (59–85), delves into CST's trinitarian anthropology.

20. Pope John Paul II's apostolic constitution *Ex Corde Ecclesiae* (August 15, 1990) notoriously stipulates in part 2, article 4, 4, that, "in order not to endanger the Catholic identity of the university or institute of higher studies, the number of non-Catholic teachers should not be allowed to constitute a majority within the institution." *Ex Corde* does not discuss how to determine if someone counts as Catholic for its purposes; presumably baptism would not suffice. Nonetheless, we agree with the basic point, brought home to us in conversation with Michael Schuck, that it is *people*—both Catholics and those of other Christian denominations and other faiths—who bring traditions like CST alive. In other words, if a college or university lacks a significant core

of faculty and staff and administrators for whom CST resonates and makes sense, a resource like it is next to useless. Further, perhaps it is even potentially harmful if it is merely instrumentalized for political ends.

21. John Paul II, *Ex Corde Ecclesiae*, part 1, 13.

22. Francis Oakley, *From the Cast-Iron Shore: In Lifelong Pursuit of Liberal Learning* (Notre Dame, IN: University of Notre Dame Press, 2019), 409. Oakley, who was president of Williams College from 1985 to 1993, contrasts "a Durkheimian understanding of the social and institutional world as an objective and alien facticity" with his own "counterintuitive Weberian assumption that institutional life is a fragile social construct, the product of human creativity and fraught, therefore, with human meaning" (409).

23. See Vatican II's decree on the apostolate of the laity, *Apostolicam Actuositatem* (November 18, 1965), 1. Similarly, the Council's constitution on the Church in the modern world, *Gaudium et Spes* (December 7, 1965), 43, enjoins the laity to see to it that the "the divine law is inscribed into the life of the earthly city."

24. David Hollenbach, SJ, "The Catholic University under the Sign of the Cross: Christian Humanism in a Broken World," in *Finding God in All Things: Essays in Honor of Michael J. Buckley, SJ*, ed. Stephen Pope and Michael Himes (New York: Crossroad, 1996), 279–98, at 287–88.

25. See Bernard G. Prusak, "Independent Boards of Trustees at Catholic Colleges and Universities, Fifty Years Later: Findings and Reflections from Six Holy Cross Schools," *Journal of Catholic Higher Education* 37, no. 1 (2018): 3–27.

26. The Ignatian Colleagues Program, administered by the Association of Jesuit Colleges and Universities (AJCU), represents an exception to this rule. See https://www.ignatiancolleagues.org.

27. Steinfels, *A People Adrift*, 11. Compare the Association of Jesuit Colleges and Universities, "Some Characteristics of Jesuit Colleges and Universities: A Self-Evaluation Instrument" (2012), 7, available online at ajcunet.edu: "The majority of our lay people come without adequate formation or interest in learning about and implementing the mission beyond humanistic concerns, like 'care of the person' or a 'commitment to service.'"

28. Claudia Goldin, "Journey across a Century of Women" (2020 Martin S. Feldstein Lecture, National Bureau of Economic Research, July 21, 2020), https://www.nber.org. The subsequent quotations in the paragraph come from the same lecture.

29. Goldin cites, along with multiple data sets, two news articles that illustrate her argument: Deb Perelman, "In the Covid-19 Economy, You Can Have a Kid or a Job. You Can't Have Both," *New York Times*, July 2, 2020, and Claire Cain Miller, "Women Did Everything Right. Then Work Got

'Greedy,'" *New York Times*, April 26, 2019, both available online at nytimes .com.

30. See Rakesh Kochhar and Jesse Bennett, "U.S. Labor Market Inches Back from the COVID-19 Shock, but Recovery Is Far from Complete," Pew Research Center, April 14, 2021, available online at pewresearch.org. See further Jessica Grose, "Women Are the 'Shock Absorbers' of Our Society," *New York Times*, October 14, 2020, available online at nytimes.com.

31. See Jillian Kramer, "The Virus Moved Female Faculty to the Brink. Will Universities Help?" *New York Times*, October 6, 2020, available online at nytimes.com.

32. See, e.g., Pope Pius XI, *Quadragesimo Anno* (May 15, 1931), 71: "Mothers, concentrating on household duties, should work primarily in the home or in its immediate vicinity. It is an intolerable abuse, and to be abolished at all cost, for mothers on account of the father's low wage to be forced to engage in gainful occupations outside the home to the neglect of their proper cares and duties, especially the training of children." See even *Gaudium et Spes* 52: "The active presence of the father is highly beneficial to [children's] formation. The children, especially the younger among them, need the care of their mother at home. This domestic role of hers must be safely preserved, though the legitimate social progress of women should not be underrated on that account." Luciana Reali provides further citations in "Women in Catholic Social Thought: The Creation of a New Social Reality," *Journal of Catholic Legal Studies* 44, no. 2 (2005): 461–78. It likely is not remarked enough that, to date, magisterial teaching has been composed by male clerics. See in this regard the project "Women Engaging the Catholic Social Tradition," online at www.womenengagingcst.org. For a quite different perspective, see John Finnis, "A Radical Critique of Catholic Social Teaching," in Bradley and Brugger, *Catholic Social Teaching: A Volume of Scholarly Essays*, 548–84, at 554–55.

33. For a simple example, consider the controversy over the Jesuit James Martin's anodyne book, *Building a Bridge: How the Catholic Church and the LGBT Community Can Enter into a Relationship of Respect, Compassion, and Sensitivity* (New York: HarperCollins, 2017). Martin is now persona non grata in some Catholic circles, despite Pope Francis's affirmation of his ministry. See also Martha Nussbaum's thoughtful reflections entitled "Marley's Burden: A Ghost Story," *Boston College Magazine* 65, no. 4 (Fall 1996): 31–35. Nussbaum notes, gratefully, that at Catholic institutions "notions of intrinsic value and of the human being as an end provide a common language in which we can, without preliminary skirmishing, converse" (31). But she observes that "no issue is more divisive on Catholic campuses, both in social life and curricular matters," than homosexuality (35). As a genuine question: How much has that changed since 1996?

34. See, e.g., William J. Byron, SJ, "The 10 Building Blocks of Catholic Social Teaching," *America*, October 31, 1998, available online at americamagazine.org; Robert P. Maloney, SM, "Ten Foundational Principles in the Social Teaching of the Church," *Vincentiana* 43, no. 3 (1999), available online at depaul.edu; and Beyer, *Just Universities*, 40–41.

35. We do not claim, however, that a student has a duty to participate in ways that represent the group or groups with which she or he identifies, particularly if those groups are not well-represented in the class.

36. The groundbreaking text is Miranda Fricker's *Epistemic Injustice: Power and the Ethics of Knowing* (Oxford: Oxford University Press, 2007). The person whose contributions to classroom discussion are brushed aside and discounted suffers what Fricker terms testimonial injustice.

37. To have a claim right, as Stephen Darwall nicely explains, "includes a second-personal authority to resist, complain, remonstrate, and perhaps use coercive measures of other kinds...if the right is violated." In other words, a claim right gives you "a standing to make a special demand against people who might step on your feet—you have the authority to resist, claim compensation, and so on." See Darwall's *The Second-Person Standpoint: Morality, Respect, and Accountability* (Cambridge, MA: Harvard University Press, 2006), 18.

38. As Stephen Pope notes, CST from Leo XIII through John Paul II (and now Benedict XVI and Francis) has "selectively incorporated, sometimes to the consternation of purists [and at some risk of incoherence—BP and JRB], both modern natural rights theories as well as the older views of medieval jurists and Scholastic theologians," who did not understand *ius* in terms of so-called subjective rights (rights on the part of the subject), but as what is objectively right, or in other words just or fair, in a given set of circumstances. See Stephen J. Pope, "Natural Law in Catholic Social Teachings," in Himes, *Modern Catholic Social Teaching*, 41–71, at 48–49. Compare Kevin L. Flannery, SJ, "The Moral Principles Governing the Immigration Policies of Polities," in Bradley and Brugger, *Catholic Social Teaching: A Volume of Scholarly Essays*, 365–86, at 383–84.

39. See Dana Goldstein, "Detroit Students Have a Constitutional Right to Literacy, Court Rules," *New York Times*, April 27, 2020, available online at nytimes.com, with a link to the Sixth Circuit's ruling, which overturns that of a district court.

40. Pope John Paul II, *Centesimus Annus* (May 1, 1991), 33.

41. Pope Francis, *Evangelii Gaudium* (November 24, 2013), 53.

42. United States Conference of Catholic Bishops, "Seven Themes of Catholic Social Teaching," online at usccb.org.

43. See, at greater length, Gerald J. Beyer, "Worker Justice as a Pro-Life Issue," in *Voting and Faithfulness: Catholic Perspectives on Politics*, ed. Nicholas P. Cafardi (Mahwah, NJ: Paulist Press, 2020), 153–78.

44. This is a point that Onora O'Neill makes emphatically and eloquently in her *Towards Justice and Virtue: A Constructive Account of Practical Reasoning* (Cambridge: Cambridge University Press, 1996), 128–34.

45. Social justice, as we understand it, has to do with social action: the (re-)organization of the social systems in which people live and work. We have learned in this regard from William Ferree, SM, *Introduction to Social Justice* (New York: Paulist Press, 1948), which enthusiastically explicates and comments on Pope Pius XI's encyclicals *Quadragesimo Anno* and *Divini Redemptoris* (March 19, 1937). See further Christine Firer Hinze, "Commentary on *Quadragesimo anno* (*After Forty Years*)," in Himes, *Modern Catholic Social Teaching*, 151–74, at 167, and Samuel Gregg, "*Quadragesimo anno* (1931)," in Bradley and Brugger, *Catholic Social Teaching: A Volume of Scholarly Essays*, 90–107, at 93–98.

46. Pope Pius XI, *Quadragesimo Anno* 71.

47. Pope Pius XI, *Divini Redemptoris* 53.

48. Compare Martin Schlag, "Are Businesses Responsible for the Moral Ecology in Which They Operate?," in *Business Ethics and Catholic Social Thought*, ed. Daniel K. Finn (Washington, DC: Georgetown University Press, 2021), 163–79.

1

WHAT STUDENTS? WHICH MISSION?

Laura Nichols

WHAT WOULD JESUS NOTICE if he walked into Catholic colleges and universities today? Like the temple cleansing that brought to light the ways that the use of the temple had gone astray from its purpose, this volume provides fodder as Catholic colleges and universities (CCUs) consider our situation as individual institutions and as a larger cohort of CCUs within the U.S. higher education landscape. Catholic higher education and higher education in general face a crisis as high demand and need for postsecondary education collide with rising tuition, increasing education debt, demographic changes, and college closings. CCUs, as private, nonprofit institutions, have not escaped these realities. At the same time, CCUs possess a wealth of experience and resources to meet the needs of this moment, and this volume provides an avenue to consider Catholic higher education anew, in light of Catholic social thought (CST).

As we know, mission statements highlight the values that undergird an organization. They help to socialize new members, to remind all constituents of the values, goals, and ideals upon which structural components of organizations are built, and to guide important decisions. A mission statement often includes an institution's founding values as well as its aspirations for the future. External pressures, however, might cause an organization to engage in what organizational theorists refer to as "decoupling" from mission as a means of survival.[1] This can occur when organizations adopt practices that conflict with their main purpose, often resulting in day-to-day operations that differ from stated missions. Decoupling can cause problems at the organizational level, and newer research suggests that it might also negatively affect those who work at such organizations, increasing employee cynicism and even contributing to negative behaviors at odds with the stated mission of the organization.[2]

To understand decoupling from mission at CCUs, this chapter analyzes demographic data regarding the students whom a range of types of CCUs enroll. My aim is to examine the current state of CCUs in the United States, consider how they have evolved, and assess the extent of decoupling from mission that has occurred as indicated by the characteristics of students. The chapter's focus aligns with the directive in Pope Paul VI's 1971 apostolic letter *Octogesima Adveniens* that "it is up to the Christian communities to analyze with objectivity the situation which is proper to their own country, to shed on it the light of the Gospel's unalterable words, and to draw principles of reflection, norms of judgment, and directives for action from the social teachings of the Church."[3]

I start by analyzing institutional data for all CCUs in the United States, as well as subsets that include those ranked highly by external entities. I then examine CCUs that have successfully maintained their earlier missions of providing avenues of social mobility for students. I pay particular attention to the enrollment of the largest segment of future college students in the United States, a demographic with whom Catholic schools have had a history of success: students who are the first in their families to attend college. Focusing on first-generation college students holds potential for addressing another impending crisis in postsecondary education, namely, the predicted drop in the numbers of U.S. students graduating from high school.[4] Currently, 58 percent of children under age eighteen in the United States have parents without college experience and would be first-generation college students, making this group even more important for enrollment outreach.[5] In the conclusion, I connect mission as expressed via student demographics to CST. As Prusak and Reed-Bouley state in the introduction to this volume, "CST might help to anchor Catholic colleges and universities in their missions as distinctively Catholic institutions." My basic question is this: How can CCUs live up to the ideals of a just society as articulated by CST?

Neoliberalism and Meritocracy: Values Antithetical to CST

Samuel Maseus and Lucy LePeau outline the key components of a neoliberal ethos that has overtaken most postsecondary institutions in the United States.[6] As we will see from data presented later in this chapter, most highly ranked CCUs show the effects of this ethos. The five neoliberalist components that Maseus and LePeau analyze are consumerism; competitive individualism, including "false beliefs in meritocracy...where every person prioritizes their own self-interest"; surveillance; precarity; and declining morality, with "an increased focus on fiscal exigency and profit-making."[7] These ways of operating directly conflict with CST's theological anthropology, which highlights the dignity and value of the human person as created by God and accordingly emphasizes access to participation in the goods of society (as Prusak and Reed-Bouley's introduction also notes). Yet educational systems, especially at the postsecondary level, are deeply invested in the myth of meritocracy, leading to admissions and other practices that conflict with CST.

Selective colleges with the highest graduation rates tout annual increases in average SAT scores and GPAs and often lavish "merit scholarships" on students as a means to entice them to attend their schools. While the tuition and scholarship/grant formulas do contribute to the common good of keeping colleges and universities full, the offers of internal aid appear to students as individual scholarships based on merit. The admissions process rewards already-advantaged students for their hard work and effort, while low-income students must navigate institutional, state, and federal bureaucracies to attempt to garner sufficient aid to afford college. As we will see, these practices result in very bifurcated student bodies at most selective CCUs, with many students from families in the upper class, few from families with limited economic resources, and a shrinking number of students from families in the middle class.

The neoliberal homage to individual effort in fact wreaks systemic harms. As Michael Sandel writes in *The Tyranny of Merit*, "The more we view ourselves as self-made and self-sufficient, the less likely we are to care for the fate of those less fortunate than ourselves."[8] In his judgment, "a perfect meritocracy banishes all sense of gift or grace. It diminishes our capacity to see ourselves as sharing a common fate. It leaves little room for the solidarity that can arise when we reflect on the contingency of our talents and fortunes."[9] Moreover, students born into wealthy families often spend their high-school years in a "high-stress, anxiety-ridden, sleep-deprived gauntlet of Advanced Placement courses, test-prep tutoring, sports training, dance and music lessons, and a myriad of extracurricular and public service activities," all to the end of competing against their peers for the few coveted spots at the most elite colleges with less than 10 percent acceptance rates.[10]

By contrast, CST calls on individuals and institutions to aspire to contribute to the common, public good. The recognition of our interdependence requires that individuals and organizations practice a "highly inclusive solidarity."[11] CST also posits a preferential option for those with the fewest resources and calls for just laws and structures to ensure that the basic needs of all are met. While other chapters address significant concerns about alignment between the mission of CST and other areas of operations, it is the demographics of the students whom Catholic colleges and universities enroll that is of concern here.

A Short History of Catholic School Development in the United States

Public and private investments in education as a public good, even during the Great Depression, contributed to social mobility and the growth of a middle class in the United States. The founders of Catholic schools in this country knew that education was key to making sure that Catholics had opportunities to become active and full members of society. In some geographic areas, Catholic schools were among the first schools. As a result, Catholic schools influenced all levels of public and private schooling.

Catholic schools were created with a two-pronged mission: to provide a place for Catholics to learn more about their faith, and to serve as a means for educational opportunities for Catholics discriminated against in the mainstream, Protestant-influenced "common" (public) schools of the time.[12] Catholic schools constituted an important opportunity structure for Catholics to participate in society amid discrimination and active campaigns against Catholics, starting with Irish American Catholics who were deemed "intellectually inferior, morally suspect, and prone to manipulation."[13]

Catholic schools spread rapidly and succeeded in providing avenues for evangelization and for the social mobility of millions of first- and second-generation Catholic immigrant families.[14] The 1940s and 1950s are considered the height of Catholic education in the United States, with large numbers of Catholic youth attending Catholic schools at some point in their K–12 educations.[15] Many of these schools were free or low cost, thanks to the availability of low-paid teachers from Catholic religious orders.

The founding missions of CCUs similarly included providing religious training, redressing discrimination against Catholics, and preparing Catholics to succeed in burgeoning occupations of the time. As historian of higher education John Thelin writes, "The hallmarks of the urban Catholic colleges were utility and upward mobility, especially for the sons of first-generation immigrants."[16] Catholic institutions expanded with the increase of Catholic immigration. By 1930, there were 126 Catholic colleges throughout the United States, 39 percent of which were for women.[17]

While Catholic schools have always served a stratum of the Catholic economic elite, at both the K–12 and postsecondary levels they mainly served low-income Catholic families. Conversely, Catholic schools that survive today are disproportionally dominated by children whose families are wealthy. Today, most Catholic K–12 students attend public schools, and the most prestigious CCUs enroll very few low-income students or those who would be the first in their families to graduate from college. (See the data below.)

The "Catholic Advantage"

The prevalence of quality free or affordable Catholic schools in the United States is one factor that explains the wealth mobility of white Catholics during the 1980s and 1990s,[18] known as the "Catholic advantage." As sociologist Lisa Keister notes,

> While not all people raised in Catholic families attended Catholic schools, the majority of those who were Catholic and elementary school age in the 1970s did. Some 60 percent of [adult] American Catholics surveyed in 1999 had attended Catholic school as a child for at least a short period of time, and 36 percent had attended seven or more years.[19]

The Catholic school system contributed to the common good of building a middle class and providing an opportunity structure for—it should be noted—mainly white Catholics to develop their human potential and contribute to society. (Consult the chapter in this volume by Tia Noelle Pratt and Maureen O'Connell.)

At the organizational level, while in the 1950s there were more than thirteen thousand Catholic elementary and secondary schools in the United States, by 2015 there were half as many.[20] These changes have influenced who attends private K–12 schools. According to education researchers studying the changing demographics of private K–12 schools,

> In 1965, 89 percent of American children who attended a private elementary school were enrolled in a Catholic school; in 2013, the comparable figure was 42 percent. By contrast, the percentage of private elementary-school students who attended a non-Catholic religious school increased from 8 percent in 1965 to 40 percent in 2013.[21]

The number of Catholics in the United States has grown from 48.5 million in 1965 to almost 68 million today,[22] but most Catholic school children attend urban public schools.[23] Further, the demographics of Catholics in the United States has changed dramatically from the mid-twentieth century. Today, 40 percent of Catholics identify as Latinx and 60 percent of Catholics under age eighteen are Latinx, with 90 percent born in the United States.[24] That is over eight million Catholic school-aged children who are Latinx. However, only 2.3 percent of K–12 Catholic Latinx youth attend a Catholic school.[25]

Catholic schools of the past provided an opportunity structure for low- and middle-income families to attend private schools. However, with the decrease in the number of Catholic schools, and increase in private schools that are not Catholic, the percentage of children from middle- and low-income families attending private schools has dropped. To quote the same education researchers,

> As a result of growing residential segregation by income, low-income families are increasingly concentrated in urban areas. In such places, one quarter of high-income families enroll their children in private schools compared to a much smaller—and declining—proportion of middle- and low-income families. As a result, both urban public schools and urban private schools exhibit less socioeconomic diversity today than several decades ago.[26]

The pandemic has accelerated Catholic school closings, further limiting access to Catholic education for students from low- and middle-income families.[27] And so, as schools have relied more and more on finding "customers" who can pay the requisite tuition, admission and financial aid practices have decoupled from a mission of providing opportunities for large numbers of students from low-income families to gain social mobility via education. Catholic schools might teach CST, but the students receiving this instruction are mainly from wealthy families and often do not identify as Catholic.

Demographics of Current Students Attending CCUs

The first takeaway of this exploration into mission and students at CCUs in the United States today is that one driver of the loss of Catholics represented in CCUs results from the predominant socioeconomic profile of the students whom many CCUs look to enroll. Much of the discussion and many of the publications around the mission of CCUs focus on the curriculum.[28] One fear is that CCUs are losing their way, especially given the loss of priests and other religious among faculty and increasingly administrators.[29] At the same time, the proportion of students at CCUs who identify as Catholic has decreased. In 2019, 47 percent of entering first-year students at CCUs identified as Catholic, compared to 55 percent ten years earlier. This percentage has been decreasing each year.[30] At the same time, we have more Catholics in the United States today than at the height of Catholic K–12 education.[31]

While the profile of current practicing Catholics in the United States is similar to that of Catholics of the past—many are low-income and are first- or second-generation immigrants—this is not reflected in the student bodies at our CCUs. Latinx Catholics, who are among the greatest numbers of current practicing Catholics, are underrepresented at CCUs. While Latinx students have always been part of the history of Catholic parishes and schools, they have often been treated as outsiders, especially at the more "elite" Catholic high schools and colleges. Instead, students in many Catholic high schools and colleges are likely to be white/European American, wealthy, and third- or more generation immigrants. Despite the growing number of Latinx Catholics,[32] only 29 of the 246 CCUs with publicly available data are federally defined as Hispanic-Serving Institutions (HSIs), that is, institutions at which at least 25 percent of undergraduate full-time students identify as Hispanic.[33] (See further Michelle Gonzalez Maldonado's chapter in this volume.)

Comparing Data on Students at Nationally Ranked and Closed/Closing CCUs

Next, let us look at data from current CCUs. All data reported in the tables and the figure in this chapter are publicly available and provided by institutions as part of federal requirements for operating as a private, nonprofit, accredited school. The data mainly come from the Integrated Postsecondary Education Data System (IPEDS). To run the analyses presented in the following tables and figure, I identified the CCUs using each school's IPEDS unique identification number. I also merged additional data from the College Scorecard and the Opportunity Insight Project to create one database of CCUs. I then used this database to analyze the demographics of students in subsets of CCUs, starting with CCUs that are ranked highly in national ranking systems.

The first set of analyses looks at the undergraduate demographics at ten nationally ranked CCUs, listed below (table 1).[34] When available,

I also compare these percentages to the rates for all four-year colleges in the United States (represented in the last row of the table).

Table 1. U.S. News Top Ten Nationally Ranked Catholic Colleges and Universities

Name of College, State	% First Gen	% Receive Pell	Median Family Income	% Parents in Top 20% Income*	% Incoming Class Transfer**
U of Notre Dame, IN	10	11	$112,232	73	2
Georgetown, DC	16	13	$78,300	73	1
Boston College, MA	13	13	$103,007	69	2
Villanova, PA	13	11	$110,409	70	1
Santa Clara U, CA	17	11	$97,113	65	3
Loyola Marymount, CA	22	17	$69,000	58	7
Fordham, NY	18	19	$97,877	51	3
Gonzaga, WA	13	13	$110,000	55	3
Marquette, WI	19	18	$96,300	58	2
University of San Diego, CA	25	18	$70,085	59	5
All Predominantly 4-Year/ BA Degree	34	39	$46,145	–	–

2020 ranking. Data from College Scorecard except *Opportunity Insight Project Data and ** transfer data from IPEDS entering class Fall 2018

As we see in table 1, many CCUs reproduce the income inequality that has become so extreme in the United States today. The most highly ranked CCUs enroll a very small proportion of their student bodies who would be first in their families to attend college or are low-income and receive need-based Pell grants. Ten percent of the University of Notre Dame's undergraduate student body in the fall of 2018 were first in their families to attend college and 11 percent received Pell grants. University of San Diego and Loyola Marymount University have the highest proportion of first-generation and Pell students of the CCUs in table 1, but they are still under the national average of 34 percent (first-generation) and 39 percent (Pell) for students at all four-year colleges. Further, at all the nationally ranked CCUs, more than half of the undergraduate student bodies have parents in the top 20 percent of income in the United States (i.e., 51% of the student body at Fordham, to the highest proportions of 73% at Notre Dame and Georgetown).

While the greatest proportion of students aspiring to go to college in the United States today are first-generation college students, they make up a very small proportion of students entering four-year colleges, especially selective colleges. And this can translate to climate issues as students from radically different social classes and experiences come together for the first time and attempt to build community in classrooms, residence halls, and cocurricular activities. Imagine being the first in your family to attend college where over 80 percent of students come from families with knowledge and acumen for navigating college. Further, very few of the students at the top ten CCUs would even be considered middle class.

Now let us consider the same data points at Catholic colleges that have recently closed or are closing.[35] In table 2, we see that the proportions of students who are first in their families or receive Pell grants are much higher at closed or closing CCUs than the ten profiled in table 1. And, for the most part, the median income of families is much lower.

Table 2. Recent Catholic College Closings and Demographics of Undergraduate Students

Name of College, State (Year of Closure)	% First Gen	% Ugrad Pell Recipients	Median Family Income	% Incoming Class Transfer**
College of St. Joseph, VT (2019)	54	55	$26,570	10

Holy Family College, WI (2020)	48	45	$28,127	10
Marygrove College, MI (2019)	41	63	$17,164	N/A
Notre Dame de Namur, CA (2021)—closed to undergraduate enrollment	46	45	$39,259	13
Saint Joseph's College, IN (2017)	34	30	$73,855	N/A
St. Catharine College, KY (2016)	45	47	$49, 666	N/A
Data from College Scorecard as of June 2020 or latest data available				

Catholic colleges that are closing or have closed have much higher proportions of first-generation and Pell-recipient students than colleges that are ranked in the top ten. What will happen to the students who previously would have gone to now-closed colleges? This is particularly a concern given that CCUs are more successful than public and private non-Catholic colleges in graduating students who are first in their families to go to college, as well as students who identify as Latinx—the college students of the future.[36]

Success of CCUs in Enrolling and Graduating First-Generation Students

Schools that are already successful in enrolling and graduating first-generation college students can provide a blueprint for other CCUs. The figure below plots all 246 CCUs with data available on the

Figure 1. CCUs, Enrollment, and Graduation Rates

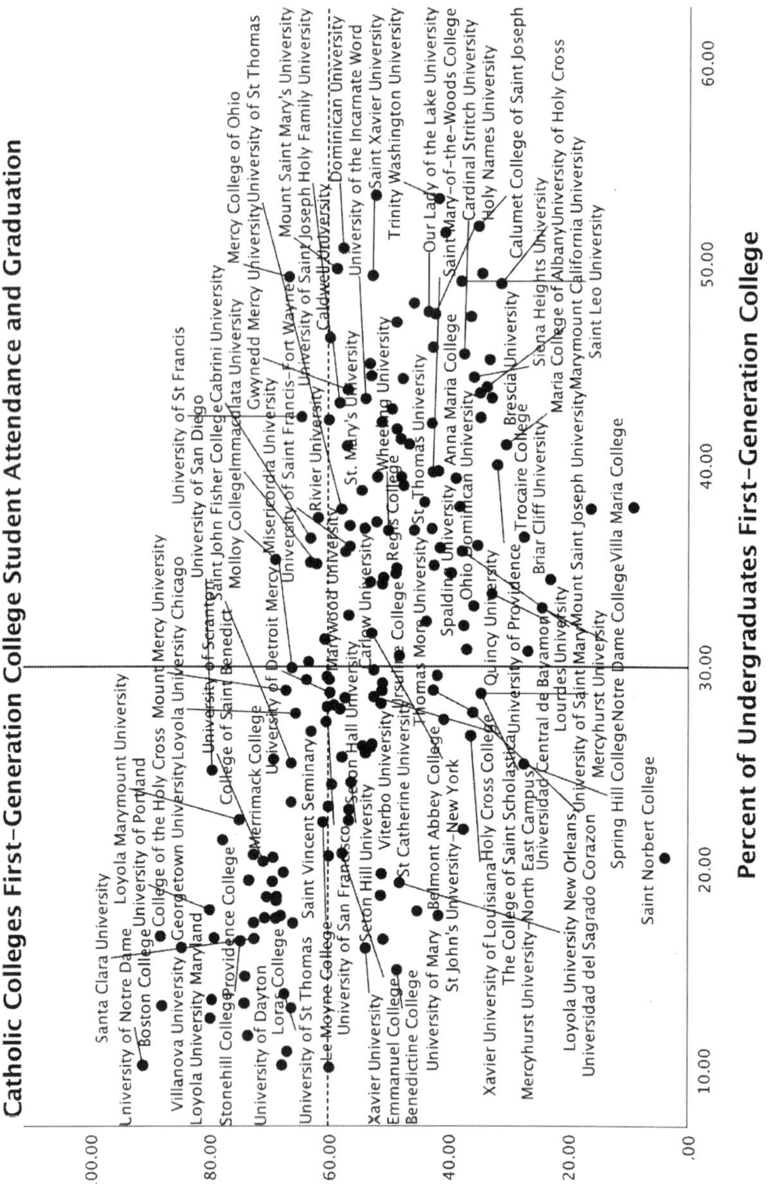

Catholic Colleges First-Generation College Student Attendance and Graduation

Percent of Undergraduates First-Generation College

Percent of First-Generation Students Graduate in 6 or Fewer Years

percentage of first-generation undergraduate students, along with six-year graduation rates for this same group of students.

In the figure above, the CCUs to the right of the solid vertical line have undergraduate student populations in which a third or more are first in their families to attend college (defined as neither parent having any college experience). In other words, the CCUs that are farthest to the right enroll the highest proportions of their undergraduate students who are first in their families to attend college. Those schools in the top right box have both relatively high proportions of first-generation students and strong graduation rates for those same students. Colleges in the box on the bottom, to the right, and below the dotted line have high enrollment of first-generation students but less than a 60 percent six-year graduation rate for those same students. A small number of CCUs has low proportions of first-generation college students and low rates of graduation of those same students.

Moving clockwise around the figure, the box on the top left of the figure includes CCUs that have low proportions of first-generation college students, but high rates of graduation of those students. All the top ten ranked CCUs in the United States, in table 1, are in this quadrant. What is going on here? Likely a multitude of factors. First, these schools tend to have very high graduation rates in general, and they are likely "creaming" first-generation college students who have the most resources to attend college full-time and live away from home, come from well-resourced high schools, and have the social and individual capital and time to navigate the multitude of financial aid application requirements to fund their educations. The structure of the CCUs themselves, including size, staffing dedicated to student success, and the critical mass of students with the resources to get to a timely graduation, are likely also factors.

If more CCUs want to live out their missions and address the impending demographic crises facing postsecondary schools in the U.S., it makes sense to pay attention to CCUs that already enroll and graduate high proportions of first-generation students. When we take a closer look at those CCUs that have 30 percent or more of their student bodies who are first-generation college students and that have high rates of graduation of first-generation students (60 percent or more graduating in six or fewer years)—we see there are nine schools with the highest graduation rates, as depicted in table 3.

Table 3. Characteristics of Undergraduates at CCUs with over a Third First-Generation College Students and High Rates of Bachelor Degree Completion

College, State	% First Gen	% First Gen Graduate 6 < Years	% Pell	% Parents in Top 20% Income	% Incoming Class Transfer**
Cabrini University*, PA	36	63	40	42	4
Our Lady of the Elms*, MA	35	63	47	24	22
DePaul University, IL	30	63	33	44	9
Immaculata University*, PA	35	62	29	35	8
Iona University, NY	31	61	32	41	3
Mercy College*, OH	49	67	41	N/A	28
Molloy College*, NY	35	69	32	N/A	9
Rivier University*, NH	37	62	30	N/A	6
University of St. Francis*, IL	42	64	36	35	16

N/A=Data not available; *college started by female religious order

Of the nine colleges, seven were founded by religious orders of women. At least for those CCUs for which there are data available, there is a similar proportion of students who qualify for and receive Pell funding and students whose families are in the top 20 percent of the income quartile: in other words, an undergraduate student body that is more balanced in terms of socioeconomic status than at the CCUs represented in Table 1. All the schools are in the Midwest or East. Some schools also have very high proportions of transfer students. This is to be expected, as many first-generation students need to attend economical two-year schools close to home and then transfer for their bachelor's degree.[37]

Retooling CCUs for the Students of the Future

It must be acknowledged that the call of this chapter, and the issues raised in this whole volume, are not easily solved. Holding our institutions to standards rooted in CST that are different from the powerful neoliberal forces that dominate postsecondary education in the United States is a tall order. Further, present and imminent demographic changes will only exert greater stress on our schools, especially those modeled on (the nostalgia of) a four-year, residential college experience. The pull to compete with other CCUs to enroll even higher proportions of students born into wealthy families will continue to make it difficult for CCUs to operate in ways that are consonant with the Catholic values and ideals that we teach and proclaim in our mission statements. Yet CCUs do have advantages that make them well-poised to meet this moment.

First, we have experience enrolling and graduating the demographic of students who are the future of college students: students who would be the first in their families to attend college, including a high proportion of first- and second-generation immigrants and students from low-income families. Second, though youth today are much less likely than in the past to claim a religious affiliation, new immigrant parents make up a larger proportion of today's practicing Catholics, providing a means to reach future students.[38] Third, research suggests that future students will seek colleges close to home.[39] CCUs are spread throughout the United States, many located in urban areas with high proportions of young people looking for educational opportunities.

Undocumented students constitute another population that some CCUs have worked to enroll and graduate.[40] To the point, in Pope Francis's encyclical *Fratelli Tutti*, there is a reminder to protect individuals, including students, who may not possess documentation of citizenship: "No one, then, can remain excluded because of his or her place of birth, much less because of privileges enjoyed by others who were born in lands of greater opportunity. The limits and borders of individual states cannot stand in the way of this."[41]

If CCUs do nothing to alter the influence of capitalism and corporatization on our practices,[42] then CCUs will continue to decouple from mission and be stratified similarly to the demographics of the U.S. population as a whole and higher education in general. Richer CCUs will dominate the rankings, hoard resources, and educate mainly students from wealthy families. These schools also risk admissions practices that prioritize legacy applicants, thereby disadvantaging first-generation students, ironically much as early Catholics to the United States were excluded from elite, non-Catholic schools.[43] Poorer CCUs, serving greater numbers of first-generation and underresourced students, will struggle to survive and in perhaps many cases will not. I suggest two main ways to "recouple" mission with the students of the future: (1) better use of data to understand the students whom we enroll and the students we are missing, and (2) an honest reckoning as to our histories as CCUs in the United States. Further, creative leadership is necessary to harness the power of our networks and to help CCUs collaborate and have a stronger basis from which to live out and enact mission rooted in CST. (See in this regard the chapters by James L. Heft, SM, and Matt Mazewski.)

The Role of Data in Promoting Mission

Data can help us to question if we have been living true to our missions in the students whom we enroll. Fortunately, there is much data available, and recent census numbers can also help us understand the demographics of our local communities. IPEDS, the College Scorecard, and the Opportunity Insight Project (data used in this chapter and others in this volume), as well as institutional data, all illuminate to what extent CCUs provide opportunities for students to achieve social mobility, or if we are instead reproducing inequality in educating mostly those from upper-class families. There are numerous students who aspire to go to college and would be the first in their families to attend, as well as students who may be languishing in larger public institutions,[44] and this is true at all levels of Catholic education, not just postsecondary education. Networks of schools such as Nativity middle schools and Cristo Rey high schools provide engines for mobility and opportunity for students to transition to the next level of quality education.[45]

We can also use data, in conjunction with local dioceses, parishes, community colleges, for-profit colleges, and public and Catholic high schools, to understand the students currently being shut out of our CCUs, and then innovate alternative pathways for them. Determining the number of aspiring first-generation local students can be a data challenge, but it is possible. In addition, current initiatives can give us insight on how to reach such students, including creating two-year schools to go along with our four-year schools, such as the impressive work of Loyola University Chicago in establishing Arrupe College.[46] Another avenue is to focus energy on improving partnerships with local two-year colleges and certificate granting programs, which is likely more cost-efficient than creating new schools. Giving preference to students now shut out of most CCUs will require retooling for schools that have been operating on the assumption that students want and can afford a residential, four-year experience.

In states with declining populations, this work will be more difficult unless partnerships are built with other CCUs with higher demand. As the data in table 1 demonstrated, some CCUs enroll a very small proportion of transfer students each year. A transition to enrolling more transfer students will require time to allocate resources to appropriate departments and services for this new group of future students.[47]

Data will also help us to reckon with the current structures in our schools and states that privilege some groups over others and that play into false notions of meritocracy. This reckoning might include a review of admissions practices to look at how financial aid decisions are made and if we communicate decisions about aid differently if they are "merit"-based over "need"-based. If aid is presented as the result of individual accomplishment in the case of merit scholarships, but aid based on need is the result of family circumstances, students may be getting different messages about their value to their college. The reckoning in question will also require analysis of the students who are missing from our schools—not just those who apply and go somewhere else, but students who live in our local communities who may not apply to our schools or attend college at all.

Understanding, Expressing, and Addressing Our Institutional Histories

To be prepared for the students of the future and authentically reaffirm mission, CCUs must also face our histories as institutions that were created to address discrimination against early Catholic immigrants, mainly from Europe, but benefited from enslavement and the colonization and displacement of Indigenous communities when many CCUs were formed. What is required includes ongoing education at all levels of our institutions, from trustees to faculty, staff, and every new student. We should learn about the role CCUs played in providing opportunities for new immigrants of the times, while also supporting slavery, violating the human rights of those who were living peacefully on the sites of our institutions, and profiting from the labor and lives of those brought to the U.S. forcibly. A number of CCUs have begun to research and engage in discussions about the histories of our schools and to attempt to address the harms they inflicted. Examples of such initiatives include Georgetown University's engagement with descendants of the human beings it sold and consideration of descendant status in admission decisions, as well as Santa Clara University's partnership with indigenous groups once living where the school is located.[48]

This work requires the marshalling of experts across our schools and solidarity with community members and descendants of those whose lives and legacies CCUs harmed. This is one important way to be wary of the potential unintended consequences of decoupling mission from practice and to be alert to the harm of, as two critics write,

> creat[ing] institutions that reward agendas and efforts that conform to core tenets of neoliberal logics, ensuring that even work that is designed to advance equity often simultaneously reinforces neoliberal rationalities, thereby reifying the very systems that they are designed to disrupt, deconstruct, and combat.[49]

Conclusion: Mission and CST

Arguably, Catholic schools in the United States have done a better job teaching Catholic values than providing an opportunity structure for most present-day Catholics and others with limited access to quality education to attend Catholic schools. Although many of the mission statements of CCUs reflect a commitment to CST and Catholic identity more broadly,[50] a number of CCUs in the United States have followed the path of corporatized higher education in terms of funding, enrollment, and administrative practices, especially at the most highly ranked schools. This trend is not unique to CCUs: scholars have found that, while many colleges espouse missions that tout social justice agendas rooted in equity, their practices are guided by neoliberal agendas.[51]

The use of tuition to cover the majority of costs, especially at the secondary and postsecondary levels, has put Catholic education out of reach for many Catholic families in the United States. And as we saw from the data presented in this chapter, some CCUs look very much like other selective private, nonprofit schools in enrolling high proportions of privileged students and thereby reproducing current social class structures. On the other hand, CCUs that enroll a greater proportion of first-generation and students from low-income families continue the earliest mission of Catholic education of providing an opportunity structure for social mobility for those otherwise excluded, particularly young people born into poverty or first- or second-generation immigrants. But this mission comes at a great financial risk, as we saw in data on the demographics of CCUs that have recently closed or are closing.

Recoupling mission with the students we enroll may require CCUs to collaborate. As Matt Mazewski suggests in his chapter, there are models of resource sharing that could be activated to work against dog-eat-dog capitalism. Such models could be instituted across CCUs sponsored by the same religious congregation, or maybe collaboration could take place regionally. Initiatives such as the Moving the Needle Project, a collaboration among five CCUs, the Association for Catholic Colleges and Universities, and the education consulting firm Credo, represent a start.[52] Such collaborations might be the only way to save some of our CCUs that are serving the students with the most financial and educational need—our college students of the future—but have the least economic resources to do so.

To bring CST more fully into practice at all CCUs in the United States will take courage. The stakeholders committed to this challenge must disrupt the corporatization of higher education and the influences of advanced capitalism that demand the pursuit of prestige, rankings, and wealth for survival and instead find innovative ways to create organizations that serve the common good by enrolling more students who might otherwise be excluded from the benefits of higher education. This challenge will require the collection and use of data to interrogate current practices within our institutions and the will and wherewithal to innovate and realize long-standing missions anew.

Questions for Consideration and Discussion

1. Nichols provides evidence that Catholic education in this country has historically served society by providing an opportunity structure for economic advancement and social mobility for first-generation and low-income students. Is this a worthy mission for CCUs today? What are its advantages and disadvantages? To what extent is this goal consistent with your institution's self-understanding, mission, and strategic plan? To what extent is it feasible?
2. Nichols analyzes significant demographic changes that affect Catholic higher education. How has the decline in the percentage of Catholic young people who attend Catholic elementary and high schools affected your institution's recruitment pipelines, curricula, and cocurricula? What are the effects of the fact that less than half of first-year students at CCUs currently identify as Catholic? Is there a need at your institution to reenvision what it means to be a Catholic college or university when so many students at CCUs do not identity as Catholic? If there is such a need, what would you change?
3. What can colleges and universities learn from the CCUs listed in table 3 that already enroll and graduate high proportions of first-generation and low-income students?
4. What is your institution's history regarding educating mainly white immigrant Catholics while benefiting from slavery and the dis-

placement of Indigenous communities? What has been and can be done to educate your campus community about this history? What other measures can or should be taken in this regard?

5. In the introduction to this volume, Prusak and Reed-Bouley claim that Catholic social thought can serve as an anchor for CCUs in these turbulent times. Nichols focuses on Catholicism's theological anthropology and resulting principle of the common good as touchstones for the goal of educating first-generation and low-income students. What elements of Catholic social thought (e.g., symbols, stories from your founding, lives of holy women and men, principles, biblical narratives) do you or could you draw upon to articulate your own institution's commitment to educating first-generation and low-income students (assuming that your institution embraces that commitment)?
6. As you conclude your discussion of this chapter, what are three to five initiatives you might affirm or undertake on your campus with respect to enrolling and graduating first-generation and low-income students? Or would you take issue with this goal? If so, why?

Notes

1. See John W. Meyer and Brian Rowan, "Institutionalized Organizations: Formal Structure as Myth and Ceremony," *American Journal of Sociology* 83, no. 2 (1977): 340–63.

2. See Tammy MacLean, Barrie E. Litzky, and D. Kip Holderness, "When Organizations Don't Walk Their Talk: A Cross-Level Examination of How Decoupling Formal Ethics Programs Affects Organizational Members," *Journal of Business Ethics* 128, no. 2 (2015): 351–68, at 364. See also Michael Delucchi, "Staking a Claim: The Decoupling of Liberal Arts Mission Statements from Baccalaureate Degrees Awarded in Higher Education," *Sociological Inquiry* 70, no. 2 (2000): 157–71.

3. Pope Paul VI, *Octogesima Adveniens* (May 14, 1971), 4, www.vatican.va.

4. Peace Bransberger, Colleen Falkenstern, and Patrick Lane, "Knocking at the College Door: Projections of High School Graduates," Western Interstate Commission for Higher Education, December 2020, https://files.eric.ed.gov/fulltext/ED610996.pdf.

5. National Center for Education Statistics, "State of Education" (2020), https://nces.ed.gov.

6. Samuel D. Maseus and Lucy A. LePeau, "Navigating Neoliberal Organizational Cultures: Implications for Higher Education Leaders Advancing Social Justice Agendas," in *Higher Education Administration for Social Justice and Equity: Critical Perspectives for Leadership*, ed. Adrianna Kezar and Julie Posselt (New York: Routledge, 2019), 209–24.

7. Maseus and LePeau, "Navigating Neoliberal Organizational Cultures," 212.

8. Michael J. Sandel, *The Tyranny of Merit: What's Become of the Common Good?* (New York: Farrar, Straus and Giroux, 2020), 59.

9. Sandel, *Tyranny of Merit*, 25.

10. Sandel, *Tyranny of Merit*, 178.

11. Gerald J. Beyer, *Just Universities: Catholic Social Teaching Confronts Corporatized Higher Education* (New York: Fordham University Press, 2021), 37.

12. See Anthony S. Bryk, Valerie E. Lee, and Peter B. Holland, *Catholic Schools and the Common Good* (Cambridge, MA: Harvard University Press, 1993). For a summary of the mission and influence of the earliest schools, see also Michael T. Rizzi, "We've Been Here Before: A Brief History of Catholic Higher Education in America," *Journal of Catholic Higher Education* 37, no. 2 (2018): 153–74, esp. 155.

13. Erika Lee, *America for Americans: A History of Xenophobia in the United States* (New York: Basic Books, 2019), 57.

14. Benjamin Justice and Colin Macleod, *Have a Little Faith: Religion, Democracy, and the American Public School* (Chicago: University of Chicago Press, 2016).

15. See enrollments over time, updated annually, at the National Catholic Education Association, https://www.ncea.org.

16. John R. Thelin, *A History of American Higher Education* (Baltimore: Johns Hopkins University Press, 2004), 142.

17. John S. Brubacher and Willis Rudy, *Higher Education in Transition: A History of American Colleges and Universities* (New Brunswick, NJ: Transaction Publishers, 1997), 75.

18. Lisa A. Keister, "Upward Wealth Mobility: Exploring the Roman Catholic Advantage," *Social Forces* 85, no. 3 (2007): 1195–225.

19. William V. D'Antonio, James D. Davidson, Dean R. Hoge, and Katherine Meyer, *American Catholics: Gender, Generation, and Commitment* (Walnut Creek, CA: AltaMira Press, 2001), as cited in Keister, "Upward Wealth Mobility," 1199.

20. Hosffman Ospino and Patricia Weitzel-O'Neill, "Catholic Schools Serving Hispanic Families: Insights from the 2014 National Survey," *Journal of Catholic Education* 19, no. 2 (2016): 54–80.

21. Richard J. Murnane, Sean F. Reardon, Preeya P. Mbekeani, and Anne Lamb, "Who Goes to Private School?" *Education Next* 18, no. 4 (2018): 58–66, available (though without pagination) at https://www.educationnext.org/who-goes-private-school-long-term-enrollment-trends-family-income/.

22. Center for Applied Research in the Apostolate, "Frequently Requested Church Statistics," http://cara.georgetown.edu/frequently-requested-church-statistics/.

23. Margaret F. Brinig and Nichole Stelle Garnett, *Lost Classroom, Lost Community* (Chicago: University of Chicago Press, 2014).

24. See United States Census Bureau, Current Population Survey 2013, https://www.census.gov/programs-surveys/cps.html.

25. See Ospino and Weitzel-O'Neill, "Catholic Schools in an Increasingly Hispanic Church," and Sarah M. Ovink, *Race, Class, and Choice in Latino/a Higher Education: Pathways in the College-for-All Era* (New York: Palgrave Macmillan, 2017).

26. Murnane et al., "Who Goes to Private School?"

27. See National Catholic Educational Association, "Data Brief: Catholic School Enrollment and School Closures, Post-COVID-19," February 9, 2021, https://www.ncea.org/NCEA/Who_We_Are/About_Catholic_Schools/Catholic_School_Data/NCEA/Who_We_Are/About_Catholic_Schools/Catholic_School_Data/Catholic_School_Data.aspx?hkey=8e90e6aa-b9c4-456b-a488-6397f3640f05.

28. See, e.g., the articles in the *Journal of Catholic Higher Education* 34, no. 1 (2015), originating from a fall 2014 conference at King's College (PA) on "The Idea of a Catholic College."

29. See, e.g., Beyer, *Just Universities*.

30. Data can be found in *The American Freshman: National Norms*, prepared each year by the Cooperative Institutional Research Program at UCLA, https://www.heri.ucla.edu/monographs/TheAmericanFreshman2019.pdf.

31. Data for Catholic school enrollment starting in 1919 show that the largest number of students enrolled in K–12 Catholic education was in the fall of 1960, when over 5 million students attended Catholic elementary and secondary schools. This number has dropped to about 1.6 million today. See enrollments over time, updated annually, at the National Catholic Education Association website, https://www.ncea.org.

32. See Michael Lipka. "A Closer Look at Catholic America," Pew Research, September 14, 2015, https://www.pewresearch.org/fact-tank/2015/09/14/a-closer-look-at-catholic-america/, and Center for Applied Research in the Apostolate at Georgetown University, "Hispanic Catholics: Fact Sheet," https://cara.georgetown.edu/staff/webpages/Hispanic%20Catholic%20Fact%20Sheet.pdf.

33. See the official definition at https://sites.ed.gov/hispanic-initiative/hispanic-serving-institutions-hsis/.

34. See Farran Powell and Josh Moody, "See Which Catholic University Is Highest Ranked," *U.S. New & World Report*, April 14, 2021, https://www.usnews.com/education/best-colleges/slideshows/explore-the-highest-ranked-catholic-national-universities. Data in this table come from three sources. The College Scorecard provides data on the proportion of undergraduate students who are first-generation college and receive Pell grants, as well as students' families' median income. The Opportunity Insights Project provides data on the percentage of students enrolled whose families were in the top 20 percent of family income. For a full description of the measures, see Raj Chetty, John N. Friedman, Emmanuel Saez, Nicholas Turner, and Danny Yagan, "Mobility Report Cards: The Role of Colleges in Intergenerational Mobility," *Working Papers* 2017-059, Human Capital and Economic Opportunity Working Group, https://ideas.repec.org/p/hka/wpaper/2017-059.html. Finally, the Department of Education (IPEDS data) provides the percent of the 2018 class who were transfer students. The term "first-generation college student" includes students whose parents have no college experience.

35. Thanks to Nadine T. Jalandoni, director of research at the Association of Catholic Colleges and Universities, for providing this information in September 2020.

36. See Laura Nichols, "The Role of Catholic Schools in Reducing Educational and Economic Inequality," *Integritas* 9, no. 4 (2017): 1–25.

37. See Heather Adams, "It Takes a Village (or an Entire State) to Transform Transfer," *Inside Higher Ed*, June 24, 2021, https://www.insidehighered.com/blogs/tackling-transfer/it-takes-village-or-entire-state-transform-transfer.

38. See Gregory M. Eirich, "Parental Religiosity and Children's Educational Attainment in the United States," in *Religion, Work and Inequality*, ed. Lisa A. Keister, John McCarthy, and Roger Finke (Bingley, UK: Emerald Group Publishing, 2012), 153–81.

39. See Abigail Wozniak, "Going Away to College? School Distance as a Barrier to Higher Education," EconoFact, March 22, 2018, https://econofact.org/going-away-to-college-school-distance-as-a-barrier-to-higher-education.

40. See Michael M. Carnes, "Alma Mater, Mater Exulum: Jesuit Education and Immigration in America: A Moral Framework Rooted in History and Mission," in *Undocumented and in College: Students and Institutions in a Climate of National Hostility*, ed. Terry-Ann Jones and Laura Nichols (New York: Fordham University Press, 2017), 84–103.

41. Pope Francis, *Fratelli Tutti* (October 3, 2020) 121.

42. By "corporatization," I mean, following Gerald Beyer, "an institution that is characterized by processes, decisional criteria, expectations, orga-

nizational culture, and operating practices that are taken from, and have their origins in, the modern business corporation." See *Just Universities*, 14–15.

43. See Deborah L. Coe and James D. Davidson, "The Origins of Legacy Admissions: A Sociological Explanation," *Review of Religious Research* 52, no. 3 (2011): 233–47, at 242. See also Matthew S. Kraatz, Marc J. Ventresca, and Lina Deng, "Precarious Values and Mundane Innovations: Enrollment Management in American Liberal Arts Colleges," *Academy of Management Journal* 53, no. 6 (2010): 1521–45.

44. For example, for the cohort of students who started college in 2012, only 62 percent had a degree in six years if they started at a public college, versus 74 percent of those who started at a private, nonprofit. See Doug Shapiro, Afet Dundar, Faye Huie, Phoebe K. Wakhungu, Ayesha Bhimdiwala, and Sean E. Wilson, "Completing College: A National View of Student Completion Rates—Fall 2012 Cohort (Signature Report No. 16)," National Student Clearinghouse Research Center, December 2018, https://nscresearchcenter.org/wp-content/uploads/SignatureReport16.pdf, 12. Students who start at two-year institutions have even lower rates of degree completion.

45. See Mickey L. Fenzel, *Improving Urban Middle Schools: Lessons from the Nativity Schools* (New York: State University of New York Press, 2009) and Laura Nichols, *The Journey Before Us: First-Generation Pathways from Middle School to College* (New Brunswick, NJ: Rutgers University Press, 2020).

46. See Stephen N. Katsouros, *Come to Believe: How the Jesuits Are Reinventing Education (Again)* (Maryknoll, NY: Orbis, 2017) and G. R. Kearney, *More Than a Dream: How One School's Vision Is Changing the World* (Chicago: Loyola Press, 2008).

47. For information on connecting data to transfer initiatives, see Abby Miller, Sue Clery, and Amy Topper, *Assessing the Capacity of IPEDS to Collect Transfer Student Data*, National Postsecondary Education Cooperative, https://nces.ed.gov/ipeds/pdf/NPEC/data/NPEC_Paper_IPEDS_Transfer_Students_Data_2018.pdf.

48. See "Georgetown Reflects on Slavery, Memory, and Reconciliation: For Descendants," https://www.georgetown.edu/slavery/descendants/, and Lauren Loftus, "Reconciliation," *Santa Clara Magazine*, July 1, 2019, https://magazine.scu.edu/magazines/summer-2019/reconciliation/.

49. Maseus and LePeau, "Navigating Neoliberal Organizational Cultures," 211.

50. See Kathleen Maas Weigert, Kurt Schlichting, and Jay Brandenberger, "Institutional Commitment to the Catholic Social Tradition: Implicit or Explicit?" *Journal of Catholic Higher Education* 37, no. 1 (2018): 29–51.

51. See Adrianna Kezar and Julie Posselt, *Higher Education Administration for Social Justice and Equity* (New York: Routledge, 2020).

52. See the announcement on the website of the higher education consulting firm Credo, "Association of Catholic Colleges and Universities and Credo Announce 1st Cohort for Student Success," May 13, 2021, https://www.credohighered.com/blog/association-of-catholic-colleges-and-universities-credo-announce-1st-cohort-for-student-success. The CCUs involved are Assumption College (MA), Gwynedd Mercy University (PA), Newman University (KS), Mount St. Mary's University (MD), and University of St. Francis (IL).

2

"CONTRARY TO THE TENETS OF CHRISTIAN SOCIAL JUSTICE"

Racism and Catholic Social Thought in Catholic Higher Education

Tia Noelle Pratt and Maureen O'Connell

Each of the approximately 250 institutions of Catholic higher education in the United States has a unique identity rooted in its mission and often the distinctive charism of its founding religious order. Despite thoughtfully crafted mission statements that articulate institutions' identity and values, metrics of equality and equity provide evidence of the ways racism is embedded throughout the structures of these colleges and universities. For example, regarding admissions, the Association of Catholic Colleges and Universities (ACCU) reports that, as of 2018, Black, Indigenous, People of Color (BIPOC) students made up 43 percent of the roughly 850,000 undergraduates in Catholic institutions in the United States.[1] However, Gerald Beyer notes that minority students are "concentrated in less selective Catholic institutions," which have fewer resources to dedicate toward student success, leaving elite institutions more racially homogenous than less selective institutions.[2] In terms of graduation rates, while 80 percent of Catholic institutions report higher graduation rates than the national average, including for Black and Hispanic populations, the ACCU acknowledges in a 2017 report that "Catholic higher education is not immune to the gap in degree obtainment" that plagues the sector more broadly, in which Black students graduate at a rate nearly 20 percent lower than their white counterparts.[3] With respect to college debt, the average white graduate will have repaid 95 percent of student loans twenty years after graduation, whereas the average Black graduate will still owe 95 percent at that point.[4] Although the ACCU does not report the racial demographics of executive leadership (as it does for gender), the Association of Jesuit Colleges and Universities (AJCU) announced its first Black president among its twenty-eight member schools in 2020, which leads us to conclude that Catholic institutions likely fall below the benchmark of 14 percent of racial minorities in executive leadership in the broader sector as of 2020.[5] Beyer's analysis of the most recent data available from the Postsecondary Education Data System indicates that Black faculty make up less than 4 percent of tenure track or tenured faculty in Catholic colleges and universities with tenure systems; Latino or Hispanic faculty make up just over 4 percent.[6] No central clearing house exists for assessing curricular commitments to diversity, equity, and inclusion, itself a problematic indicator of levels of commitment in light of the adage "what you measure grows."[7]

It would be tempting to think that this evidence of racial inequity is merely a reflection of contemporary dynamics of racism in higher education writ large, and that if Catholic institutions are not immune, they are not particularly responsible. While the former may be true, we contend that it is more accurate to say that Catholic higher education has benefited from the dynamics of racism in the wider society, and more specifically the dynamics of racism *within* the Church itself, in order to expand Catholic higher education's reach, to solidify its brand, and to attract students. To that end, Catholic institutions of higher education carry a level of responsibility for our present social reality. Our goal is to help identify that responsibility and suggest ways of rectifying the harm.

Because we understand that some reading this volume may be exploring issues of race and racism in Catholic higher education for the first time, after an autobiographical analysis showing how being steeped in Philadelphia's Catholicism influenced our educations and experiences of race and racism, the chapter offers an exegesis of three key models that shape our analysis: race relations, racial justice, and anti-racism. Subsequently, we analyze a case study in light of these models to identify how the thorny dynamics of racial inequity in the past have set the conditions for more of the same in contemporary Catholic higher education and how a failure to acknowledge that past assures it will continue to repeat itself. We conclude by offering some recommendations for creating an anti-racist system and community within Catholic higher education.

Our Catholic Education Stories: Maureen O'Connell's Path to This Chapter

I grew up in a suburban neighborhood, which shared a county line with the northern reaches of Philadelphia, and am deeply tethered to Catholic spaces there, since my siblings and I attended the same Catholic elementary school as our parents and their siblings. I am a thorough product of Catholic education in the archdiocese, including a private suburban high school sponsored by the Religious Sisters of Mercy and then an undergraduate degree from Saint Joseph's University. The Catholic Church's commitment to educating white Catholics in the Archdiocese of Philadelphia made my own education, including my advanced degree from a Jesuit institution in another diocese, possible and practically debt-free. My immigrant great-grandparents belonged to a Catholic parish that ensured a spot for their children in Philadelphia's Catholic primary and secondary schools. My high school-educated grandparents achieved the goal of a college education for their sons in Philadelphia's Catholic universities, whose mission focused on educating the "sons of immigrants." My father created an admissions legacy for me and my siblings at his increasingly elite alma mater of Villanova University, even if we instead attended its storied rival, Saint Joseph's. My siblings and I coupled his advanced degree-level earnings with merit-based aid that our private Catholic secondary educations helped us secure, which in turn ensured we would graduate from college without debt; and my brother can now dedicate more of his own debt-free, advanced-degree earnings to college savings for my double legacy niece and nephews when they head to college less than a decade from now.

Research on my family's history in Philadelphia, dating back to the antebellum period, has helped me to recognize just how thoroughly white my Catholic educational experience was, including and certainly most notably for this chapter my Catholic higher education in Philadelphia.[8] There were the obvious markers of whiteness, many of which linger in most Catholic institutions of higher education in the Philadelphia metropolitan area: a predominantly white student body and a supermajority white faculty and senior administrators; a Eurocentric curriculum; a largely racially segregated student body, especially during Catholic liturgy and rituals. But there were also more subtle markers, undertows of whiteness, in my Catholic higher education that ebbed the campus community, particularly its white members, away from movements of social change. These have only become evident to me as I have joined other white Catholics who attempt to respond to the invitations, if not demands, for racial equity in Catholic communities. One of those undercurrents includes a missionary sensibility when it comes to understanding and responding to racial inequity. In other words, through an emphasis on faith that does service, I learned to love the neighbor with charity but not necessarily by asking what factors might be *making* them poor. I learned to see economic and racial differences through the lens of need and deficit, which only reinforced a sense of my own sufficiency and capabilities. Another undercurrent of whiteness in my educational experience was a form of Christian humanism that understood white humans as both the norm and the exemplar. I certainly learned of the contributions of "exhibits" of Black excellence, to borrow from historian Ibram Kendi.[9] But I also learned to silo those Black exhibits—whether via isolated pockets in the curriculum or appendages to syllabi, or via separate student clubs and leadership opportunities—in a way that would ensure that white supremacy would remain intact. I also learned to settle for de facto explanations of racial segregation and inequality—for example, the view that such separations and inequalities were the result of personal preferences for sameness or poor personal choices with bad economic consequences—that whitewashed a history of structural and de jure causes at the hands of government and ecclesial authorities.[10] I learned through silence and inaction that the Church—its hierarchy, institutions, teaching, and so on—are exempt from critical questioning about current realities. So not only did I *not* learn how to be curious and analytical about racial inequality, but I also learned how to compartmentalize the disruptive things I did learn and experience when it came to racial inequality.

In short, while it would be hard to argue that my degree from a Catholic institution of higher education is not one of the reasons for my social mobility, current professional success, and financial stability, it is also hard not to pin my underdeveloped capabilities for anti-racism on my Catholic college experience as well. I am also struck by how little has changed between being an undergraduate myself and teaching undergraduates today.

Our Catholic Education Stories: Tia Noelle Pratt's Path to This Chapter

I was educated in Philadelphia's Catholic schools from first grade through my bachelor's degree. While I left Philadelphia for my graduate studies, I did not leave the Catholic school system, receiving my master's and doctoral degrees from a Jesuit university. I grew up in Philadelphia's "Catholic Bubble," meaning my education and much of my social life took place in Catholic spaces. However, as an African American, I was exposed to life outside of the bubble as well. The immediate family of my childhood in Philadelphia—my mother, her siblings, and my grandparents, my grandfather's sister, and her family, as well as my great-grandmother, her siblings in Philadelphia, and their families—were all practicing Catholics. However, my grandmother's siblings and their families were not Catholic. Because there are so few African American Catholics relative to the number of African Americans and the number of Catholics in the United States, it is highly likely that, like me, African American Catholics will have family members and others they are close to who are not Catholic.

I spent the first part of my childhood as a member of a predominantly Black parish, one of many in Philadelphia that has closed or merged over the last few decades. So the idea that there are "no Black Catholics" or that being Black and Catholic is an anomaly was not part of my early experience. My grandfather is originally from New Orleans, and that part of my family—his many aunts, uncles, cousins, and their families—has been Catholic for the hundreds of years for which we have records, and most likely for hundreds of years before that. Because of those family members, I knew New Orleans to be a bastion of Black Catholics in the United States. Additionally, growing up in one of Philadelphia's predominantly Black parishes meant that I was exposed to Philadelphia's other predominantly Black parishes as well. Consequently, I knew that there was a structural component, that is, parishes in numerous cities, to Black Catholics' place in the Catholic Church.

I spent the first part of my childhood believing that everyone knew this same reality I knew about Black Catholics. Then, the summer I was twelve years old, my mother bought a house, and we moved. It was only to the next zip code over and still in West Philadelphia. Yet we moved from a predominantly Black neighborhood to a predominantly white neighborhood. As she had since I was in first grade, my mother registered me to attend our parish elementary school. What was different this time is that I went from a school where all the children were Black to a school where I was the first Black child ever to attend the school—in 1989. Years later, when I earned my PhD, one of the teachers from the school told me how proud she was of me and that I "showed them."

What I didn't know until that conversation was that there had been teachers in the school who didn't want me there because they thought I would "bring down the school." Me—a chubby twelve-year-old who still wore her hair in braids every day! I was about as much of a danger to the school as six-year-old Ruby Bridges had been with her white ankle socks and ribbons in her hair. Nevertheless, although our childhoods were decades apart, we both experienced white adults who considered us a threat. The key difference was that I did not need armed federal marshals escorting me to school. Someone must have had the forethought to tell those teachers that, as a Catholic child who had received all my sacraments to date and lived in the parish, they could not keep me out of the school. Yes, at that time, my new school required that all students be Catholic and live in the geographic boundaries of the parish. My former school had given up those requirements long before. Catholic schools in white neighborhoods protect their whiteness by refusing to admit non-Catholics and not evangelizing newcomers when the neighborhood changes. Thus, Black folks are kept out of both Catholic churches and Catholic schools.[11] As neighborhoods inevitably change, this practice means that, after a few decades, churches close. Because I was born with a sociologist's mind and have been Black all my life, I knew—yes, at twelve—that there might be kids who didn't want to talk to me or parents who didn't want their kids to talk to me. And the fact that there were teachers who felt that way in 1989 shows the extent to which whiteness will go to protect itself.

Three Models: Race Relations, Racial Justice, and Anti-Racism

In light of our experiences in Catholic higher education, we recognize that conceptualizing Catholic social thought (CST) primarily in terms of the seven principles of Catholic social teaching spelled out by the United States Conference of Catholic Bishops both centers the conversation in whiteness and limits our understanding and responses to racism.[12] It misses cultures of white dominance and the structural realities of racism. Consequently, this chapter, like in fact this volume, is about broadening the concept of CST and amplifying its efficacy in the context of Catholic higher education. To this end, let us briefly clarify three models of understanding racism: interpersonal, systemic, and white supremacy. These models conceptualize racism differently, but they all concern anti-Blackness—a specific form of racism that targets Blackness because of its hypervisibility in U.S. society.[13] Interpersonal racism couches racism in the context of encounters between individuals or groups of individuals of different races shaped by racial bias; it tends to be what comes to mind when most people think of racism. Systemic racism considers the ways racial identity informs how the social institutions and systems that shape civil society serve and are accountable to people; since we live our lives within the systems and institutions of society, this form of racism is inescapable for racial minorities. Yet, because it is embedded in society's systems, it is often invisible to the white people who perpetuate it and benefit from it.[14] White supremacy is a cultural reality in which whiteness and white people are valued more than other racial or ethnic groups; this has been considered the ethos of America or the central organizing framework of our collective self-understanding.[15]

With these three models of racism in mind, we offer three approaches for confronting racism in society: race relations, racial justice, and anti-racism. The race relations model focuses on personal racism. It frames racism as extreme prejudice that manifests itself as specific acts of violence that one person commits against another, such as racial slurs, racist graffiti, and other property damage. The race relations model describes racism through the common phrases *a few bad apples* or *that's just one person*. As such, the race relations model allows those who do not commit such acts to divorce themselves from any culpability for benefiting from the climate of fear and intimidation such acts create. Additionally, adherence to this model allows a denial of responsibility for the ways such fear and intimidation create the intended atmosphere that prevents marginalized groups from seeking social change. The absence of any pushback from minoritized groups allows racist practices and policies to become further embedded in societal systems. Thus, the climate of fear and intimidation is intended to keep African Americans and other marginalized people from challenging such systems.

The racial justice model elevates the understanding of racism by moving the discourse away from merely an individual level to a systemic level. The racial justice model underscores how societal systems create and perpetuate racism through policies such as redlining, voter suppression laws, and other tactics that target specific racial groups with near surgical precision. For example, when the minimum wage was first enacted as part of the New Deal, it did not apply to farmworkers and domestic workers—jobs disproportionately held by African Americans, particularly in the South.[16] After World War II, African American veterans were prohibited from using the GI Bill to attend college and from receiving low-interest home mortgages, even though they had risked their lives in service to their country in equal measure to their white counterparts. Against this background, it is easy to see why African Americans have not caught up to the level of generational wealth produced by the GI Bill nearly eighty years after the end of World War II.[17] The racial justice model allows us to see how the seemingly personal acts on which the race relations model fixates can be viewed as acts toward an entire group and not just an individual, as well as acts that reflect and sustain systems and cultures that award advantage and disadvantage based on race. Thus, the race relations model allows us to understand how acts such as attacking an Asian American senior citizen on the street or burning a historically Black Church can be prosecuted as hate crimes against an entire community.

The anti-racism model elevates the discourse beyond the other two models. Its purpose is to dismantle and then rebuild the structures that are named in the racial justice model and are rooted in the climate of fear and intimidation created by the acts of violence that the race relations model fixes on. Those doing the work of anti-racism seek, first, to break down the societal systems whose cultures of white supremacy inhibit equity in society and, second, to build new systems that are equitable and rooted in justice. This work is essential in Catholic higher education. Too often, there is a gulf between what institutions *say* they value and what their practices and policies *show* they value. To be effective, anti-racism work must be engaged in every facet of college and university life—including board leadership, curriculum, hiring, performance evaluation, contract bidding, and recruitment and retention of students and employees.

A Case Study

The racial context of our Catholic educations in Philadelphia, as well as the forms of racism and resistance to it that we just mapped out, is illuminated by the following case study.

In December 1937, Ms. Ethel Lee wrote a letter to Br. Edwin Anselm, FSC, President of La Salle College. She wrote in her role as the Secretary of the Federated Colored Catholics (FCC) of Philadelphia, the local chapter of a national organization created a decade earlier to address the issue of segregation in America's Catholic schools, particularly its colleges.[18] In that letter, the FCC inquired why La Salle had denied admission to James Richardson, a Black applicant from West Philadelphia Catholic High School for Boys, where the De La Salle Christian Brothers themselves had an active presence. Mr. Richardson had received a scholarship named for the archdiocese's Cardinal, Joseph

Dougherty, who had just launched an archdiocesan-wide appeal to raise tuition funds for any student who wished to attend one of Philadelphia's six independent Catholic colleges.[19] The second Black applicant to La Salle, Harvey Scott, was ready to pay his tuition in cash, yet was denied admission. The FCC explained to Br. Anselm that, from its perspective, La Salle's "conduct [was] far removed from the principles upon which your noble order was founded," and also seemed "contrary to the tenets of Christian social justice."[20] Moreover, these "uncatholic" actions would "serve but to prolong racial misunderstanding."[21] Philadelphia's FCC then wrote a subsequent letter to Philadelphia's Cardinal Joseph Dougherty, calling his attention to this situation and naming his hypocrisy in light of his recently launched tuition appeal while at the same permitting institutions like La Salle to deny admission to Black students.[22]

Perhaps as a result of the FCC's strategic decision to alert Dougherty, La Salle's senior administration "took up the question of admitting Catholic Negros" at the February 1938 meeting of the Community Council, akin to an executive cabinet. It was the second item addressed—after a discussion of introducing Italian language instruction. Minutes from the meeting indicate that the discussion "of admitting Catholic Negroes" was deemed important, because "similar cases" to the one at hand could arise; the refusal to admit other Black students could "possibly reach the ears of His Eminence"; and an "Interracial College Association," of which La Salle students were members, was "soliciting the aid of Catholic Colleges [on] behalf of the Catholic Negro." In light of these factors, it was "the general opinion of the Council that a favorable attitude should be adopted, if the Catholic Negro meets all the College entrance requirements."[23] La Salle admitted its first Black student in 1938 but did not graduate its first Black student until 1946. Whether admission was ever extended to James Richardson or Harvey Scott is unclear; Mr. Scott enrolled at a non-Catholic university while Mr. Richardson enrolled at Villanova University and graduated from there in 1941.

The case occurred nearly 85 years ago. Some reading this volume may believe, erroneously, that, because Mr. Richardson, Ms. Lee, Br. Anselm, and Cardinal Dougherty are deceased (in some cases for decades), the racism in the Church has passed into the annals of history. Eighty-five years really is not that long, however, especially when we consider that the anti-Blackness that prevented Mr. Richardson from enrolling at La Salle continues to persist in myriad Catholic spaces, including Catholic colleges and universities. We contend that candor with institutional histories like the ones we share is critical for disrupting the way that history continues to play out in institutions of Catholic higher education, particularly those couching current "diversity, equity, and inclusion" initiatives in the principles of CST.[24] In what follows, we map how this past has created our present reality.

The three models for understanding racism provide distinct ways of learning from the case. The Race Relations Model fixes simply on the act of discrimination by Br. Anselm against Mr. Richardson. Br. Anselm is the "bad apple" or "just one person" who discriminated against Mr. Richardson by denying him admission to La Salle College because of his race. While not incorrect, the Race Relations Model is insufficient. First, if this was simply a matter of one person discriminating against another, this matter would have never reached Br. Anselm's presidential desk. It did so because all of the people in the chain of command, starting with the admissions officer who would have first reviewed Mr. Richardson's application, believed he should not be admitted despite his academic qualifications and his scholarship named for the then-Archbishop of Philadelphia. The fact that this incident reached the president of La Salle College indicates a culture of anti-Blackness throughout the institution. Thus, the Race Relations Model is an inadequate tool of analysis.

Using the Racial Justice Model not only illuminates the scope of the anti-Black racism in this example, but it also highlights the deficiencies in the Race Relations Model. The Racial Justice Model allows us to see the systemic realities of the case. It also draws out the conflicts that can exist within systems. Mr. Richardson's scholarship, named for Cardinal Dougherty, indicated support from the Archdiocese of Philadelphia. Yet, that support was not affirmed throughout Catholic spaces, namely, La Salle College—hence, the letter from Ms. Lee.

The Anti-Racism Model compels us to acknowledge the myriad ways racism is embedded in societal systems as well as specific institutions. In the case, using the Anti-Racism Model would necessitate that La Salle completely overhaul its written policies, established practices, and admissions procedures. That overhaul would consider how to attract applicants like Mr. Richardson as well as how to retain such students once they enroll. The fact that so many higher education institutions are undertaking this work *now* indicates just how little progress has been made in the more than 80 years since Mr. Richardson was denied admission to La Salle College.

Anti-racism work is some of the most difficult work an institution—especially a Catholic higher education institution—can do. It is especially difficult in Catholic higher education because it means these institutions must admit they have not always exhibited their foundational values.[25] In Catholic higher education, this essential work can be informed through a lens of CST—if we dare to imagine CST as addressing anti-racism directly instead of alluding to it through a generously broad interpretation of the seven oft-cited principles of Catholic social teaching, none of which directly addresses racism. Attention needs to be paid to the specific *injustices* in our society—in the work at hand, anti-Blackness. Sometimes we can understand what justice requires only by a deeper understanding of experiences of injustice.[26]

History Uninterrupted: The Past Is Present

The history of Catholic higher education capitalizing on Catholic anti-Blackness is another critical dimension that needs to be contended with in Catholic higher education if we wish to chart an anti-racist path forward. While this history is worthy of a much more substantive review,[27] we use our case study to identify three historical moments that point to the interplay between structural racism and anti-Blackness in the context of the advancement of Catholic higher education for white Catholics.

First, Ms. Ethel Lee, Secretary of the Philadelphia Chapter of Federated Colored Catholics, was a member of a prominent Philadelphia Catholic family who themselves were descendants of Catholics once enslaved by Jesuits in Maryland. Because the financial future of the nation's first Catholic institution of higher education, and one of its most prominent today—Georgetown University—was made more viable by her ancestors, not as participants in that enterprise but as commodities on its balance sheet, it is not a stretch to say that the Lees, and the estimated 10,000 descendants of the 272 Jesuit-owned Catholics sold in 1838, also helped secure the future of the very idea of Catholic higher education in the United States. During the period of American slavery in the nineteenth century, many Catholic institutions relied on the unpaid labor of enslaved peoples to build physical infrastructure and to finance their enterprises, whether through the wealth accumulated through the sale of their bodies or their labor, which in some cases paid off debt and in others covered tuition costs.[28] Some of these same institutions contributed to a distinctive American Christian theology that supported racist ideas about the inferiority of Black people, justified racial segregation, and emphasized a missionary approach that prioritized the evangelization of enslaved souls over justice for enslaved persons.[29]

Second, two of the Black families named in this case, the Lees and the Richardsons, hailed from West Philadelphia, which by the 1930s had already been redlined by appraisers with the Home Owners Loan Corporation for federal disinvestment in the name of redirecting social welfare programs associated with homeownership toward the suburbs and white buyers.[30] White Catholic families and, perhaps more important, Cardinal Dougherty and his team already had planned to develop new parishes in the green-lined suburbs, from which the Lees and Richardsons would be excluded. These neighborhoods, with their predominantly white parish schools and high schools, became the pipeline that fueled Catholic institutions, especially as their residents' abilities to pay a larger share of tuition became an increasingly attractive feature of their applications.[31]

In other words, since the mid-twentieth century, Catholic colleges and universities reaped the benefits of federally mandated housing segregation by creating largely white-only admissions pipelines that tapped largely white-only suburban parish schools and high schools. The growth of these "feeder schools" is linked to federal mortgage assistance offered to white homeowners and the desire of white Catholics to escape "invasions" of peoples of color into urban parishes. As costs for Catholic higher education grew exponentially toward the end of last century and into the first decades of the twenty-first, subsequent generations of white Catholic families were better positioned to convert equity gained through federally backed mortgages into education equity, which in turn enabled Catholic institutions to meet tuition-dependent bottom lines.[32] In the same way that they had been contained in neighborhoods marked for federal disinvestment in the 1930s through the 1960s, today most Black families, who are already marginalized by a significant gap in housing equity, are less likely to have their children recruited by top-tier colleges and universities. Subsequently, those students are relegated to less elite colleges and universities—institutions with fewer institutional resources to spend on their students' success and, for that reason, lower graduation rates.[33]

Third, our case is also emblematic of the reluctance on the part of the leadership of at least one Catholic institution, as well as the reluctance of Catholic ecclesial leadership in one of the country's leading archdioceses, to take a bold and unequivocal stance in support of racial integration and equity in the context of Catholic higher education. In fact, it was only the threat of negative optics that appears to have motivated leaders at La Salle to adopt a "favorable attitude" toward Black applicants; there was no meaningful attempt to welcome, much less re-orient, the institutional culture to foster a sense of belonging for Black applicants. Like much of what we see from Catholic higher education leadership today, La Salle's institutional response was preoccupied with optics, public performance, and a concern for impact on the bottom line.

There is a contemporary corollary to the justification that La Salle's Community Council provided in 1938: "a favorable attitude should be adopted, *if* the Catholic Negro meets all the College entrance requirements." In the context of corporatized higher education, which has increased the cost of college at a private institution by 129 percent between 1988 and 2018, the qualifiers "elite" and "white" have become increasingly correlated in admissions algorithms, evidenced by the declining numbers of students of color admitted to the nation's top institutions.[34] Catholic institutions, competing against each other as well as with private and public institutions in the marketplace of higher education, are no exceptions to this emerging admissions rule.[35] (See further Laura Nichols's chapter in this volume.) In other words, as was the case in 1937, precisely at a time that a college degree is deemed critical for social mobility, Black and Latino students are largely shut out of elite Catholic institutions, whose elite status in some ways depends on their exclusion. Less exclusive institutions are equally dependent upon their tuition contributions, regardless of the likelihood of degree completion or the disproportionate debt that students of color will incur. In brief, Br. Anselm's successors at financially struggling institutions (like La Salle currently) serve as catalysts for college debt by admitting economically disadvantaged students in order to meet budget projections while not adequately accompanying them to graduation. As was the case with Ethel Lee's ancestors, whose unpaid labor made the Jesuit legacy of higher education possible, Black marginalization contributes to making Catholic higher education financially viable today.

A Virtuous Circle or a Vicious Cycle?

In the introduction to this volume, Prusak and Reed-Bouley define CST as including "magisterial teaching, scholarship, and the lived experience of faithful Catholics and other people of good will." Catholic higher education cultivates these distinct facets of Catholic discipleship from generation to generation by integrating them into Catholic classrooms and campus life with the assistance of the "Catholic intellectual tradition," which Monika Hellwig characterized as the "classic treasures to be cherished, studied, and handed on; and the way of doing things that is the outcome of centuries of experience, prayer, and critical reflection."[36] In this way, the Catholic intellectual tradition, of which Catholic colleges and universities are unique stewards, serves as a conduit for CST.

To be sure, there are many examples of Catholic institutions of higher education relying on the Catholic intellectual tradition in orchestrating a generative relationship or virtuous circle with CST as a constitutive dimension of campus life. These instances should be celebrated. But that is not the case when we consider racism. When it comes to racism, we contend that too often a predominantly white understanding of what constitutes our Catholic intellectual tradition abets our institutions in replacing the virtuous circle of the mutually informing principles, actions, dispositions, and skills of CST with a vicious cycle of silence, recalcitrance, denial, and resistance. We see evidence of this claim in the historical case study and in the current climate of American Catholic higher education.

In our observation, cultures of white supremacy in our Catholic institutions of higher education render our communities as echo chambers for the ecclesial silences regarding systemic racism. In other words, Catholic institutions are ready to follow what many Catholic scholars characterize as the tepid lead of the magisterium, particularly the U.S. Conference of Catholic Bishops, when it comes to the problems of racial injustice, rather than take more prophetic stances.[37] In our case study, the administrative leadership at La Salle College measured its institutional commitment to racial integration in the late 1930s against Cardinal Dougherty's commitment to the same. He, and many of his successors to date, tended to view the situation of Black Catholics through the lens of a paternalistic missionarism (which meets the needs of individual people who are seen as a group to be fundamentally different and sacramentally deficient) and gradualism (in which policies change only if doing so benefits the institutional Church understood primarily as white). Dougherty himself stood in a troublesome tradition of official Church teaching around Black people: one of his predecessors in Philadelphia, Bishop Patrick Francis Kendrick, wrote a moral manual in 1840 to guide American priests in ministering to Catholic slaveowners.

Furthermore, the U.S. bishops continue to limit Catholic engagement in racial justice. In the aftermath of George Floyd's murder in May 2020, discussion of the #BlackLivesMatter movement moved into a new realm of Catholic discourse with high-profile, white bishops entering the conversation. What should have been a conversation that affirmed Blacks and Blackness in the Church became instead yet another way to center whiteness and perpetuate anti-Blackness. Evidence of U.S. episcopal leaders' lack of prophetic witness on this issue and their prioritization of white comfort over justice is not limited to our 85-year-old case. The contemporary episcopate provides evidence of the same.

For example, in July 2020, Archbishop William Lori of Baltimore published an article in *America* magazine entitled, "Archbishop Lori: How Church Teaching Can Help Explain Why 'Black Lives Matter.'"[38] The anti-Blackness begins in the very title. As one of us, Tia Noelle Pratt, commented in an article in *Commonweal*, the title conveys that the archbishop must *explain* why Black lives matter,[39] as if the fact that Black people are human beings who exist in this Church and this world is not enough. We know that the humanity of Black lives was not always recognized by the Roman Catholic Church,[40] and in the article Archbishop Lori makes himself the arbiter of whether or not Black humanity should be of any importance to those who have always mattered—whites and, in this case, white Catholics. He observes that the phrase "Black Lives Matter" is self-evident to many, but "divisive and partisan" to others. According to him, "the question before *us as Catholics* [emphasis added] is this: Is there a truth reflected in these words that transcends partisan platforms and ideological constructs, a truth that indeed resonates with the Gospel values that flow from our faith?" The "us" in this sentence is not Black Catholics; neither is it Native, Asian-American, Pacific Islander, or Latinx Catholics. Rather, the "us" in the sentence, the people he addresses, are his fellow white Catholics because whiteness, for him and so many others, is synonymous with "Catholic." This is the very essence of white supremacy. In the very next sentence, Archbishop Lori doubles down on this point by writing, "what should these three words mean for *us* [emphasis added] as Catholics?"

Archbishop Lori continues: "The words 'Black Lives Matter' should prompt *us* [emphasis added] to examine *our own* [emphasis added] consciences with regard to racism and spur *us* [emphasis added] on to advocate and work for racial justice." Once again, the word *us* is doing a lot of work. It is clear that Archbishop Lori is addressing only white Catholics and does not acknowledge that BIPOC Catholics are even part of the Church's tapestry. If Archbishop Lori had only stated that his piece was directed at white Catholics because BIPOC Catholics understand the destructive power of racism in a way whites will never be able to, this criticism would not be necessary. Instead, the archbishop of an archdiocese intimately connected to African-American Catholics (Baltimore) demonstrates absolutely no regard for the African-American Catholics in his episcopate or elsewhere. He chooses to embody the position of the white moderate refusing to push the limits of white comfort—his own or anyone else's. With this insulting response to African-Americans' demand for liberation as a benchmark, it is no wonder that Catholic higher education has fallen so woefully short in meeting calls for racial justice in its ranks.

Catholic higher education also figures as rocky soil where grassroots movements for racial justice are concerned, especially when we consider the institutional reluctance, if not outright resistance, to student-led movements for racial equity on many Catholic campuses. To return to our case study, in 1937 the Federated Colored Catholics invoked the emerging elements of CST in making their appeals for racial equity to La Salle's leadership.[41] In filling the silences around racial inequity in magisterial teaching, they embodied CST, as did the white student members of the Catholic Collegiate Interracial Council that La Salle leadership referenced. However, those efforts were not considered embodiments of Catholic identity in the 1930s, since they received little institutional investment at the college and diocesan levels.

We might ask similar questions today in light of the reception to movements for equity on Catholic campuses, particularly around racial equity.[42] In their June 24, 2020, public call to action posted on Black Perspectives (a blog of the African American Intellectual History Society), ten Black faculty and administrators from African American studies programs at nine Catholic institutions across the country challenged the sufficiency of public statements of solidarity from the leaders of Catholic higher education posted in the weeks following the police murders of George Floyd and Breonna Taylor. "Statements and apologies without clear plans for transformation and accountability are empty," they noted. "Worse, such incomplete approaches exacerbate conditions long in need of remedy."[43] Drawing attention to the collective power of Catholic campus communities, they rooted their action plan in principles of CST, such as the common good and the preferential option for the marginalized. Then they called for institutional commitments to remediate a variety of structures on campus that question the value of Black lives, including changes to campus policing, partnerships of mutuality with surrounding neighborhoods, just compensation for laborers, honest reckonings with campus histories, prioritizing Black needs in budgeting processes, and support for protesting students and faculty. As such, these colleagues embody CST, informed by the Catholic intellectual tradition. Their decision to post their statement outside the confines of Catholic higher education, and our challenge in finding evidence that their ideas gained any traction, provide further evidence of the vicious cycle of silence, recalcitrance, denial, and resistance. That the ACCU launched a Consortium of Diversity Officers in Catholic Higher Education in 2019 is certainly a positive step toward interrupting the vicious cycle we identify; centering that work on the voices of minoritized students, faculty, and colleagues, as opposed to predominantly white academic leadership, board members, and even bishops, will be critical for the efficacy of this initiative.[44]

Finally, Catholic higher education perpetuates the inherent whiteness of the canon of the Catholic intellectual tradition in treasuring Eurocentric classics and handing on Eurocentric methods of critical reflection and models of prayer. In the case discussed above, perhaps the blinders of a narrowly defined Catholic intellectual tradition kept the growing edge of CST around racial integration on the periphery and prevented mission-based racial integration from capturing the moral imagination of the college's leadership team. During La Salle College's Christian Brothers' Community Council meeting in 1939, robust discussion about adding Italian language instruction to the curriculum preceded the discussion of admitting Black students!

We recognize similar blinders and failed imaginations in contemporary institutional responses to Black colleagues' calls for institutional commitments to valuing Black lives on campus. For example, in the wake of 2020's reckoning with systemic racism, Loyola University Maryland decided to remove Flannery O'Connor's name from one of its dormitories and name the building instead for Servant of God Sr. Thea Bowman, FSPA. In making this change, the university cited racism in O'Connor's personal correspondence as well as "the need for residence halls to be a 'home and haven for those who live there'" with eponyms that reflect Jesuit values. However, limiting the controversy to Flannery O'Connor and "cancel culture" can be considered a "failure of imagination."[45] Renaming the residence hall is an opportunity to reflect on O'Connor's outsized place in the Catholic literary imagination and to reimagine the Catholic Church in the United States. Similarly, we invite reflection on reimagining the entire Catholic intellectual tradition, including CST. There is room in the Catholic literary tradition for more than Flannery O'Connor, and Catholic colleges and universities have a role to play in making that room.

Creating a Virtuous Circle of Anti-Racism in Catholic Higher Education

In "Letter from Birmingham Jail," Rev. Dr. Martin Luther King Jr. wrote that he had "almost reached the regrettable conclusion" that African-Americans' "great stumbling block in the stride toward freedom" was not members of violent white supremacist organizations, whom he referred to as "the White Citizen's Counciler or the Ku Klux

Klanner." Rather, it was "the white moderate who is more devoted to 'order' than to justice; who prefers a negative peace which is the absence of tension to a positive peace which is the presence of justice." Dr. King elaborates by saying that the white moderate "constantly says, 'I agree with you in the goal you seek, but I can't agree with your methods of direct action'" and "paternalistically believes he can set the timetable for another man's freedom," namely, "a 'more convenient season.'"[46] Contemporary white moderates say that they agree with the idea of "Black Lives Matter," but not the organization.[47] What is this if not paternalistically "set[ting] the timetable for another [person's] freedom"? Is Catholic higher education trying to do the same?

Those who say "Dr. King was about peace" when they really mean "I don't like that you're making me uncomfortable" have corrupted his message and likely do not know that one of King's six steps for nonviolent social change is direct action. In other words, disrupting societal systems and making privileged people uncomfortable is an essential piece of nonviolent social change.[48] Freedom cannot result from a blueprint designed and implemented by those who are already free. A vibrant, radical movement is thereby twisted, whitewashed, and made altogether milquetoast and ineffective. Consider the USCCB's use of the term "The Movement for Black Lives" in place of "Black Lives Matter."[49] This change in language is slight enough to be almost unnoticeable. Of course, that is the point. This seemingly benign alteration of wording would at first appear inconsequential. In fact, it allows for a complete reframing of the narrative. The USCCB's framing of the movement is not one that confronts racism in its many forms. Rather, it is another "gentle accompaniment" of white Catholics whose refusal to be uncomfortable is at the root of the continued perpetuation of white supremacy in the Church and its affiliated institutions.

Even though the diagnosis is bleak, we contend that Catholic higher education in the United States is in the unique position to offer more than gentle accompaniment. Rather, we can make significant and impactful change where racial equity and justice are concerned, turning to CST to cultivate transformation. And while doing so for the sake of the integrity of our institutions should be motivation enough, we also believe that integrating the resources afforded us by CST will bring the institutional stability and viability that racial segregation of the past century has falsely promised.

How, then, do we integrate the facets of our shared identities as well as of the members of our campus communities in Catholic institutions?

First, Catholic institutions of higher education can push the envelope where CST on racism is concerned by serving as thought and action partners, both for Catholic ecclesial leadership and for the lay faithful. This will entail ongoing public acknowledgement of the limitations of ecclesial teaching and institutional failings of the Catholic community, including campus communities, at the local and national levels. We can only transform that about which we are truthful. From there, Catholic institutions of higher education can foster a willingness to boldly grow ecclesial teaching, perhaps identifying new applications of familiar principles or by proposing entirely new principles that directly address racism.

For example, in her book *Birth of a Movement: Black Lives Matter in the Catholic Church*, Olga Segura calls on the USCCB to "address, through a formal pastoral letter, the harm that has been done to Black Americans by the Church and apologize for how the Church has been and continues to be complicit in white supremacy."[50] True accountability, Segura submits, can happen only by centering "those who are most ignored [and] most affected by unjust, white supremacist systems of oppression."[51] Such a document would move the institutional Church away from the individualistic orientation of the Race Relations Model to the Racial Justice Model's systemic orientation. Certainly, Catholic institutions of higher education can host and participate in such truth-telling initiatives, incorporating a variety of skill sets available in our campus communities to ensure meaningful impact. Moreover, if this pastoral letter is to accomplish the goals Segura sets out, it must also elevate ecclesial discourse to the Anti-Racism Model by giving clear direction on how to dismantle the white supremacy that continues to be embedded in the Church.[52] Again, members of our campus intellectual communities can bring a host of theoretical and practical knowledge to this dismantling work. Achieving this gargantuan, but not impossible, task requires first listening to those who have been oppressed and then entering into a dialogical relationship with those who have experiential and academic wisdom to share. In short, it would require embracing synodality not just between the pope and the bishops, but also between the bishops and the people. Catholic campus communities can be nodes of such generative and liberating synodality.[53]

Along these same lines, Catholic theologian MT Dávila recently posted on Twitter: "Do you think it is time for Catholic social teaching to have a specific principle called racial justice?" She went on to point out that "the entirety of the CST documentary heritage comes to us post the conquest of the Americas, and yet none of the magisterial documentation deals directly with it." Such a principle might serve as a "corrective to the dynamics of conquest and extraction."[54] The time has come for such a principle, and who better than communities of contemplation and action fostered by Catholic higher education to help develop this principle and bring it to life?

The pastoral letter that Segura calls for, as well as the expansion of Catholic social teaching that Dávila recommends, could and *should* be one and the same. The 2018 pastoral letter *Open Wide Our Hearts: The Enduring Call to Love* does not do the job. Though it was the first pastoral letter to address racism in nearly forty years, this long-overdue treatment of racism disappoints in two major ways. First, it limits the analysis of racism to the Race Relations Model, where discourse on racism has stagnated for far too long. Additionally, the process of creating and disseminating the letter was done backward. Instead of holding listening sessions to hear the concerns of lay Catholics, and then using that information to inform the letter, the USCCB's Ad Hoc Committee on Racism did the opposite. Only after the letter was written, approved by the full USCCB, and published did the Ad Hoc Committee on Racism conduct listening sessions. Once again, the bishops attempted to impose ideas on the faithful by choosing hierarchy over synodality, thereby communicating a disregard for the experiences of Catholics by not allowing those experiences to inform Church teaching.

Unsurprisingly, the blueprint for what Segura and Dávila discuss already exists. In a 2020 interview with *Our Sunday Visitor*, theologian M. Shawn Copeland outlined what such a pastoral letter might look like should she be asked to draft one:

> I would build on the notion of racism as a moral evil and a sin as taught in "Brothers and Sisters to Us," but stress that racism is not merely about rogue individuals who act viciously toward others. Racism forms part of the fabric of

> our social structures because it is embedded in our consciousness, in our thinking, in our action.[55]

In these two sentences, Copeland shows us what moving from the Race Relations Model to the Racial Justice Model looks like in the form of magisterial teaching. Her own affiliation at a Catholic university points to the role Catholic campus communities can play in fostering and implementing these ideas.

Until the bishops undertake the type of constructive action advocated by Segura and Dávila, it is up to the rest of us—namely the editors of, contributors to, and readers of this volume—to broaden CST by engaging it and living it in communities also trying to broaden their commitment to belonging. Catholic colleges and universities can be settings where this type of engagement can occur by amplifying the knowledge produced by scholars who work in this area and by inviting the local community to connect to that knowledge through lectures, workshops, and community-centered learning opportunities.

In order to engage in these action steps in distinctively Catholic ways, Catholic colleges and universities can expand capabilities for this work among all members of the campus community and people who partner with us by expanding the Catholic intellectual tradition beyond its current white parameters to include the wisdom of communities of color long excluded from it. Doing so will help heighten our awareness of the latent connection between what we teach, how we teach it, and why we teach. (See Anna Moreland and Mark Shiffman's chapter in this volume on the role of the liberal arts, as well as Vincent Miller's chapter on integral ecology as a catalyst for transdisciplinary scholarship and teaching.)

Earlier, we invoked Monika Hellwig's definition of the Catholic intellectual tradition as "classic treasures to be cherished, studied, and handed on; and the way of doing things that is the outcome of centuries of experience, prayer, and critical reflection." We propose an alternative paradigm, one that helps us see that these treasures are more than academic treatises and magisterial documents, and that our ways of handing them on can and should change if we wish to put our tradition at the service of fostering racial equity and justice. The sociologist Nancy T. Ammerman uses the lens of "culture and identity" to discuss the unique attributes that distinguish congregations from one another. Ammerman defines culture as "who we are and the world we have created to live in. It is the predictable patterns of who does what and habitual strategies for telling the world about the things held most dear."[56] She goes on to say that we can consider culture and identity by examining "activities, artifacts, and accounts," i.e., the things we do, the things we make, and the stories we tell about both.

For example, if we apply Ammerman's paradigm to the Metropolitan Museum of Art's Costume Institute's spring 2018 exhibition, "Heavenly Bodies: Fashion and the Catholic Imagination," we can appreciate the artifacts that were displayed as themselves embodiments of the Catholic intellectual tradition, in particular in how they expressed and shaped the Catholic imagination.[57] These creations should be considered alongside Michelangelo's *Pietà*, according to Ammerman's understanding of the artifacts created by and through religion. (As an aside, the rarely seen items on loan from the Vatican were accompanied by designs that invoked Catholic imagery by Gianni Versace, Dolce & Gabbana, Yves Saint Laurent, and John Galliano. The fact that the designers featured are white highlights the canon of whiteness discussed throughout this chapter.)

Examining the Catholic intellectual tradition from the perspective of activities, artifacts, and accounts might help us to recognize the latent impulses of anti-racism in our own Catholic tradition and to use our tradition to cultivate the dispositions and practices of anti-racism. Thinking about the Catholic intellectual tradition through the lens of "activities" would allow us to recognize a long and often forgotten history of marches and public actions, prayerful silence and disruptive laments, spoken word art and mural-making. With an eye on activities—otherwise put, what students are able to *do* in light of their exposure to the Catholic tradition and not simply what they *know*—we might dedicate more attention in our curricula and other learning spaces to introducing students to civic engagement, participatory action research, or community-based learning through a variety of pedagogies of social change. Embracing the "artifacts" approach to our Catholic intellectual tradition would deepen our appreciation for the material dimensions of our shared experiences on campus or interrupt us with the realization that such shared experiences may actually be lacking. We might pay more attention to the kinds of art displayed around campus and where that art is encountered, the names given to residence halls, the ritual aspects of our gatherings, and the physical touchstones of belonging on our campuses. For example, we might develop walking tours of our campus to introduce members of our communities to the complicated narratives of social change movements that have unfolded there.[58] Finally, approaching our Catholic intellectual tradition as "accounts" can help us prioritize our capabilities for telling and hearing stories, particularly painful or interruptive ones, in ways that build empathy, trust, and shared commitment to transformation. Attention to whose story counts or how we are accounting for contradictions in our institutional narratives can be tools for building equity. Catholic institutions might consider, for example, implementing Truth, Racial Healing, and Transformation practices, initiatives, and centers on their campuses.[59] In short, applying Ammerman's paradigm to the Catholic intellectual tradition heightens our awareness of the latent connections among what we teach, how we teach it, and, perhaps most important, why we do so.

Ultimately, we need to acknowledge that what is generally understood as the Catholic intellectual tradition is steeped in the canon of whiteness to which Catholic institutions dedicate much social, political, and economic capital. This entrenched whiteness is part of why systemic racism is so deeply embedded in Catholic higher education and the Church broadly understood. Breaking free of systemic racism requires reimagining the Catholic intellectual tradition along with CST. Flannery O'Connor, James Joyce, Michelangelo, Hildegard of Bingen, and Beethoven are just a few of the luminaries associated with the Catholic intellectual tradition. But there is every reason to include others, such as Louise Erdrich, Toni Morrison, Thea Bowman, FSPA, and Gianni Versace. Erdrich's and Morrison's writings invoke a very specific image of Catholicism that is informed by their experiences as Native American and African American women, respectively.[60] Sr. Thea Bowman famously told the U.S. Conference of Catholic Bishops, "I come to my Church fully functioning. I bring myself, my Black self, all that I am, all that I have, all that I hope to become, I bring my whole history, my traditions, my experience, my culture...as a gift to the Church."[61]

It is long past time for the Church and Catholic higher education to stop dismissing the gift of Blackness. De-colonizing the Catholic intellectual tradition increases capabilities for empathy and also points us toward perspectives and imaginations that have been overlooked or undervalued. To do so requires a willingness to dissipate the canon of whiteness that pervades Catholic higher education. It also depends on broadening the ranks of those who get to assert what counts as part of the intellectual canon. This will happen not only by diversifying faculty but also by retaining them long enough that they become incorporated into the pipeline of leadership through tenure, promotion to full professor, and advancement into senior leadership positions.

Conclusion: Expanding the Tenets of Christian Social Justice

If the initiatives we have presented here have any chance of success, then Catholic higher education institutions must turn the mirror on themselves. Announcing that an institution is now anti-racist is not enough. The institutions of Catholic higher education must be willing to apply the same level of critical self-reflection on themselves that they ask students and employees to undertake as individuals. When that happens, institutions will cease being stuck at the level of the Race Relations Model. Accomplishing that will first require institutions to ask themselves about the Mr. Richardsons and Br. Anselms in their respective histories. To move forward on the path toward anti-racism, they must then seek partnerships with the Ethel Lees and Federated Colored Catholics of our day who are committed to bringing integrity to institutional missions and embodying CST where racial equity is concerned. Finally, they must use the resources of an expanding Catholic intellectual tradition to recover, analyze, and grow from artifacts, accounts, and activities that spark truth and transformation about who they are, who they hope to become, and the work they are doing in their own campus communities to arrive there. By doing this, Catholic higher education will take on anti-racism with the integrity that the work demands, instead of merely performative lip service to anti-racism goals.

Questions for Consideration and Discussion

1. Pratt and O'Connell share their Catholic education stories at the beginning of the chapter. What do they reveal about racism in the Church and society? How do these stories compare with yours?

2. Pratt and O'Connell cite current demographic information regarding enrollment, graduation rates, debt, and leadership in Catholic higher education as evidence of how the history of anti-Blackness continues into the present. What are the comparable statistics at your institution?
3. The chapter refers to three models for responding to racism: Race Relations, Racial Justice, and Anti-Racism. Which model is predominant at your institution? Are there incidents or issues that you can recall to which your campus responded in one of these three ways? What does your institution need to do in order to move to (or move deeper into) an anti-racism model?
4. Pratt and O'Connell show how Catholic colleges and universities in Philadelphia benefit materially from past and present anti-Blackness in society and the Catholic Church, including geographic segregation and the development of pipelines for white students. How was or is this the case for your institution? What has your institution done to counter anti-Blackness as a specific form of racism? What work remains to be done?
5. Pratt and O'Connell invite readers to find and follow their institution's "Black@" Instagram account as a way to gain insight regarding racial dynamics on their campuses. What does this account (if it exists for your institution) reveal? Where else could you be listening for or listening to the voices of people of color in your campus community?
6. According to Pratt and O'Connell, "conceptualizing Catholic social thought (CST) primarily in terms of the seven principles of Catholic social teaching...both centers the conversation in whiteness and limits our understanding and responses to racism." For "[i]t misses," they go on, "cultures of white dominance and the structural realities of racism." They thus call for re-imagining CST "as addressing anti-racism directly," and they endorse MT Dávila's call for a new principle directly concerned with racial justice. What are the limits of oft-cited CST principles in redressing racism and anti-Blackness in particular? Why is solidarity, for example, insufficient? If we start by considering the injustice of racism, what "principles," or virtues, do we need to counter it beyond those already recognized in conventional accounts of CST?
7. According to Pratt and O'Connell, "what is generally understood as the Catholic intellectual tradition is steeped in the canon of

whiteness to which Catholic institutions dedicate much social, political, and economic capital." Do you agree with this claim? What counts as evidence for it? Is there evidence for it on your campus, or in your institution's curriculum? How might your institution "dissipate the canon of whiteness" and "stop dismissing the gift of Blackness"?

8. Pratt and O'Connell observe that "anti-racism work is some of the most difficult work an institution—especially a Catholic higher education institution—can do." As you conclude your discussion of this chapter, consider the most important steps your institution has taken to dismantle racism on campus. What are the most significant anti-racist steps you could undertake in the future, and who might help lead those efforts? What do you need to do as a community to support and sustain those efforts and the people leading them?

Notes

1. Association of Catholic Colleges and Universities, "Catholic Higher Education FAQs," https://www.accunet.org/Catholic-Higher-Ed-FAQs #Diverse.

2. Gerald J. Beyer, *Just Universities: Catholic Social Teaching Confronts Corporatized Higher Education* (New York: Fordham University Press, 2021), 180.

3. Association of Catholic Colleges and Universities, "Graduation Rates: Catholic Higher Education Exceeds National Averages," https://www.accunet.org/Portals/70/Docs/Publications/FastFacts-graduationrates.pdf?ver=p4GHVbm1ooDVloJjveM_FQ%3d%3d. The fact that we had difficulty finding aggregate data for graduation rates by race for Catholic institutions is problematic when it comes to determining just how wide this gap is.

4. Laura Sullivan, Tatjana Meschede, Thomas Shapiro, and Fernanda Escobar, "Stalling Dreams: How Student Debt is Disrupting Life Changes and Widening the Racial Wealth Gap," Brandeis University, Institute on Assets and Social Policy, September 2019, https://www.insidehighered.com/sites/default/server_files/media/Stalling%20Dreams.pdf; and Melanie Hanson, "Student Loan Debt by Race," https://educationdata.org/student-loan-debt-by-race. For more on contributing factors to the wealth inequality that higher education generates, see Dorothy Brown, "College Isn't the Solution for the Wealth Gap. It's Part of the Problem," *Washington Post*, April 9, 2021, https://www.washingtonpost.com/outlook/2021/04/09/student-loans-black-wealth-gap/.

5. Adam Pritchard, Sarah Nadel-Hawthorne, Anthony Schmidt, Melissa Fuesting, and Jacqueline Bichsel, *Administrators in Higher Education Annual Report: Key Findings, Trends, and Comprehensive Tables for the 2019–20 Academic Year*, CUPA-HR, https://www.cupahr.org/surveys/results/.

6. Beyer, *Just Universities*, 174.

7. In some instances, we extrapolated from the broader sector of American higher education since no collective body, clearinghouse, or agency conducts a racial analysis of Department of Education data for Catholic institutions as a subset of institutions. This lacuna in the data analysis could be an indicator of reluctance to engage in structural change.

8. See Maureen H. O'Connell, *Undoing the Knots: Five Generations of American Catholic Anti-Blackness* (Malden, MA: Beacon Press, 2021).

9. Ibram X. Kendi, *Stamped from the Beginning: The Definitive History of Racist Ideas in America* (New York: Bold Type Books, 2017), 92–103.

10. Richard Rothstein makes this point about the housing sector in the United States in *The Color of Law: A Forgotten History of How our Government Segregated America* (New York: Liveright, 2017).

11. For the history of residential segregation in urban Catholic parishes, see John McGreevy, *Parish Boundaries: The Catholic Encounter with Race in the 20th Century Urban North* (Chicago: University of Chicago Press, 1998); Katie Walker Grimes, *Christ Divided: Antiblackness as Corporate Vice* (Minneapolis: Fortress Press, 2017); and O'Connell, *Undoing the Knots*.

12. See United States Conference of Catholic Bishops, "Seven Themes of Catholic Social Teaching," https://www.usccb.org/beliefs-and-teachings/what-we-believe/catholic-social-teaching/seven-themes-of-catholic-social-teaching.

13. For a detailed description of anti-Blackness and anti-Black racism, particularly in Catholic academia, see Katie Grimes, "Antiblackness," *Theological Studies* 81, no. 1 (2020): 169–80.

14. See Joseph Barndt, *Becoming an Anti-Racist Church: Journeying toward Wholeness* (Minneapolis: Fortress Press, 2011), 117; and Joe R. Feagin, *Systemic Racism: A Theory of Oppression* (New York: Routledge, 2006).

15. Eddie Glaude, *Democracy in Black: How Race Still Enslaves the American Soul* (New York: Broadway Books, 2016), 29–50. Joe Feagin describes this in terms of the "white racial frame," which he suggests is dominant in American history and culture. See Feagin, *The White Racial Frame: Centuries of Racial Framing and Counter-Framing* (New York: Routledge, 2010).

16. Ira Katznelson, *When Affirmative Action Was White: An Untold History of Racial Inequality in Twentieth-Century America* (New York: W.W. Norton & Company, 2005), 55.

17. Katznelson, *When Affirmative Action Was White*, 113–31.

18. For a history of the Federated Colored Catholics, particularly their founder, Thomas Wyatt Turner, see Cyprian Davis, "Black Catholics in the Civil Rights Movement in the Southern United States: A.P. Tureaud, Thomas Wyatt Turner, and Earl Johnson," *U.S. Catholic Historian* 24/ 4 (2006): 69–81.

19. Not including the St. Charles Borromeo Seminary, there are now eleven Catholic colleges and universities located within the five counties of southeastern Pennsylvania that comprise the Archdiocese of Philadelphia.

20. Letter from Ethel Lee to Br. Edwin Anselm, FSC, December 3, 1937, 80.5257, Dougherty Correspondence, Catholic Historical Research Center of the Archdiocese of Philadelphia.

21. Ethel Lee to Br. Edwin Anselm, FSC, December 3, 1937.

22. Letter from Ethel Lee to Cardinal Joseph Dougherty, January 19, 1938, 80.5257, Dougherty Correspondence, Catholic Historical Research Center of the Archdiocese of Philadelphia.

23. Community Council Meeting Minutes, February 16, 1938, La Salle University Archives.

24. Black Perspectives, "A Call to Action to Catholic University Communities," June 24, 2020, https://www.aaihs.org/a-call-to-action-to-catholic-university-communities/. See also Jessie Remedios, "Via Instagram, Catholic Colleges Face Racial Reckoning," *National Catholic Reporter*, July 29, 2020, https://www.ncronline.org/news/accountability/instagram-catholic-colleges-face-racial-reckoning. We also encourage readers to find and follow your institution's "Black@" Instagram account to gain more insight regarding dynamics on your campus.

25. It is important to acknowledge that there is only one Catholic Historically Black College and University (HBCU) in the United States, Xavier University of Louisiana (XULA). Founded by St. Katharine Drexel as a ministry of the Sisters of the Blessed Sacrament, XULA has always existed for the benefit of African-Americans. Yet, the history of St. Katharine Drexel's order shows that even this work has not always lived up to established ideals. See Cyprian Davis, *The History of Black Catholics in the United States* (New York: Crossroad, 1990).

26. Compare Miranda Fricker, *Epistemic Injustice: Power and the Ethics of Knowing* (Oxford: Oxford University Press, 2007), vii–viii.

27. For a history of the relationship between slavery and American higher education, see Craig Wilder, *Ebony and Ivy: Race, Slavery, and the Troubled Heart of American Universities* (New York: Bloomsbury Press, 2014); Jeannine Hill Fletcher, "Grace of the Ghosts: Ancestors, Activists and the Making of Theologians" (Paper presented at the American Theological Society Annual Meeting, Virtual Gathering, March 20, 2021); and the Jesuits'

Slavery, History, Memory, and Reconciliation Project, https://www.jesuits.org/our-work/shmr/.

28. See various subsites of the Slavery, History, Memory, and Reconciliation Project; see also the work of the Society of the Sacred Heart's Committee on Slavery, Accountability and Reconciliation, https://rscj.org/history-enslavement.

29. Willie James Jennings, *The Christian Imagination* (New Haven, CT: Yale University Press, 2017); Jeannine Hill Fletcher, *The Sin of White Supremacy: Christianity, Racism and Religious Diversity in America* (Maryknoll, NY: Orbis, 2017).

30. For more on the history of federally supported housing segregation in communities across the country, see Rothstein, *The Color of Law*.

31. Rick Selzer notes that Catholic elementary and high school closures have narrowed enrollment pipelines at CCUs. Furthermore, white first-year enrollment at CCUs declined from 78 percent in 2010 to 66 percent in 2019. See "Narrowing Enrollment Pipeline Pressures Roman Catholic Colleges," *Inside Higher Ed*, March 5, 2021, https://www.insidehighered.com/quicktakes/2021/03/05/narrowing-enrollment-pipeline-pressures-roman-catholic-colleges.

32. See Rothstein on the equity impact of housing segregation in *The Color of Law*, and Beyer on changing tuition costs in *Just Universities*, 169–206.

33. Beyer, *Just Universities*, 180, citing Diane Cardenas Elliot, "Student Heterogeneity and Diversity at Catholic Colleges," *Journal of Catholic Higher Education* 31, no. 1 (2012): 61–81, at 77–79.

34. The Postsecondary National Policy Institute reports that as of Fall 2019 African-American students made up 2.1 of the 16.6 million undergraduate students enrolled in colleges and universities across the country, "but they were not equally represented at different institution types," which include two- and four-year programs in private, public, and for-profit institutions. See "African-American Students in Higher Education," June 12, 2020, https://pnpi.org/black-students/. For enrollment data as of Fall 2018 on post-secondary education at large and by institution type, see the National Center for Education Statistics at the Institute of Education Sciences, "The Condition of Education 2020," May 2020, 141, https://nces.ed.gov/pubsearch/pubsinfo.asp?pubid=2020144. See also Vimal Pital, "Black Students Have Less Access to Elite Public Colleges than Four Years Ago," *Chronicle of Higher Education*, July 21, 2020, https://www.chronicle.com/article/black-students-have-less-access-to-selective-public-colleges-now-than-20-years-ago-report-finds; and Valerie Strauss, "Elite Colleges Still Giving Wealthy and Connected Students a 'Legacy Admissions' Edge During Pandemic," *Washington Post*, March 21, 2021, https://www.washingtonpost.com/education/2021/03/21/elite-colleges-still-give-wealth-connected-students-a-legacy-admissions-edge/.

35. Beyer, *Just Universities*, 80.

36. "The Catholic Intellectual Tradition: Overview," Association of Catholic Colleges and Universities, https://www.accunet.org/About-Catholic-Higher-Ed-Catholic-Intellectual-Tradition.

37. For critical assessment of the U.S. bishops' teaching and witness on racial justice, see Bryan Massingale, *Racial Justice and the Catholic Church* (Maryknoll, NY: Orbis, 2010); Grimes, *Christ Divided*; Olga M. Segura, *Birth of a Movement: Black Lives Matter and the Catholic Church* (Maryknoll, NY: Orbis, 2021), 44–52 and 67–81.

38. William E. Lori, "Archbishop Lori: How Church Teaching Can Help Explain Why 'Black Lives Matter,'" *America*, July 27, 2020, https://www.americamagazine.org/faith/2020/07/27/archbishop-lori-how-church-teaching-can-help-explain-why-black-lives-matter.

39. Tia Noelle Pratt, "'I Bring Myself, My Black Self': Sr. Thea Bowman's Challenge to the Catholic Church," *Commonweal*, November 3, 2020, https://www.commonwealmagazine.org/i-bring-myself-my-black-self.

40. While never a secret, Catholic slaveholding has received increased scholarly and public attention in recent years. Key works include Adam Rothman and Elsa Barraza Mendoza, ed., *Facing Georgetown's History: A Reader on Slavery, Memory, and Reconciliation* (Washington, DC: Georgetown University Press, 2021); Kelly Schmidt, "Enslaved Faith Communities in the Jesuits' Missouri Mission," *U.S. Catholic Historian* 37, no. 2 (2019): 49–81; Thomas J. Murphy, SJ, *Jesuit Slaveholding in Maryland, 1717–1838* (New York: Routledge, 2001); Thomas Ulshafer, PSS, "Slavery and the Early Sulpician Community in Maryland," *U.S. Catholic Historian* 37, no. 2 (Spring 2019): 1–21; Stafford Poole, CM and Douglas J. Slawson, CM, *Church and Slave in Perry County, Missouri:1818–1865* (Lewiston, NY: The Edwin Mellen Press, 1986).

41. Karen L. Johnson, "Beyond Parish Boundaries: Black Catholics and the Quest for Racial Justice," *Religion and American Culture: A Journal of Interpretation* (Summer 2015): 264–300; Lincoln Rice, *Healing the Racial Divide: A Catholic Racial Justice Framework Inspired by Dr. Arthur Falls* (New York: Pickwick Publications, 2014).

42. The "Black@" social media posts at a variety of Catholic institutions that appeared during summer and fall 2020 point to a myriad of examples of ongoing institutional resistance to meaningful structural and cultural change to undo racism.

43. Black Perspectives, "A Call to Action to Catholic University Communities." For news coverage, see Brian Roewe, "Catholic University Leaders Call for Their Institutions to Address Systemic Racism," *National Catholic Reporter*, June 25, 2020, https://www.ncronline.org/news/justice/catholic-university-leaders-call-their-institutions-address-systemic-racism.

44. For more on the ACCU's Consortium of Diversity Officers, see https://www.accunet.org/diversity-officers. That the group's first meeting involved reflection on the recent U.S. bishops' pastoral letter, however, underscores our previous point about following the tepid lead of the American hierarchy.

45. Tia Noelle Pratt, "'I Bring Myself, My Black Self.'"

46. Martin Luther King Jr., "Letter from Birmingham Jail," April 16, 1963, https://www.africa.upenn.edu/Articles_Gen/Letter_Birmingham.html.

47. Segura, *Birth of a Movement*, 90–91.

48. See The King Center, https://thekingcenter.org/about-tkc/the-king-philosophy/.

49. See USCCB, https://www.usccb.org/reflections-movement-black-lives-blm.

50. Segura, *Birth of a Movement*, 50.

51. Segura, *Birth of a Movement*, 50–51.

52. Eric Martin, "The Catholic Church Has a Visible White-Power Faction," *Sojourners*, August 2020, https://sojo.net/magazine/august-2020/catholic-church-has-visible-white-power-faction.

53. See Brian Flanagan, *Stumbling in Holiness: Sin and Sanctity in the Church* (Collegeville, MN: Liturgical Press, 2020).

54. MT Dávila, https://twitter.com/mtdavila/status/1384247084673507331, April 19, 2021.

55. M. Shawn Copeland, "What Would a Systematic Theology of Racism Look like from the U.S. Church?" interview with Brian Fraga, *Our Sunday Visitor*, November 6, 2020, https://osvnews.com/2020/11/06/what-would-a-systematic-theology-of-racism-look-like-from-the-u-s-church/.

56. Nancy T. Ammerman, "Culture and Identity in the Congregation," in *Studying Congregations: A New Handbook*, ed. Nancy T. Ammerman, Jackson W. Carroll, Carl S. Dudley, and William McKinney (Nashville, TN: Abingdon Press, 1998), 78–104.

57. "Heavenly Bodies: Fashion and the Catholic Imagination," https://www.metmuseum.org/exhibitions/listings/2018/heavenly-bodies/art-and-fashion-images.

58. See Scott Myers-Lipton, *Change! A Student Guide to Social Action* (New York: Routledge, 2017).

59. See Association of American Colleges and Universities, "Truth, Racial Healing and Transformation Campus Centers," https://www.aacu.org/initiatives/truth-racial-healing-transformation-campus-centers.

60. Pratt, "'I Bring Myself, My Black Self.'"

61. United States Conference of Catholic Bishops, "Sr. Thea's Address to U.S. Bishops," June 1989, https://www.youtube.com/watch?v=uOV0nQkjuoA&t=15s.

3

¡PRESENTE! THE LATINX FUTURE OF CATHOLIC HIGHER EDUCATION

Michelle Gonzalez Maldonado

In a moment marked by debates on the role of race and the study of racial inequality in the history and life of the United States, the Latinx population remains a complex, growing group that challenges simplistic reductions of identity today. One only has to look at the 2020 presidential election, which revealed that it is extremely difficult, if not impossible, to make broad generalizations about the Latino/a community as a whole.[1] The internal diversity masked by the broad category of Latino/a, whether based on geography, nation of origin, economic class, gender identity, or race, reveals a population that at times seems to have very little that it shares collectively across the board. If we must give ourselves a single name, we cannot even agree on what it is, with *Hispanic*, *Latino/a*, and *Latinx* being used by different age groups and generations in different parts of the United States. As it happens, Latino/as would overwhelmingly rather be categorized by their nation of origin, Cuban-American in my case, than describe themselves in these panethnic terms. In the following, I nevertheless use all the terms above.

For the Catholic Church in general, and institutions of Catholic higher education in particular, the growing Latinx population offers a study in contrasts. On the one hand, we are often credited with "saving the Catholic Church" here in the United States through our membership and younger demographics. On the other hand, we are leaving the Church consistently, either shifting to Protestant, most notably evangelical, churches or leaving organized religion altogether and becoming part of that growing category of "nones" who do not affiliate with institutional Christianity. As noted by the Pew Forum in 2014, one in four Hispanic adults is a former Catholic, and 18 percent are religiously unaffiliated.[2] Forty-six percent of Latino/as between age eighteen and twenty-nine describe themselves as religiously unaffiliated.[3] We are dramatically underrepresented and underserved by Catholic higher education. One only has to look at our numbers, whether it be students, faculty, or administrators, to see a world where Latino/as are not and never have been a demographic priority in Catholic colleges and universities (CCUs).

This chapter makes two arguments: (1) not only is it incumbent upon CCUs to accompany and support Latinx students more effectively, but (2) the failure, to date, to do so puts the futures of these institutions in jeopardy. The Latinx population is the youngest and fastest growing racial ethnic group in the country and in the Church. Accordingly, colleges and universities that claim to be Catholic, yet ignore their prospective and current Latinx students, are not in fact a reflection of the Church itself.

I begin by exploring the complexities in naming Latinx communities, which reflects the challenges of attending adequately to the diversity that the term *Latinx* encompasses. Then the chapter moves to analyzing the resources within Catholic social thought (CST) pertaining to race and diversity. I focus on the U.S. bishops' November 2018 pastoral letter, "Open Wide Our Hearts: The Enduring Call to Love." The chapter concludes by offering suggestions for future initiatives within Catholic higher education that will support the enrollment and success of Latinx students.

Latinx, Latino/as, and Hispanics

Although the panethnicity of *Latinidad* (loosely translated as Latino/a-ness) must always be heavily contextualized by geography and nation of origin, we cannot reject the political, cultural, and social currents that steer the U.S. understanding of Latinx peoples as a whole. As noted by Christina Mora,

> Ultimately, Hispanic panethnicity has become a salient form of collective identification in America. This is true despite the fact that organizations frame Hispanic/Latino panethnicity in various ways, and despite the fact that the category remains ambiguous to many. We should be cautious of any statements that depict Hispanics as a homogenous community with little internal variation. At the same time, however, we should not dismiss the social currents that are attempting to unify subgroups and the potential impact that Hispanic/Latino solidarity can have on American institutions.[4]

Latino/as are the largest racial/ethnic group in the United States and have the lowest educational attainment in higher education. The majority of Latino/as who attend college attend community colleges and have high attrition rates, though the number in four-year colleges is growing. At least two-thirds of Latino/as who are in four-year colleges attend Hispanic Serving Institutions, at which at least 25 percent of the student body identifies as Hispanic.

In 2016, Latino/as made up 17.6 percent of the U.S. population, and projections show that by 2060 they will be 28.6 percent of the U.S. population. According to the U.S. Department of Education, by 2029 Latino/as will constitute 27.5 percent of public-school enrollment. Latinx youth, and Latino/a people as a whole, are overwhelmingly U.S. citizens and U.S. born. They make up over 40 percent of first-generation college students, the largest percentage of any racial/ethnic group. The majority of Latino/as work while they are in college, and close to 50 percent receive Pell grants. The majority of degrees awarded to Latino/as students are at public universities.[5] Nationally, 5 percent of faculty are Hispanic (in degree seeking postsecondary institutions), and only a little over 3 percent of professors are Latinas. According to a 2017 study by the American Council on Education, only 3 percent of chief academic affairs officers are Latinx.[6]

More than 40 percent of Catholics are Latino/a; of Catholics under the age of eighteen, 60 percent are Hispanic. Despite these numbers, less than 4 percent of Latino/a children are enrolled in Catholic elementary schools, while Latino/a students make up about 17 percent of the population at Catholic high schools.[7] In brief, the demographics of Latino/as in the Church do not mirror their presence in our educational institutions. As Frances Contreras notes, this is a missed opportunity: "Catholic institutions, because of their longstanding success with Latino students in the K–12 sector, and high college completion rates in the postsecondary sector, represent a viable higher education option to meet the needs of select high achieving Latino students in the US."[8] Admittedly, this significant gap in population versus enrollment must be contextualized in light of the alarming decline in all students seeking Catholic education in the United States.[9] Some initiatives are attempting to counter this trend, such as the Nativity and Cristo Rey schools, which are "networks of Catholic middle and high schools that have been created to address the specific needs of low-income students."[10] As Laura Nichols notes in her chapter in this volume, these programs demonstrate that Catholic schools can play a pivotal role in facilitating economic mobility and reducing wealth inequality in the United States.

With respect to CCUs, only 13.7 percent of students enrolled in those institutions are Latinx.[11] As Hosffman Ospino notes, geography is a significant factor. A high percentage of Latino/a students live in the South and West, whereas the majority of CCUs are located elsewhere in the country.[12] The map of Association of Jesuit Colleges and Universities (AJCU) schools indicates a heavy concentration of schools in the Northeast and the absence of schools in the Southwest and in Florida, two areas that are home to a heavy percentage of Latino/as. In addition, Latino/a families face financial obstacles, some actual and some perceived, in attending a private college or university. In many Latin American countries, Catholic education is seen as exclusively for the wealthy. For many working-class Latinx families, the idea of attending a private CCU in the United States seems out of reach.[13] Latino/a families are not alone in this perception: as a 2019 EAB Enrollment Services study indicates, the third most common word parents associate with Catholic higher education is *expensive*.[14]

Another reason for low enrollment numbers is the abovementioned complexities of defining the Latino/a community as a whole, which has implications for recruitment and retention efforts. Colleges and universities cannot treat Latino/a communities as a homogenous group and thus may need to use discrete strategies and terminology based on geographic region and nation of origin.[15] We do not make it easy for higher education in that we, as a collective, cannot agree on even how to name ourselves. For example, I use the terms *Latinx*, *Latino/a*, and *Hispanic* interchangeably. In South Florida, where I am from, the term *Hispanic* is often used. However, I quickly learned during my years in California that this term was unacceptable there, since it was interpreted as embracing our Spanish heritage but rejecting the influences of African and Indigenous peoples on our culture, history, and identity. The term *Latinx* has risen to prominence in the academy and is less cumbersome in speech than *Latino/a*; however, I find it highly problematic. Not only is it unconventional in both English and Spanish; more to the point, it is not embraced, used, or even known by the majority of Latino/as in this country.[16] At the same time, I recognize that, as Ed Morales writes, "*Latinx* intends to describe the in-between space which Latinx love, which allows us to cross racial boundaries more easily and construct identities, or self-images, that include a wide variety of racial, national, and even gender-based identifications."[17] My use of the three terms, *Latino/a, Hispanic*, and *Latinx*, is a nod to the fluidity and complexity of the construction of our communal identity.

To add another layer of complexity to the conversation, though Latino/as are often inaccurately characterized as a single racial group in this country, it has to be remembered that, in fact, Latino/as embody all races. Latino/as are often referred to as "people of color," a move that eclipses Latina/o racial diversity and white-skin privilege within Latino/a communities. There are Latino/as of Indigenous and Asian descent, and there are white, black, and brown Latino/as. (The number of Latino/as identifying as black is growing.[18]) In addition, many Latino/as define as mixed race. Both *mestizaje* and *mulatez* refer to the racial hybridity of some Latinx peoples, with the former referring to the mixture of Indigenous and Spanish, and the latter referring to Spanish and African. As scholars have noted, Latin American and Caribbean countries do not operate under the same black-white dualism in which racial identity is constructed in the United States.[19] Instead, Latinx people come from cultures and countries that have much more nuanced racial hierarchies.[20] Latino/as do not enter into discussions of the black-white binary here in the United States without their own constructions of race from their Latin American backgrounds.[21]

Finally, it is also problematic to treat Latino/as as an ethnic group. As Laura Gómez thoughtfully reminds us,

> For one thing, the tendency to think of Latinos in ethnic terms perpetuates the idea that Latinos are perpetual foreigners rather than bona fide Americans. To speak of the immigrant but never the (native) American is fundamental to the racial logic of Latino subordination....Another problem with viewing Latinos from an ethnic rather than a racial frame is that doing so pits them against African Americans in a way that supports white supremacy.[22]

The challenges to naming a single, unified identity outlined here also play out in Catholic higher education.

Latino/as in Catholic Higher Education

Within higher education, the Latino/a "question" or "issue" is contextualized in conversations involving diversity, inclusion, and equity. At its best, *diversity* refers to how individuals and communities contribute to the intellectual and institutional culture: in other words, not only demographics, but also intellectual trajectories. *Inclusion*, on the other hand, refers to the ways in which colleges and universities saturate diversity in their demographics, curriculum, and identity. Finally, *equity* points to a recognition of the achievement gaps and challenges for certain populations in our communities. In other words,

> Diversity is an understanding of how individual and group differences contribute to the diverse thoughts, knowledge, and experiences that are the foundation of high-quality liberal education. Inclusion is an active, intentional, and ongoing engagement with diversity across the curriculum, co-curriculum, and our communities to increase awareness, content knowledge, cognitive sophistication, and empathic understanding of the complex ways individuals interact with systems and institutions. Equity prioritizes the creation of

> opportunities for minoritized students to have equal outcomes and participation in educational programs that can close the achievement gaps in student success and completion.[23]

Diversity, inclusion, and equity must be lifted up together. Inclusion, for example, is an empty promise if its primary focus is to include the excluded into a system that has historically marginalized them. The system itself has to change.

The question is what we can do as Catholic colleges and universities to become more reflective of our present Church, its future, and the future in general of higher education. Latinx Catholicism is consistently underserved and underrepresented in the Church, as starkly highlighted by Brett Hoover's observation that only 6 percent of Masses celebrated across the country are in Spanish, "despite the fact that more than 12 percent of Americans speak Spanish as their first language."[24] These inequalities are reproduced within CCUs, where Latinx students often do not see their Catholicism affirmed and celebrated.[25]

Our efforts need to be multitiered and comprehensive. At a base level, we need a radical shift in the manner in which we construct our Catholic intellectual tradition. I often wonder when I see Jesuit colleges and universities commemorate the martyrdom at the University of Central America (UCA) in El Salvador if these same institutions include these figures in their intellectual identity. We rightly mourn the murder of Ignacio Ellacuría, SJ, yet how many Jesuit colleges and universities have students read Ellacuría—a difficult task, I admit—in their courses? Similarly, how many Latin American and Caribbean thinkers are included in curricula at our institutions outside of courses that are specifically tagged to cover these geographic regions? As Paul Ortiz points out, "Those interested in the origins of democratic traditions in this country must look to Latin America, the Caribbean, and Africa as often as they look to Europe."[26] What I am suggesting is an epistemic shift in how our institutions design their courses. The goal would be to include Latino/a contributions in the canon across the curriculum; such contributions have often been undervalued and even excluded, leading to a truncated understanding of significant topics. Such a shift, however, requires strong leadership and dialogue among faculty, administration, and students. The process of determining which authors are included in the curriculum and how they are taught can be fraught.

Similarly, many CCUs do a great job of providing service opportunities in Latin America and the Caribbean, but to what extent do we draw from these regions in our intellectual autobiography? Or are these just poor brown peoples whom we encounter on service trips?[27] We cannot reduce our engagement with the broader Americas exclusively to our social justice traditions; they must also be a part of our intellectual traditions. Otherwise, our countries of origin, and Latinx people generally, are cast as intellectually and culturally deficient. We must confront the ways in which we create an intellectual culture that mirrors the internalized oppression that so many Latinx students face in our classrooms. As Dean Brackley remarks, part of Ellacuría's legacy was to challenge CCUs to take a moral stand on the critical issues and crises in our contemporary world.[28] This includes examining the impact of race and identity on Catholic higher education.

Race and Catholic Social Thought

The common good is at the foundation of CST.[29] Humans do not exist as highly isolated individuals, but rather as the community that is humanity. The scriptural basis of the common good is the assertion in the Book of Genesis that humans are created in the "image of God." Yet God in the Christian tradition is triune. Christians' *imago Dei* is in the image of the Trinity. The Trinity reveals a God that is one but threefold, a God who is constituted by the relationships among the three persons of the Trinity. Relationality is what reflects the image of God within humanity. It is through relationships that humans most concretely reflect God's image.

Because CST has a communitarian basis, its morality includes positive obligations toward others, on both personal and societal levels (civil, political, economic). Often, when people hear the words duty or obligation, they think of things they unfortunately "have" to do. This is not the attitude CST encourages. Our obligations toward others, ideally, are something we want to do. In other words, Catholics should want to be in solidarity with their fellow human beings and to empower them. Catholics embrace the fact that their love of God is reflected in their love of neighbor.

A second key component of CST is the preferential option for the poor, a theological concept first elaborated by Latin American liberation theologians and ecclesial leaders in the 1960s and 1970s. Latin American liberation theologies understand poverty as scandalous to God, for God wants all of God's creation to flourish. In situations of oppression, God is not neutral. This preferential option for the poor is due to the situation of oppression. The poor are in no way closer to God or holier per se; instead, their context demands liberation. The preferential option for the poor emerges from the conviction that, as oppressed and alienated, the poor offer a vision of hope that counters and overcomes these conditions, for while forgotten by us the poor are embraced by God. Latin American theologians ground their insights in the Hebrew and Christian Scriptures, arguing that the God they reveal is on the side of the oppressed.

In addition to revealing something about God taking sides, the poor reveal something about God's presence and about our society. "The existence of the poor attests to the existence of a Godless society, whether one explicitly believes in God or not. This absence of God is present when someone is crying out. The absence of God is present in the poor person. The poor are the presence of the absent God."[30]

The theologian M. Shawn Copeland expands this construction of the sacred when she argues that poverty, through race, is the entry point for understanding the sacred: "Poor is the color of God because God has made the liberation of poor, excluded, and despised persons a divine goal. To say that poor is the color of God is to say that God has made the condition of the poor, excluded, and despised God's own."[31] She grounds her claim in Scripture and in the example of Jesus assuming the condition of poverty during his life. It makes sense to associate poverty with race when one examines the demographics of the poor in the United States. For Copeland, one cannot understand poverty without also seeking to understand race. The fact of the matter is that class inequality impacts minoritized populations disproportionately.

As I noted above, the U.S. bishops' November 2018 pastoral letter, "Open Wide Our Hearts," is a resource for thinking about issues of race in the United States. The document warrants attention both for what it says and for what it does not say. There is much to praise about this document, starting with its mere existence. This letter is a follow-up to the bishops' 1979 letter on racism entitled "Brothers and Sisters to Us." I am very much of the school of thought that, while we can see a trajectory of social justice movements and historical moments actively combatting racism in this country, we can also see a simultaneous growing agenda seeking to maintain racism in all its forms. Correctly, then, "Open Wide Our Hearts" begins with a sense of urgency: "The persistence of the evil of racism is why we are writing this letter now. People are still being harmed, so action is still needed."[32]

The document opens by defining racism and connecting it to sin:

> Racism arises when—either consciously or unconsciously—a person holds that his or her own race or ethnicity is superior, and therefore judges persons of other races or ethnicities as inferior and unworthy of equal regard. When this conviction or attitude leads individuals or groups to exclude, ridicule, mistreat, or unjustly discriminate against persons on the basis of their race or ethnicity, it is sinful.[33]

Racism is sinful because it violates justice. The letter defines justice as right relationship with God, God's creation, and each other.[34] The theological ground for opposing racism is our egalitarian creation as humans in the image of God.[35] Ultimately, to be a racist is to deny the full humanity of fellow human beings.

As its title suggests, the document is a call to a conversion of the heart that will lead to social change and the reformation of our institutions.[36] We are called to humility, for only then will our hearts be open to the long road of conversion. Part of embracing this humility is acknowledging, as a nation, our original sin of racism. The letter accordingly recounts the history of racist attitudes, practices, and policies toward Native Americans, African Americans, and Latino/as.[37] With respect to the U.S. Latinx community, the bishops note,

> Since the Mexican-American War, Hispanics from various countries have experienced discrimination in housing, employment, healthcare, and education. Hispanics have been referred to by countless derogatory names, have encountered negative assumptions made about them because of their ethnicity, have suffered discrimination in applying for college, for housing, and in registering to vote.[38]

The bulk of the bishops' analysis of institutional racism is outward looking, citing the water crisis in Flint, Michigan, repeated incidents of police violence toward unarmed Black men, and the overwhelming number of people of color in our prison system. In a section on "Acknowledging Sin," the letter turns to the Catholic Church's own participation in the racist history of the United States. This section makes up, however, less than two pages and a mere three paragraphs,[39] suggesting the bishops' failure to reckon fully with the institutional Church's complicity. (See further analysis of this document in the chapter in this volume by Tia Noelle Pratt and Maureen O'Connell.) As Catholic ethicist and priest Brian Massingale argues in his book *Racial Justice and the Catholic Church*, the U.S. Church is an institution where whiteness is normative.[40] If that were not the case, why would the USCCB have cultural diversity subcommittees for African Americans, Hispanics, Asian and Pacific Islanders, and Native Americans? Apparently, the bishops consider white or Euro-American Catholicism as the norm rather than as one among many dimensions of U.S. Catholicism's diversity.

Just as "Open Wide Our Hearts" emphasizes racism in society rather than in the Church itself, CCUs tend to focus their efforts to redress racism on their surrounding communities (through community service learning, study abroad, scholarship on racism in society, and other similar projects) rather than on the college or university itself. Both are needed. Like the institutional church, CCUs must interrogate their normative whiteness, as well as acknowledge and repent for their past and present participation in racist structures. Otherwise, they will never become welcoming homes to historically underrepresented populations, implement effective strategies to include and graduate Latinx constituents, or reflect Latinx intellectual contributions and realities.

Ways Forward

Successful approaches to educating Latinx students in Catholic higher education are characterized by comprehensive attention to the entire student experience—from targeted partnerships with Latinx communities and Catholic high schools that enhance pipelines for recruitment and retention of first-year and transfer students, to development and implementation of culturally relevant curricula and cocurricula, to support for graduates as they support the institution in turn as alumni/ae. Concrete suggestions for CCUs to consider, among others,[41] include providing scholarships earmarked for the recruitment and retention of Latinx students, improving on-campus and off-campus leadership opportunities that engage Latinx students, promoting recruitment and advancement of Latinx faculty and staff, attending to curricular changes that demonstrate Latinx scholars' contributions across the curriculum, and engaging in ongoing evaluation and scholarship regarding these initiatives. Moreover, in our efforts to create a community of belonging that is appealing to Latinx youth, we must ensure that Latinx students see themselves in the identity and culture of our institutions, and not just during Hispanic Heritage month or on El Día de los Muertos. Centering Latinx contributions to various disciplines, for example, has been shown to be a significant factor in creating a culture of belonging and improving graduation rates for Latinx students. Indeed, a recent study by K. Jurée Capers of the characteristics that facilitate high graduation rates for Latinx college students found that representation (i.e., percentage of Latinx students, faculty, and staff) was not as positively correlated as other factors. Capers thus recommends,

> Institutions may consider improving their structural representative behaviors (i.e., adopting culturally related curricula, courses, services, or resources) as this appears to be an important predictor of Latinx completions. With proper investments, appropriate application of resources, and a committed mission to serve underserved students, non-HSIs can also help to improve the completion rates for Latinx students.[42]

There are several CCUs that are beginning this important work and whose initiatives are illustrative of the comprehensive approaches more CCUs could take to ensure diversity, inclusion, and equity for Latinx students. What follows is a brief description of some concrete initiatives undertaken at three universities located in different areas of the country and sponsored by different religious congregations. All are responding to the growing Latinx Catholic population in light of CST.

The differences among the universities' approaches illustrate various ways forward that build upon particular institutions' strengths and characteristics.

First, Barry University in Miami, Florida, has multiple public-facing initiatives that highlight the university's commitment to anti-racism work and to creating an inclusive community. With a student body that is 30 percent Latinx and 30 percent Black, Barry also represents a Catholic university where the majority of the student population is nonwhite.[43] Barry's Anti-racism and Equity Coalition is a university-wide team of faculty, staff, and students charged with celebrating diversity and promoting anti-racism work on campus.[44] Barry's Institute for Hispanic/Latino Theology offers a Certificate in U.S. Hispanic Latino(a) Theology, centering the Latino/a faith experience as central to the ministry and intellectual tradition of the Roman Catholic Church.

In a similar vein, the University of Notre Dame has multiple initiatives focused not only on the recruitment and enrollment of Latinx students, but also on support of research and curricular innovations involving Latinx histories and identities. Started in 1999, the Institute for Latino Studies promotes Latinx Studies through a major and minor, leadership training, research support, and community building initiatives.[45] Notre Dame's Latino Studies Scholars Program offers merit-based leadership scholarships. In 2012, the University founded the Latino Enrollment Initiative (LEI), which "identifies and assists Catholic schools with substantial unmet capacity (open seats), favorable demographic potential—namely, a growing number of Latino families in the surrounding area—and motivated principals by offering a framework to transform schools to attract and serve Latino families."[46] The LEI provides summer trainings and institutes for schools to meet these goals. These visible initiatives, at the intersection of student, curricular, and research support, offer a comprehensive engagement with Latinx communities.

In 2016, Marquette University began the process of becoming a Hispanic Serving Institution. Marquette's recent five-year benchmark demonstrates the progress it has made in this institutional priority, which "speaks to the very heart of our values as a Jesuit institution: to serve the traditionally underserved, to provide care for each of our students, and to strive for inclusive excellence."[47] This initiative has been marked by engaging the Spanish-speaking community, working with Latinx organizations in higher education, providing precollege bridge programs, strategic enrollment management recruitment, targeted financial aid, student support, faculty/staff support, faculty/staff diversity hiring initiatives, and curricular innovations. Marquette's institutional evaluation of this initiative is publicly accessible through its website.[48]

In short, until we recognize that Latinx students are key to our mission, our identity, and our future, we will continue to treat them merely as a necessary demographic to save us from the looming enrollment crisis. As Hosffman Ospino writes, "Do we want a strong church? Then let's educate Hispanic children now and give them the best possible tools, so they can be the next generation…of teachers, theologians and college presidents."[49] The three Catholic universities' initiatives highlighted here offer multiple tools for success. CCUs that prioritize such initiatives not only demonstrate their congruence with CST, but also contribute to ensuring a well-educated Church and society.

Questions for Consideration and Discussion

1. Maldonado observes that less than 14 percent of students enrolled in Catholic colleges and universities are Latinx. What are your institution's enrollment and graduation rates for Latinx students? What are your institutional strengths and challenges in this respect? Are enrolling and graduating Latinx students institutional priorities?
2. Maldonado claims that "diversity, inclusion, and equity must be lifted up together." In what ways does your institution promote diversity, inclusion, and equity? What barriers exist?
3. Maldonado challenges leaders to structure Catholic higher education so that it more adequately reflects the demographics of the Catholic Church, but also so that it serves Latinx students better than does the rest of the current Church. Does your campus community celebrate and critically examine Latinx intellectual, spiritual, artistic, and other contributions within the curriculum and cocurriculum? What are strengths and weaknesses of your campus in this respect?
4. Maldonado observes that CCUs tend to focus their racial justice efforts on their surrounding communities rather than on the college

or university itself. Is that the case for your campus? In what ways could your institution improve its work for racial justice both on campus and in the community?

5. According to Maldonado, "Successful approaches to educating Latinx students in Catholic higher education are characterized by comprehensive attention to the entire student experience." Consider the several suggestions that Maldonado makes in this regard. Is your institution doing comparable work? Or what work does your institution need to do here? Further, what are the perspectives of Latinx students, faculty, and staff on these questions?
6. Maldonado points to several elements of CST, including human dignity, the common good, and the preferential option for the poor, as principles that can anchor Catholic higher education with respect to educating Latinx students. In what ways do these principles facilitate or obstruct conversations on your campus? What elements of Catholic social thought (e.g., symbols, stories from your institution's founding, lives of holy women and men in your tradition, principles, biblical stories) do you or could you draw upon to articulate a shared and compelling narrative in support of the Latinx present and future in Catholic higher education?
7. As you conclude your discussion of this chapter, what are three to five ways you can affirm current initiatives and enact positive change on your campus with respect to promoting diversity, inclusion, and equity for Latinx community members? Or would you take issue with this goal? If so, in what ways?

Notes

1. Geraldo Cadava, *The Hispanic Republican: The Shaping of an American Political Identity, from Nixon to Trump* (New York: Ecco Press, 2020); Ed Morales, *Latinx: The New Force in American Politics and Culture* (New York: Verso, 2018). See also Gregory A. Smith, "8 Facts about Catholics and Politics in the U.S.," Pew Research Center, September 15, 2020, https://www.pewresearch.org/fact-tank/2020/09/15/8-facts-about-catholics-and-politics-in-the-u-s/.

2. Pew Research Center, "The Shifting Religious Identity of Latinos in the United States," May 7, 2014, https://www.pewforum.org/2014/05/07/the-shifting-religious-identity-of-latinos-in-the-united-states/.

3. Pew Research Center, "Latinos Who Are Unaffiliated (Religious 'Nones')," *U.S. Religious Landscape Study* 2014, https://www.pewforum.org/

religious-landscape-study/religious-tradition/unaffiliated-religious-nones/racial-and-ethnic-composition/latino/.

4. G. Christina Mora, *Making Hispanics: How Activists, Bureaucrats, and Media Constructed a New American* (Chicago: The University of Chicago Press, 2014), 169.

5. See the preceding citation and Michelle Camacho Liu, "Investing in Higher Education for Latinos: Trends in Latino College Access and Success," National Conference of State Legislatures, July 2011, https://www.ncsl.org/documents/educ/trendsinlatinosuccess.pdf.

6. American Council on Higher Education, "Race and Ethnicity in Higher Education," 2019, https://www.equityinhighered.org/indicators/postsecondary-faculty-and-staff/proportion-of-white-college-and-university-administrators/.

7. Hosffman Ospino and Patricia Weitzel-O'Neill, "Catholic Schools Serving Hispanic Families: Insights from the 2014 National Survey," *Journal of Catholic Education* 19, no. 2 (2016), https://files.eric.ed.gov/fulltext/EJ1089742.pdf and https://www.ncronline.org/blogs/distinctly-catholic/hispanics-catholic-schools.

8. Frances Contreras, "Latino Students in Catholic Postsecondary Institutions," *Journal of Catholic Education* 19, no. 2 (2016): 81–111, at 82.

9. Center for Applied Research in the Apostolate, "Frequently Requested Church Statistics," https://cara.georgetown.edu/frequently-requested-church-statistics/.

10. Laura Nichols, "The Role of Catholic Schools in Reducing Educational and Economic Inequality," *Integritas* 9, no. 4 (Spring 2017): 1–25, at 5.

11. Association of Catholic Colleges and Universities, "Catholic Higher Education FAQs," https://www.accunet.org/Catholic-Higher-Ed-FAQs#Diverse.

12. Maria Luisa Torres, "Why Increased Enrollment of Latino Students in Catholic Schools Benefits Both Schools and Students," *America*, February 23, 2018, https://www.americamagazine.org/politics-society/2018/02/23/why-increased-enrollment-latino-students-catholic-schools-benefits-both.

13. Michael Sean Winters, "Hispanics & Catholic Schools," *National Catholic Reporter*, March 8, 2016, https://www.ncronline.org/blogs/distinctly-catholic/hispanics-catholic-schools.

14. Sarah Parrott, "How 2,600+ Students and Parents Perceive Catholic Colleges Today," EAB, February 4, 2019, https://eab.com/insights/blogs/enrollment/how-2600-students-and-parents-perceive-catholic-colleges-today/. The number one word was *conservative* and number two was *traditional*.

15. For a study that demonstrates the significance of considering panethnicity in analyzing student and institutional characteristics that contribute to higher graduation rates, see Lucy Arellano, "Capitalizing Baccalaureate

Degree Attainment: Identifying Student and Institution Level Characteristics that Ensure Success for Latinxs," *Journal of Higher Education* 91, no. 4 (2020): 588–619.

16. See Luis Noe-Bustamante, Lauren Mora, and Mark Hugo Lopez, "About One-in-Four U.S. Hispanics Have Heard of Latinx, but Just 3% Use It," Pew Research Center, August 11, 2020, https://www.pewresearch.org/hispanic/2020/08/11/about-one-in-four-u-s-hispanics-have-heard-of-latinx-but-just-3-use-it/.

17. Morales, *Latinx*, 4–5.

18. Christine Tamir, "The Growing Diversity of Black America," Pew Research Center, March 25, 2021, https://www.pewresearch.org/social-trends/2021/03/25/the-growing-diversity-of-black-america/.

19. Edward Telles, *Pigmentocracies: Ethnicity, Race, and Color in Latin America* (Chapel Hill: University of North Carolina Press, 2014).

20. Gabriel Haslip-Viera, "White Privilege and the Ideology of White Supremacy in the Spanish-Speaking Caribbean, Its Diaspora and Latin America, 1492–Present," in *White Latino Privilege: Caribbean Latino Perspectives in the Second Decade of the 21st Century*, ed. Gabriel Haslip-Viera (New York: Latino Studies Press, 2018), 9–72.

21. See Nestor Medina, *Mestizaje: Remapping Race, Culture, and Faith in Latino/a Catholicism* (Maryknoll, NY: Orbis, 2009).

22. Laura E. Gómez, *Inventing Latinos: A New Story of American Racism* (New York: The New Press, 2020), 13–14.

23. Tia Brown McNair, Estela Mara Bensimon, and Lindsey Malcom-Piqueux, *From Equity Talk to Equity Walk: Expanding the Practitioner Knowledge for Racial Justice in Higher Education* (Hoboken, NJ: John Wiley & Sons, 2020), 6–7.

24. Brett C. Hoover, "Still Unaccommodated: Why Are Hispanic Catholics Treated Unequally?" *Commonweal*, July 10, 2021, www.commonwealmagazine.org.

25. CCUs are beginning to sponsor initiatives to share best practices. See, for example, Melissa Cedillo, "How to Better Minister to Latinx College Students," *National Catholic Reporter*, July 27, 2021, https://www.ncronline.org/news/justice/how-better-minister-latinx-college-students.

26. Paul Ortiz, *An African American and Latinx History of the United States* (Boston: Beacon Press, 2018), 7.

27. The debate over the value of service trips or "voluntourism" continues in higher education and professional schools. See, for example, Sharon McLennan, "Medical Voluntourism in Honduras: 'Helping' the Poor?" *Progress in Development Studies*, March 26, 2014, https://journals.sagepub.com/doi/abs/10.1177/1464993413517789, and Nicole S. Berry, "Did We Do Good? NGOs, Conflicts of Interest and the Evaluation of Short-Term

Medical Missions in Sololá, Guatemala," *Social Science and Medicine* 120 (November 2014): 344–51, https://pubmed.ncbi.nlm.nih.gov/24834868/. For critiques of how these learning experiences can reinforce racism within CCUs as well as suggestions for anti-racist practices, see Robbin D. Crabtree, "Talking Back: Asking Hard Questions about the Impact of International Service Learning," *Conversations on Jesuit Higher Education* 31, no. 17 (2007): 39–42; Roger Bergman, *Catholic Social Learning: Educating the Faith That Does Justice* (New York: Fordham University Press, 2011); and Jennifer Reed-Bouley and Eric Kyle, "Challenging Racism and White Privilege in Undergraduate Theology Contexts: Teaching and Learning Strategies for Maximizing the Promise of Community Service-Learning," *Teaching Theology and Religion* 18, no. 1 (2015): 20–36.

28. Christopher Kerr, "Enduring Impact of the Martyrs," *Conversations on Jesuit Higher Education*, November 11, 2019, http://www.conversationsmagazine.org/columns/2019/11/11/enduring-impact-of-the-martyrs?rq=martyr.

29. See Todd David Whitmore, "Catholic Social Teaching: Starting with the Common Good," in *Living the Catholic Social Tradition: Cases and Commentary*, ed. Kathleen Maas Weigert and Alexia K. Kelley (Lanham, MD: Rowman & Littlefield, 2005), 59–85.

30. Franz J. Hinkelammert, "Liberation Theology in the Economic and Social Context of Latin America: Economy and Theology, or the Irrationality of the Rationalized," in *Liberation Theologies, Postmodernity, and the Americas*, ed. David Batstone, Eduardo Mendieta, Lois Ann Lorentzen, and Dwight N. Hopkins (New York: Routledge, 1991), 27.

31. M. Shawn Copeland, "Poor Is the Color of God," in *The Option for the Poor in Christian Theology*, ed. Daniel G. Groody (Notre Dame, IN: University of Notre Dame Press, 2007), 226.

32. United States Conference of Catholic Bishops, "Open Wide Our Hearts: The Enduring Call to Love" (Washington, DC: USCCB, 2018), 7, https://www.usccb.org/resources/open-wide-our-hearts_0.pdf.

33. USCCB, "Open Wide Our Hearts," 3.

34. USCCB, "Open Wide Our Hearts," 9.

35. USCCB, "Open Wide Our Hearts," 4.

36. USCCB, "Open Wide Our Hearts," 7.

37. USCCB, "Open Wide Our Hearts," 10–17.

38. USCCB, "Open Wide Our Hearts," 15.

39. USCCB, "Open Wide Our Hearts," 21–22.

40. Bryan N. Massingale, *Racial Justice and the Catholic Church* (Maryknoll, NY: Orbis, 2010).

41. See, e.g., Sarah Brown, "Building Diverse Campuses: 4 Key Questions and 4 Case Studies," *Chronicle of Higher Education*, July 7, 2021, https://

www-chronicle-com.csm.idm.oclc.org/chronicle-intelligence/report/building-diverse-campuses-4-key-questions-and-4-case-studies.

42. K. Jurée Capers, "Representation's Effect on Latinx College Graduation Rates," *Social Science Quarterly* 100, no. 4 (June 2019): 1112–28, at 1123.

43. The most recent public data indicate that 25 percent of Barry's student body self-identifies as white. See https://www.barry.edu/institutional-research/quick-facts.html.

44. See Justice Equity Diversity Inclusion Consortium, Barry University, https://www.barry.edu/arec/.

45. See Institute for Latino Studies, University of Notre Dame, https://latinostudies.nd.edu/.

46. See Alliance for Catholic Education, Latino Enrollment Institute, https://ace.nd.edu/catholic-school-advantage/latino-enrollment-institute.

47. See "Hispanic-Serving Institution Progress," Marquette University, https://www.marquette.edu/diversity/hispanic-serving-institution-progress.php.

48. See Marquette's institutional research report at "Diversity and Inclusion Dashboards: Achievement," Marquette University Institutional Research and Analysis, https://www.marquette.edu/institutional-research-analysis/interactive-reports/achievement-dash.php.

49. Maria Luisa Torres, "Why Increased Enrollment of Latino Students in Catholic Schools Benefits Both Schools and Students," *America*, February 23, 2018, https://www.americamagazine.org/politics-society/2018/02/23/why-increased-enrollment-latino-students-catholic-schools-benefits-both.

4

EDUCATING FOR WHAT?

Liberal Arts in a Preprofessional World

Anna Bonta Moreland and Mark Shiffman

What are colleges and universities for? Should they prioritize the cultivation of individual talents for the student's personal benefit, or should they look above all to the promotion of justice and solidarity in the social and political spheres? Should the curriculum maximize free choice and self-direction, or should it direct students toward things most worth learning? In this chapter, we suggest that a rehabilitated sense of the liberal arts that draws upon the resources of Catholic social thought (CST) can address these important questions in a nonbinary way. But first, we outline things as they stand.

Introduction: Liberal Arts in Crisis

Today the liberal arts are experiencing an unprecedented crisis of confidence, emerging from pressures external to the academy and internal to disciplinary inquiry. External pressures include economic anxiety,[1] rising tuition costs,[2] and declining numbers of students who decide to major in the liberal arts.[3] Compared to "professional training…and scientific research where results are tangible…, the Arts are seen increasingly as a luxury."[4] In every college within the modern university, students are herded toward the job market, preparing them for conventional professions and financial success. Students, especially those in elite academic environments, experience intense pressure to "build their brand" rather than unlock their desires and talents and marry them to a profession that serves the common good.[5] Among Harvard University's 2020 graduating class entering the workforce, over 60 percent indicated they would go into the lucrative fields of consulting, finance, or technology, with only 3 percent opting for public service/nonprofit sectors.[6] These trends are repeated within Catholic universities like Villanova, where we teach: in 2021, only 2 percent of the graduating class opted for postgraduate service opportunities.

Internal pressures within departments that have traditionally housed the "liberal arts" include fights over the core curriculum, departmental turf wars, arguments within disciplines over what constitutes the canon, and deep ideological divisions among the faculty. There is, in fact, little disciplinary agreement in many liberal arts departments, such that departmental documents have become increasingly procedural to hide the lack of agreement on such foundational questions as what material students should learn in the discipline and how that material should be taught.

The effect of these pressures on the student's experience of liberal learning is often utterly debilitating. At prestigious institutions, career counseling usually begins in the student's first weeks on campus, continually reinforcing students' anxieties about their future prospects and forcefully communicating a mostly implicit message: you will be a disappointment and a failure if you refuse to follow as prestigious a career as you can. The relentless pragmatism of resumé building habituates students to think they just cannot spare time for liberal learning. At less prestigious institutions, students often choose majors that promise lucrative salaries and employment security because they want to ensure they can repay student loans.

It was from the beginning, and should continue to be, the responsibility of a college or university to inculturate students into a process of intellectual, moral, and human transformation through reflection on basic questions. William Deresiewicz, in his 2015 book *Excellent Sheep*, examines at length how elite institutions and their careerist pragmatism fail to prepare students for these basic questions. The results are conformity, mediocrity of soul and imagination, lack of purpose and meaning, and a failure to cultivate intellectual independence.

Though not himself a religious believer, Deresiewicz nonetheless finds that the alternative that he champions is best served by drawing upon a religious lexicon:

> We might propose, then, that you should arrive at college as at the beginning of a *pilgrimage*—a movement toward the truth and toward the self. That you should come to seek *conversion*, though you know not yet to what belief or way. That you should approach ideas as instruments of *salvation*, driven by a need to work things through for yourself, so that you won't be *damned* to go through life at second hand, thinking other people's thoughts and dreaming other people's dreams....We are born once....But then if we are granted such *grace*, we are *born again*. For what does it profit a man if he gains the *world* and loses his mortal *soul*?[7]

It is no accident that Christian terms serve to articulate this corrective to the failures of higher education. These terms express a conception of the human person written into the DNA of the university itself. Founded in medieval Europe, the institution of the university originally took shape around a Christian understanding of the fulfillment of the human person through moral and intellectual formation.

The contemporary Catholic college or university can draw from rich philosophical and theological traditions to fulfill this task of formation and development. In continuity with the Christian humanist vision central to the university's original mission, CST understands the human person as fundamentally oriented toward "total truth and the absolute good."[8] This principle lies at the very heart of CST: "A just society can become a reality only when it is based on the respect of the transcendent dignity of the human person."[9] The Catholic college or university, by taking this transcendent dignity as its ordering principle, can thereby both breathe life and purpose back into the liberal arts and harmonize the aims of individual development and social responsibility, liberation and formation, humane learning and career preparation.

Liberal Arts and the Origin of the University

The two great educational theorists Hugh of St. Victor and John of Salisbury, writing at the time of the birth of the Universities of Paris, Bologna, and Oxford in the twelfth century, gave forceful expression to the Catholic vision of transcendent dignity: according to them, growth in knowledge of the created natural and moral orders advances our pursuit of the true and the good. As the medieval historian Brian FitzGerald observes,

> For Hugh, a comprehensive vision of the divine presence within the natural world leads him to seek a legitimate and proper place for all forms of knowledge, balancing the new and the old, the sacred and the secular...to gain greater awareness of the divine image within. John, on the other hand, places the arts at the service...of society....For Hugh and for John, education develops man's natural capacities, making him more aware of who he is and what he is called to be.[10]

In the four major fields of the university curriculum, special attention was given to the natural world and the human place in it in the study of medicine, while the right ordering of society was the focus of law or jurisprudence. These fields were like two sides of an arch, for which the threshold was provided by philosophy, understood as an art of orderly questioning, and the keystone was provided by theology, exploring God's self-revelation of the deep principles holding everything together.[11] The major fields of knowledge were thus understood to be related to one another in an organic order. FitzGerald observes, "Underlying such an ordered system is a belief in the unity of all knowledge, the interrelationship of the liberal arts, and their importance for an understanding of the divine."[12]

These disciplines developed sophisticated habits of critical reflection, attuning students more faithfully to the created order and developing in them a keener sensibility to truth, to beauty, and to goodness.[13] It was thus an education designed to make students more fully human. For Hugh, all the choices we make are "acts of interpretation, fraught with moral and spiritual dimensions, about the true meaning of things."[14] It was precisely by seeking the things to be loved for their own sake and for God's that this education was profoundly practical, illuminating every choice made in pursuit of a fulfilling life.

The political implications of this humanism were made explicit. The thirteenth-century Augustinian philosopher Giles of Rome, who was considered the greatest teacher at the University of Paris, recognized the importance of education for forming students for civil freedom: "If the lord of a kingdom does not promote study nor wish his subjects to become knowledgeable, then he is no king but a tyrant."[15] By implication, the failure to promote liberal education—the education that liberates human beings by forming them for liberty—prepares the ground for tyranny.

The university itself sought to model a community that upholds human dignity. As a result, the pursuit of knowledge was seen as interpersonal. When today we refer to the word *universities*, we mean institutions of advanced learning. We mean a series of buildings with—preferably—a winning football or basketball team. But when medievals used the term *universities*, they did not refer to institutions, but to people: the guilds of masters and students. It was not until the fifteenth century that *university* became the common term for the school or place of study.[16]

The origin of the term *university* implies that at the center of any intellectual inquiry lies a *relationship* between student and teacher. Love of wisdom is infectious. We become attracted to wisdom by seeing others fall for it. The student-teacher relationship is nourished by the relations among the students themselves and among the faculty. Without these intellectual communities, the disciplines grow stale. The pursuit of wisdom is found more than anywhere else in lifelong conversations, in community. Intellectual friendship, then, is at the heart of university life, as ideas ultimately come to life in human beings.

Catholic universities should reflect the fact that in this religious tradition the organizing principle is the person of Christ.[17] So at a Catholic university, the relationship between student and teacher is ultimately tied to the relationship, explicit or implicit, of each to Christ. In his first encyclical *Deus Caritas Est*, Pope Benedict XVI captures this spirit when he writes, "Being Christian is not the result of an ethical choice or a lofty idea, but the encounter with an event, a person, which gives life a new horizon and a decisive direction."[18] CST sees in this radical relationship of personal encounter, not the grounding of a separate identity defined over against other identities, but the very universality of the mission of Christian humanism:

> The universality and integrality of the salvation wrought by Christ makes indissoluble the link between the relationship that the person is called to have with God and the responsibility he has towards his neighbor in the concrete circumstances of history. This is sensed, though not always without some confusion or misunderstanding, *in humanity's universal quest for truth and meaning*....In [the human person's] inner dimension are rooted, in the final analysis, the commitment to justice and solidarity, to the building up of a social, economic and political life that corresponds to God's plan.[19]

Indeed, all the features we have noted in the medieval university find their life-giving root in this relationship to the person of Christ who is also the Logos ordering creation: the organically interrelated order of all knowledge; the humanizing love of the Creator's truth, beauty, and goodness shining through the created order all the more as we come to know it better; the meaning such love and knowledge gives to our choices; the dignity of freedom that comes with understanding those meanings; the responsibility to respect and foster the social, economic, and political dimensions of that dignity in ourselves and our neighbors; the deeply interpersonal engagements inseparable from the pursuit of all these things. The university's original Catholic inspiration endows it with all these features.

This reflection on the medieval university is no exercise in nostalgia. It is a reminder of the key features proper to Catholic higher education. Today, CST orients itself by these same principles to engage constructively with the conditions of the modern world. This makes it an indispensable resource for understanding the mission of the Catholic university as an institution concerned with human dignity. Its liberating intellectual, moral, and spiritual formation protects against the ignorance, indoctrination, and despair of truth that prepare the social ground for tyranny.[20]

Capturing the Medieval Spirit in the Modern University

Three cornerstones of CST, the principles of human dignity, solidarity, and the common good, offer the modern Catholic college or university the portals through which this medieval pedagogy can reanimate the liberal arts. The need to highlight our responsibilities to our neighbor "in the concrete circumstances of history" has animated and shaped CST since its beginnings in *Rerum Novarum*, Pope Leo XIII's 1891 encyclical whose very title indicates that it is a reflection upon "new things."[21] Those new things have included such distinctly modern trends as liberalism, socialism, industrial capitalism, and totalitarianism—all of which have cast shadows on the aims of education.

In opposition and resistance to the narrow ideological tendencies found in these trends, CST has insistently reminded persons of goodwill of the primacy of our transcendent dignity. The *Compendium of the Social Doctrine of the Church*, published in 2004, warns especially against two related dangers of viewing the person solely through the reductive lens of social and political ideologies: instrumentalization of the person and neglect of the moral and spiritual dimensions of free and responsible agency.

Regarding instrumentalization, the *Compendium* insists, "*The person cannot be a means for carrying out economic, social or political projects* imposed by some authority, even in the name of an alleged progress of the civil community as a whole or of other persons, either in the present or the future." Such reduction fails to recognize the dignity of the human being "as a *person*, that is to say, as an *active* and *responsible* subject of his own growth process, together with the community to which he belongs."[22]

This teaching clearly implies a nonbinary answer to one of our initial questions: the true cultivation of the individual and the true promotion of justice and solidarity are inseparable goals. The *Compendium* is explicit on this point:

> *Removing injustices promotes human freedom and dignity*: nonetheless, "the first thing to be done is to appeal to the spiritual and moral capacities of the individual and to the

> permanent need for inner conversion, if one is to achieve the economic and social changes that will truly be at the service of [the human person]."[23]

As we have seen, Deresiewicz stresses the idea of conversion in his conception of liberal education, but his understanding of conversion seems to be informed mainly by the expressive individualism of the American Transcendentalists. CST, on the other hand, grounded in Christian humanism, conveys a vision of conversion that is inseparably both spiritual and solidaristic.

The "concrete circumstances of history" in the early twenty-first century, of course, differ significantly from those of the late nineteenth. The *Compendium* accordingly highlights some of the "new things" threatening dignity and solidarity in our time:

> The first of the great challenges facing humanity today is that of *the truth itself of the being who is man*....A second challenge is found in *the understanding and management of pluralism and differences at every level*....The third challenge is *globalization*, the significance of which is much wider and more profound than simple economic globalization.[24]

How do these three challenges—the truth of the human being, pluralism, and globalization—look today, nearly two decades after the *Compendium* raised concerns about them? Clearly, they have all had visible impacts on the study of the liberal arts in universities. Let us consider those impacts in the reverse order.

Globalization

In his 2020 book *The Tyranny of Merit*, political theorist Michael Sandel raises concerns about the complicity of American higher education and "market-driven globalization" (along with "the technocratic turn of contemporary politics, and the oligarchic capture of democratic institutions") in creating or exacerbating "the inequalities of income and social esteem we witness today."[25] Sandel is anxious about the corrosive effects on one of the central concerns of CST: the common good.[26]

According to Sandel, a "market-friendly, technocratic conception of globalization…embraced by mainstream parties of the left and the right" has led to "vast inequalities of income and wealth, an economy dominated by finance, a political system in which money spoke louder than citizens, and a rising tide of angry nationalism."[27] He regards events like Brexit and the Trump election as to a large degree "an angry verdict on decades of rising inequality and a version of globalization that benefits those at the top but leaves ordinary citizens feeling disempowered," as well as "a rebuke to a technocratic approach to politics that is tone-deaf to the resentments of people who feel the economy and the culture have left them behind."[28]

As recent bribery scandals in elite university admissions highlight, top schools provide the knowledge and skills and, more importantly, the credentials that smooth the way into the successful ruling elite in this competitive globalized system. At first glance, the attempts at bribery appear to undermine the intention of competitive college admissions, which is to open the path of success to talented students regardless of wealth; but, as Sandel explains in detail, the admissions system itself already undermines its purported intention.

The function universities have increasingly undertaken of sorting students into winners and losers in the globalized economy has led to a "meritocratic arms race [that] tilts the competition in favor of the wealthy and enables affluent parents to pass their privilege on to their kids."[29] It is undeniable that elite high school attendance, standardized test performance, and the bundles of activities that give weight to college applications all benefit from the resources wealthy parents can pour into them. The result is that "higher education has become a sorting machine that promises mobility on the basis of merit but entrenches privilege and promotes attitudes toward success corrosive of the commonality democracy requires."[30] (See further Laura Nichols's chapter in this volume.)

Whatever laudable implications there may be to the increasingly common rhetoric of colleges and universities about preparing "global citizens," this priority often has a dark underside, reflecting a broader paradigm shift in institutions of higher education: "their credentialing function now looms so large that it overwhelms their educational function."[31] Within the curriculum, liberal arts education has generally been the great casualty. The rush to slap a credential on anything that looks marketable has left the liberal arts courses, whose faculty cannot agree on the meaning and motivation behind what they teach, at a severe disadvantage in this marketing arms race.

But what liberal arts faculty have not—on the whole—woken up to is the fact that these disciplines harbor the hidden resources to meet contemporary challenges. CST shows why liberal arts education is one of the most needed remedies for the deforming effects of globalization.

In the first place, when CST recognizes in our increasingly globalized world something "much wider and more profound than simple economic globalization," this refers especially to a "growing awareness of interdependence":

> The fact that men and women in various parts of the world feel personally affected by the injustices and violations of human rights committed in distant countries, countries which perhaps they will never visit, is a further sign of a reality transformed into awareness, thus acquiring a moral connotation....When interdependence becomes recognized in this way, the correlative response as a moral and social attitude, as a "virtue," is solidarity.[32]

The liberal arts have a crucial role to play in transformation of students' awareness of interdependence as an economic fact into a mature and intelligent sense of solidarity as the ground of moral responsibility.

In its development of the theme of solidarity as a virtue, CST adds a crucial element to what is an ethic often limited to compassion and protest in the kind of secular understanding one generally finds in university settings:

> *Solidarity is also an authentic moral virtue*, not a "feeling of vague compassion or shallow distress at the misfortunes of so many people, both near and far." On the contrary, it is a *firm and persevering determination to commit oneself to the common good. That is to say to the good of all and of each individual, because we are all really responsible for all.*[33]

Commitment to the common good rests upon a principle that lies at the core of the Christian understanding of the fullness of the human person: namely, charity. "Social charity makes us love the common good."[34] Charity is the desire for the good of another that is "always ready to sacrifice itself for the sake of others,"[35] a love for which Christ is the true model.

When charity animates a love of the common good in which it is possible to recognize and accept that all are responsible for all, it grounds an understanding of and respect for the dignity of the person that makes us truly attentive to others and their good. It thus carries us beyond ourselves and beyond what risks remaining a merely cathartic and scapegoating anger of protest.[36]

Any adequate response to the deleterious tendencies of globalization would necessarily involve other key CST commitments. The universal destination of goods, for example, rests upon the foundation of the doctrine of creation. The right to private property should never be divorced from our responsibility to the common good. The preferential option for the poor challenges a meritocratic sense of justice and entitlement. The principle of subsidiarity grounds a critique of both the globalizing elite's "regulation from nowhere" and the economic hazards of multinational corporations. Much might be added on these topics, all of which rest upon an understanding of the human person that CST recognizes as its crucial underpinning, elaboration of which is beyond the scope of this chapter.

Pluralism

Just as globalization and its effects on higher education have intensified over the last two decades, so also have the demands of pluralism come into greater prominence. Given this academic landscape, how should a curriculum grounded in CST truth claims be built?

The first and simplest answer is that, in a pluralistic landscape, a Catholic institution of learning needs no apology for being authentically Catholic. As Massimo Faggioli claims in *Commonweal*, the liberal-progressive wing in Catholic higher education

> has embraced deconstruction of the neo-Scholastic hegemony since Vatican II so fully that it's now suspicious of *any* Catholic institutionalism. It has been too accommodating of the identity politics that have taken root since the 1960s. It is perhaps still too closely linked to a vision of Catholic higher education laid out more than fifty years ago in the Land O'Lakes Statement, which is showing its age.[37]

One might go further and say that the Catholic college or university fails in its proper respect for pluralism if it fails to teach with integrity the distinctive "ways of thinking, moral choices, [and] culture" that belong to the tradition of its religious affiliation.[38] If the pluralistic educational landscape can be described as a "marketplace of ideas," then Catholic colleges and universities ought to offer the particular riches that are theirs. Their responsibility is to be stalls in the market-place, not to become the marketplace. This responsibility is all the more important when non-Catholic educational institutions, whether through indifference, ignorance, or hostility, are ill-equipped to display these riches in their native splendor and attractiveness.

The challenge of pluralism, then, is not that it forbids a Catholic college or university to be authentically Catholic. Rather, one of the most important challenges of pluralism for a Catholic institution lies in the role pluralism has played in the crisis of the liberal arts. If Catholic institutions, guided by core principles of CST, can address the crisis of the liberal arts, they can offer one of the best models for doing justice to the truths of pluralism while overcoming the dangers of inadequate and reductive versions of it.

CST affirms that Christians are to be "open to dialogue with all people of good will in the common quest for the seeds of truth and freedom sown in the vast field of humanity."[39] The first thing to stress here is the word *quest*. As we have already seen, CST acknowledges "humanity's universal quest for truth and meaning." Human beings are seekers, and the Catholic faithful are no exception. Already in the century before the founding of the first universities, St. Anselm gave the definitive description of Catholic thought as "faith seeking understanding."[40] Anselm also recognized the inescapable paradox involved in this quest, because it is directed toward the fullness of truth, which is the God who "dwells in inaccessible light" and "the love of Christ which surpasses all understanding."[41] The truth provided by CST and the whole theological tradition is not something that can ever simply be possessed, but is always something into which we are growing. For this reason, even while CST claims to be grounded in the most fundamental truths, the dialogue it engages in is never one-sided, but always open to additional illumination from the insights of other traditions of seeking.

It is from this perspective that we must understand the claim of CST to universality:

> *Besides being destined primarily and specifically to the sons and daughters of the Church, her social doctrine also has a universal destination.* The light of the Gospel that the Church's social doctrine shines on society illuminates all men and women, and every conscience and mind is in a position to grasp the human depths of meaning and values expressed in it and the potential of humanity and humanization contained in its norms of action.[42]

It is because they are seekers of the good and the true that all human beings have consciences and minds in a position to be receptive to the light refracted through CST.

The Catholic understanding of human beings as receptive seekers of goodness and truth, moving within a created order illuminated by its Creator, can liberate the liberal arts from the depths of their crisis. When minds of finite capacities seek to become adequate to a truth that inescapably surpasses their grasp, pluralism is to be expected. This pluralism is, of course, already present within the bounds of the Catholic tradition, but, as *Lumen Gentium* rightly puts it, the rings of pluralism widen beyond the walls of the Church.[43] There will always be partial perspectives in need of dialogue with each other. This is why the medieval universities showed an historically unprecedented tolerance of conflicting schools of thought and voices within the same educational institution.

Reflecting back on medieval universities, nineteenth-century political philosopher John Stuart Mill observed that their pedagogical methods "were intended to make sure that the pupil understood his own opinion, and (by necessary correlation) the opinion opposed to it, and could enforce the grounds of the one and confute those of the other."[44] In this pedagogy, Mill recognized a standard of dialogue superior to that practiced in the education of his own day. The same can generally be said in our time. Today, liberal arts disciplines have become unmoored from the belief that there is one truth to which potential dialogue partners are aspiring. Even if not every scholar signs on to this abandonment, it remains a matter of professional etiquette in the disciplines.

As a result, pluralism will tend to imply relativism, and freedom of opinion will tend to be interpreted as the right to "one's own truth." Difference will be taken to imply separate and unrelated "alternatives" demanding respect in their unchallenged divergences rather than needing each other as challenging correctives. Dialogue thus becomes impossible, or at least lacking in any well-grounded motivation.[45] This seems to be a central reason that liberal arts disciplines are now so much more about varieties of methods than about growing together in the understanding of truth. Without a unifying anchor in the transcendent dignity of the human being as a hopeful truth seeker, the relationship of teaching and learning ceases to be interpersonal in any meaningful sense. It becomes transactional, in either a utilitarian or a political sense. If students perceive the liberal arts to be pointless, declining enrollments should be no surprise. The Catholic college or university, informed by CST, has resources to reanchor the liberal arts in this journey of seeking truth together.

Pluralism, then, enhances a Catholic college or university to the extent that all faculty are part of one truth-seeking enterprise. Ecclesial language referring to others as "inside" or "outside" the Church should be replaced by language of direction and orientation,[46] as some who might be considered "outsiders" are actually more deeply oriented toward seeking the truth than some "insiders." The twentieth-century philosopher Simone Weil echoes this point:

> It seemed to me certain, and I still think so today, that one can never wrestle enough with God if one does so out of pure regard for the truth. Christ likes us to prefer truth to him because, before being Christ, he is truth. If one turns aside from him to go toward the truth, one will not go far before falling into his arms.[47]

Accordingly, for a college or university to be truly "Catholic," the number of faculty epistemologically committed to truth seeking is more important than high numbers of Catholic faculty. Faculty committed to seeking truth in their own disciplinary inquiry are central to the task of Catholic higher education.

The reanchoring suggested here is particularly urgent in a "post-truth" climate of public discourse in which political pluralism has increasingly become a matter of sheer divergence closed off from challenge. CST urges us to reach beyond divisions, even to people we might be inclined to see as enemies:

> They also have a claim on our respect and charity that think and act differently from us in social, political and religious matters. In fact the more deeply we come to understand their ways of thinking through kindness and love, the more easily will we be able to enter into dialogue with them. This path requires grace, which God offers to man in order to help him to overcome failings, to snatch him from the spiral of lies and violence.[48]

In the American context, different principles affirmed by CST usually find separate homes in "liberal" and "conservative" ideologies, which parcel them out in oversimplified ways. Embracing CST's challenge to share in a coherent vision beyond political divisions can inform liberal education in a way that will offer students something more satisfying than partisan rancor. Inundated by an increasingly toxic polarized public "conversation," students long for such humane sanity, but rarely find it on display in their classrooms. They can hardly be blamed for sticking to technical subjects. The failure of higher education to provide a forum in which students can freely seek social and political wisdom adds to the danger that unquestioned and extreme oversimplifications will create an atmosphere increasingly conducive to lies and violence.

The Truth of the Human Being

For the Catholic tradition, then, the call to dialogue is ultimately a response to God's extension of grace to human beings, "to invite them and receive them into communion."[49] This vocation to communion brings us to the third of the challenges emphasized in the *Compendium*: the truth of the human being. We have stressed two aspects of this truth: the human being is a hopeful truth seeker, and the natural goal of this quest is to recognize charity both as our own fulfillment and as God's character as Creator and Redeemer. The coordination of these aspects is one of the pedagogical and curricular challenges of Catholic liberal arts education. In fidelity to the Church's role as "the sign and the safeguard of the transcendent dimension of the human person,"[50] Catholic liberal arts education must foster the freedom of truth seeking while never ceasing to take its bearings from the proper destination of that seeking: the liberating embrace of charity, the love of God and neighbor. This double task must infuse and inform the liberal arts if a Catholic college or university is to be faithful to its "evangelizing and kerygmatic mission."[51]

Balancing these two principles can be carried out in a variety of ways. The pedagogy must emphasize questioning and dialogue. The curriculum must include sources divergent from, critical of, and even hostile to the Catholic tradition, while always placing them in conversation with the most deeply thoughtful and compellingly attractive representations of that tradition.

The role of liberal arts education in developing greater awareness of the truth of the human being is especially important in an educational environment that is increasingly professionalized. The disciplines that come to dominate studies in such an environment are the more technical ones, which tend to operate according to what Pope Francis has called a "technocratic paradigm." These disciplines typically train students in a "technique of possession, mastery and transformation," one that has a tendency to treat the created order as something "completely open to manipulation."[52] As the *Compendium* emphasizes, the challenge of understanding the human in our day involves numerous questions regarding the "relation between nature, technology and morality."[53] To the extent that a discipline is reduced to the merely technical and applied dimension, it not only fails to raise questions about these relationships; it also assumes, in practice, that the relationship we aspire to is one of maximum control, with minimal if any regard for the integrity of the created order. (See for further discussion Vincent Miller's chapter in this volume.)

For the sake of clarity, it is worth considering the text of the *Compendium* at greater length on this point:

> Because of the powerful means of transformation offered by technological civilization, it sometimes seems that the balance between man and the environment has reached a critical point. *Nature appears as an instrument in the hands of man, a reality that he must constantly manipulate, especially by means of technology*....Primacy is given to doing and having rather than to being, and this causes serious forms of human alienation. *Such attitudes do not arise from scientific and technological research but from scientism and technocratic ideologies that tend to condition such research*....With the progress of science and technology, questions as to their

> meaning increase and give rise to an ever greater need to respect the transcendent dimension of the human person and creation itself.[54]

Technical education separated from the liberal learning that elucidates the transcendent dimension of the human person and the beauty and goodness of creation thus tends toward a narrowed vision of the human truth, and ultimately to a deep sense of alienation. It increases our power to do and to have, but it diminishes our capacity to consider to what ends and within what limits.

The Catholic college or university, then, should not view the liberal arts and the technical disciplines as unrelated to each other, much less as in conflict or competition. Rather, looking to the wholeness of the person, it should recognize the indispensability of the liberal arts for educating even students who are pursuing more technical or business-oriented studies. "To 'have' objects and goods does not in itself perfect the human subject, unless it contributes to the maturing and enrichment of that subject's 'being,' that is to say unless it contributes to the realization of the human vocation as such."[55] Found above all in the transcendent dimension of the person, the human vocation consists especially in seeking truth and wisdom, love of God and neighbor, and responsibility to the common good in solidarity with others, particularly with those who are more vulnerable.

Putting This Vision into Practice: The Liberal Arts Reimagined

Higher education meets students where they are to ask big questions about the meaning of human life and their role in it. It is uniquely suited to help them formulate and pursue those questions, reflection about which builds resilience in an unpredictable world. Seen from a student-centered angle, the crisis of the liberal arts is rooted in the increasing failure of colleges and universities to draw upon the resources they offer to raise, deepen, and reframe these questions, and thus to make liberal learning a vital concern for the student. In his eighteenth-century *Critique of Pure Reason*, Immanuel Kant offers three foundational questions around which the liberal arts curriculum could be structured: What can I know? What must I do? What may I hope? Similarly, W. E. B. Du Bois, articulating the aims of liberal education a century later in *The Souls of Black Folk*, insists that the central concern of the college curriculum must always be "the riddle of existence," an engagement occupied primarily with "delving for Truth, and searching out the hidden beauties of life, and learning the good of living."[56] These guiding principles echo the vision of the medieval university outlined above, in which the human person in relation to God stands at the center of the curriculum.

These core questions orient students to the transcendent dimension of the human person, respect for which CST identifies as integral to higher education and to any just society. The curriculum, then, should be structured around a canon of questions, not a canon of texts. This curriculum would engage students in a dialogue across disciplines shaped by the fundamental human questions, one that does as much justice as feasible to the best contributions of Catholic art and thought as well as to diverse sources that chime with the Catholic vision and others that go against its grain. This curriculum thus avoids some of the current internal obstacles to liberal arts education detailed in the introduction to this chapter.

The core curriculum could be organized by a group of faculty from all divisions—arts, sciences, social sciences, business, engineering, and nursing—who embrace the fact that colleges and universities are in the business of student formation. Substantively, higher education should prepare students to live a fully flourishing life. Work is part of that life, of course, but the core curriculum forms the *whole student*. As Du Bois puts it, "The true college will ever have one goal—not to earn meat, but to know the end and aim of that life which meat nourishes."[57] If student formation is at the center of the core curriculum, the disciplines can be seen, once again, as organically related to each other, and grounded in humanistic inquiry. Faculty can then build cohesive pathways through the curriculum that engage Kant's foundational questions in ways that lead students into particular disciplinary inquiry, which could in turn enliven this inquiry with a stronger sense of its relevance to "the riddle of existence."

What would this reanimated sense of the liberal arts look like in contemporary Catholic higher education? As a first step, this vision would best come to fruition in a radically restructured core curriculum that is housed, not in a school or college of the liberal arts and sciences, but under the Office of the Provost or the like. It is no longer true—if it ever was—that colleges and universities are composed of "professional schools" on the one side, and schools or colleges of liberal arts and sciences on the other. As noted at the beginning of this chapter, all schools within universities today are driven by overwhelming demands of professionalization. Taking the core out of the school of liberal arts and sciences would recognize this new reality. It is not just that engineering, nursing, and business students are required to take several courses in the liberal arts because they will be better engineers, more equipped nurses, or smarter businesswomen as a result of their liberal arts education. Students in all of the schools at a university—including those in liberal arts and sciences—will become better human beings by engaging a series of questions together.

While not housed in any of the schools, the core curriculum would stream into the different disciplines, with faculty who deepen this humanistic vision as they engage students in the question of "What must I do?" or "How should I live my life?" It is true that there are vibrant pockets of this sort of formation already at work in corners of our institutions, but these are usually exceptions in a hyper-professional atmosphere. We propose a renewed vision of higher education: anchored in the principles of CST, the liberal arts ground the core curriculum and then turn students over to particular disciplinary inquiry that is suffused by those same CST principles.

Once students move into the more specialized learning of their majors, how does our vision of an integrated liberal arts curriculum suffused with CST principles emerge in the disciplines? With so many majors, minors, and concentrations to choose from, many of our students suffer from paralysis—an overabundance that leads to an inability to choose.[58] This is paired with an overwhelming anxiety that each choice about majors or internships will define their lives. In this context, after formation in the core curriculum, discernment should be central to disciplinary inquiry. This includes but is not limited to professional discernment. As they pursue their majors, students should be trained in discernment practices that will enable them to choose their professions wisely. As work is integral to a flourishing life, students should be taught to ask hard questions about the meaning of work. The principles of CST—particularly those of human dignity, the common good, and stewardship—should frame this reflection. The twentieth-century Polish philosopher Zygmunt Bauman writes that "work has acquired—alongside other life activities—a mainly aesthetic significance. It is expected to be gratifying by and in itself." But instead, as Bauman proposes, it should be measured by "the genuine or putative effects it brings to one's brothers and sisters in humanity or to the might of the nation and country, let alone the bliss of future generations."[59] Work should ennoble. It should make students better human beings.

Is there an appetite for this kind of curriculum among our current undergraduates? The sociologist Tim Clydesdale studied the results of the Lilly Endowment Grant on vocation, in which eighty-eight campuses developed creative programs on the questions of purpose:

> As pragmatic as America's students may be, the desire to positively engage with others persists: two out of every three college juniors nationally endorsed as a life goal "reducing pain and suffering in the world"..., and all 125 of this project's in-depth interviewees agreed that they wanted their lives "to make a difference." The majority of college students seek a meaningful life, and most are willing to hear any narrative of purpose that is genuinely conveyed.[60]

Clydesdale also found that the most successful programs were those that were rooted in rich theological tradition and language.[61] The core experience we propose is interpersonal, ideally housed in small seminar classes. Within this model, online learning cannot replace in-person education.

Student formation should not focus only on professional discernment. How students choose to spend their leisure time shapes and changes them just as much as what they choose to do for work. Outside of the classroom, cocurricular planning must break out of the "involvement culture" where clubs and activities have become training camps for students' resumé enhancement. Instead, colleges and universities should help students spend their leisure time wisely, in activities that are not instrumental, that are done for their own sake, and that leave them feeling energized rather than depleted. Intellectual friendship is at the center of academic life, not just in the classroom, but in the dorms, the dining halls, and the quad.

The whole curriculum should be directed toward a professional life like the one that English novelist Dorothy Sayers outlines:

> [Work] should be looked upon, not as a necessary drudgery to be undergone for the purpose of making money, but as a way of life in which the nature of [the human person] should find its proper exercise and delight and so fulfill itself to the glory of God....[I]t should, in fact, be thought of as a creative activity undertaken for the love of the work itself; and...[the human person], made in God's image, should make things, as God makes them, for the sake of doing well a thing that is well worth doing.[62]

A Catholic higher education, grounded in the principles of CST as outlined above, will prepare its students to envision work in this way. Its graduates will enter the workforce ready to further the common good of humanity in a way that dignifies the worker herself.

Conclusion

The challenges posed by the overprofessionalization of contemporary higher education are severe. They have led to dire predictions of the future of the university that regularly surface in national news media and print books. This chapter has set forth resources from Catholic traditions of inquiry—both medieval and contemporary—to offer fresh ways to incorporate the liberal arts into our institutions. Catholic social thought—most especially the principles of human dignity, the common good, solidarity, and stewardship—should guide the reconstruction of the relationship between the liberal arts and all branches of study and knowledge. Such reconstruction will offer an education that at once expands, humanizes, and prepares its students for truly successful lives.

Questions for Consideration and Discussion

1. Moreland and Shiffman present "the Catholic university" as first and foremost "an institution concerned with human dignity." Further, according to them, "the true cultivation of the individual

and the true promotion of justice and solidarity are inseparable goals" inasmuch as human beings find fulfillment in flourishing communities. What is your Catholic college or university primarily concerned with, and how is that concern manifest? In other words, where does it find expression? Is your institution genuinely, fundamentally concerned with "the true promotion of justice and solidarity"? Should it be? Why or why not?

2. According to Moreland and Shiffman, it is "the responsibility of a college or university to inculturate students into a process of intellectual, moral, and human transformation through reflection on basic questions." Does your institution's curriculum seek to transform students in those ways? Does it in fact transform students in those ways? What are the basic goals of your institution's curriculum? Further, what would you identify as "the responsibility of a college or university"?
3. Moreland and Shiffman claim both that "Catholic colleges and universities ought to offer the particular riches that are theirs" and that high numbers of Catholic faculty matter less than "the number of faculty epistemologically committed to truth-seeking." Do you think that the number of (committed, conversant) Catholic faculty matters? If you think the number matters, does your institution have enough such faculty? Further, what are the particular riches that your institution offers? What are faculty at your institution committed to? What commitments does your institution reward through promotion and advancement? Finally, how could your institution hire and promote for mission along these lines? What, concretely, would you be seeking in candidates and faculty as they advance through the ranks?
4. According to Moreland and Shiffman, "Catholic universities should reflect the fact that in this religious tradition the organizing principle is the person of Christ. So at a Catholic university, the relationship between student and teacher is ultimately tied to the relationship, explicit or implicit, of each to Christ." What is the organizing principle of the curriculum at your institution? Is encounter with Christ even on the horizon? Can it be, in our contemporary context of growing religious nonaffiliation and illiteracy? Does it need to be somehow, if your institution is to be meaningfully Catholic?

5. Compare your institution's core curriculum with the approach proposed by Moreland and Shiffman. In light of your institution's overall learning goals for students, what are the advantages and disadvantages of your approach and of Moreland and Shiffman's proposed approach?
6. How is the core curriculum regarded at your institution by students, faculty, staff, administration, and trustees? Is the language of CST employed to describe its purpose and to guide its development? Do you see CST as useful in this regard? Why or why not?
7. Bring Moreland and Shiffman's chapter into dialogue with Pratt and O'Connell's chapter. What are lines of criticism and convergence that each chapter suggests about the other? Moreland and Shiffman propose that "the curriculum…should be structured around a canon of questions, not a canon of texts." Pratt and O'Connell claim that "what is generally understood as the Catholic intellectual tradition is steeped in the canon of whiteness to which Catholic institutions dedicate much social, political, and economic capital." What are the ways in which the vision proposed by each set of authors could be integrated?

Notes

1. The Market-Edison Research Poll, a survey developed to measure Americans' economic anxiety, found that, as of October 2020, over 35 percent of Americans surveyed lose sleep over their financial situation, a record high. Economic anxiety has also been amplified by the COVID-19 pandemic, which has led many colleges and universities to consolidate if not eliminate liberal arts programs entirely. Some small liberal arts colleges closed in 2020 as a result of the pandemic, but even larger universities have moved to eliminate faculty, majors, and whole departments, most often in the humanities. To name just three, as of February 2021, the University of Kansas announced the closure of its humanities department; the University of Vermont announced the elimination of twenty-three programs in its college of liberal arts; and Marquette University announced plans to cut 225 faculty and staff, many of whom come from liberal arts programs. See Janet Nguyen, "Americans on Shaky Ground Financially, Speaking Out More on Racism, Poll Finds," Marketplace, October 15, 2020, https://www.marketplace.org/2020/10/15/americans-on-shaky-ground-financially-speaking-out-more-on-racism-covid-19-pandemic/; Colleen Flaherty, "U of Kansas Will Cut Humanities Department," *Inside Higher Ed*, February 23, 2021, https://www.insidehighered

.com/quicktakes/2021/02/23/u-kansas-will-cut-humanities-department; Anne Galloway, "UVM to Eliminate 23 Programs in the College of Arts and Sciences," *VTDigger*, December 3, 2020, https://vtdigger.org/2020/12/03/uvm-to-eliminate-23-programs-in-the-college-of-arts-and-sciences/; and Rich Kremer, "Marquette to Cut 225 Faculty And Staff Positions by July 2022," Wisconsin Public Radio, December 10, 2020, https://www.wpr.org/marquette-university-cut-225-faculty-and-staff-positions-july-2022.

2. From 2009–2010 to 2018–2019 academic years, tuition at four-year colleges has risen 12 percent in constant dollars, 24 percent in current dollars. See U.S. Department of Education, National Center for Education Statistics, *Digest of Education Statistics: 2019*, table 330.10, https://nces.ed.gov/programs/digest/d19/tables/dt19_330.10.asp?current=yes.

3. The number of students choosing to major in the humanities has fallen sharply over the past decade. The number of bachelor's degrees conferred on students in the fields of liberal arts and sciences and humanities from 2009–2010 to 2018–2019 has decreased by 5 percent, even as the total number of bachelor's degrees conferred has risen 18 percent over the same period. Particular disciplines, such as English and philosophy and religious studies, have fared even worse, with drops in conferral of degrees of 26 percent and 23 percent, respectively. See U.S. Department of Education, National Center for Education Statistics, *Digest of Education Statistics: 2019*, table 322.10, https://nces.ed.gov/programs/digest/d20/tables/dt20_322.10.asp (calculations done by authors).

4. Gavin D'Costa, "On Theologizing Theology within the Secular University," *Transformation* 22, no. 3 (July 2005): 148–57, at 152.

5. See Gerald J. Beyer's *Just Universities: Catholic Social Teaching Confronts Corporatized Higher Education* (New York: Fordham University Press, 2021) for a compelling account of the corporatization of American higher education, esp. 11–46.

6. Kristine E. Guillaume and Jamie D. Halper, "After Harvard," in "The Graduating Class of 2020 by the Numbers," *The Harvard Crimson*, May 22, 2020, https://features.thecrimson.com/2020/senior-survey/after-harvard/.

7. William Deresiewicz, *Excellent Sheep: The Miseducation of the American Elite and the Way to a Meaningful Life* (New York: Free Press, 2014), 85–86 (emphasis added).

8. Pontifical Council for Justice and Peace, *Compendium of the Social Doctrine of the Church* (Vatican City: Libreria Editrice Vaticana, 2004), 130.

9. Pontifical Council, *Compendium* 132.

10. Brian D. FitzGerald, "Medieval Theories of Education: Hugh of St Victor and John of Salisbury," *Oxford Review of Education* 36, no. 5 (October 2010): 575–88, at 585.

11. "The arts faculty was a prerequisite to the three higher faculties of theology, medicine and law....But in a very special way the study of arts was geared to the study of theology." See James A. Weisheipl, OP, "The Structure of the Arts Faculty in the Medieval University," *British Journal of Educational Studies* 19, no. 3 (October 1971): 263–71, at 263. The arts curriculum included not only the traditional trivium and quadrivium, in which all matriculating students were expected to have some grounding already, but also "the 'three philosophies,' namely natural philosophy, moral philosophy and metaphysics" (267).

12. FitzGerald, "Medieval Theories of Education," 576.

13. "European universities established themselves from the beginning as educational institutions where professors were free to take opposing positions." The ancient philosophical schools and the monastery and cathedral schools that preceded the university in the West as the central educational institutions, by contrast, were almost always "dominated by a single teacher or a single theory." See Harold J. Berman, *Law and Revolution: The Formation of the Western Legal Tradition* (Cambridge, MA: Harvard University Press, 1983), 126.

14. FitzGerald, "Medieval Theories of Education," 578.

15. Translated by Mark Shiffman from Giles of Rome (Egidio Colonna), *De Regimine Principum Libri III* (Darmstadt: Scientia Verlag Aalen, 1967), book 3, part 2, chap. 8, 471.

16. Francis Oakley, *Community of Learning: The American College and the Liberal Arts Tradition* (New York: Oxford University Press, 1992), 17.

17. Cf. Michael J. Buckley, SJ, "Newman and the Restoration of the Interpersonal in Higher Education" (Santa Clara Lecture, Santa Clara University, November 14, 2006), https://www.scu.edu/media/ignatian-center/santa-clara-lecture/scl-0611-buckley-1.pdf. Throughout this section, we draw from Buckley's lucid *The Catholic University as Promise and Project* (Washington, DC: Georgetown University Press, 1998).

18. Pope Benedict XVI, *Deus Caritas Est* (December 25, 2005), 1.

19. *Compendium* 40, emphasis added.

20. As Pope Francis observes, ideologies find fertile ground for their unopposed sway in "young people who have no use for history, who spurn the spiritual and human riches inherited from past generations, and are ignorant of everything that came before them." See Francis's encyclical *Fratelli Tutti* (October 3, 2020), 13, quoting his postsynodal apostolic exhortation *Christus Vivit* (March 25, 2019), 181.

21. Catholic social thought, of course, finds its roots in the biblical tradition, but most ecclesial histories mark the beginning of what we have come to term CST with this nineteenth-century encyclical. See further the editors' introduction to this volume, n2.

22. *Compendium* 133.

23. *Compendium* 137 (emphasis in original), citing the Congregation for the Doctrine of the Faith's instruction *Libertatis Conscientia*.

24. *Compendium* 16.

25. Michael J. Sandel, *The Tyranny of Merit: What's Become of the Common Good?* (New York: Farrar, Straus & Giroux, 2020), 184.

26. See especially *Compendium* 164–70. Sandel himself recognizes the distinct value of CST for addressing the issues he raises, especially regarding the dignity of work, apropos of which he draws upon both the encyclical *Laborem Exercens* and the USCCB's 1986 pastoral letter *Economic Justice for All*. See *The Tyranny of Merit*, 210.

27. Sandel, *The Tyranny of Merit*, 20, 56.

28. Sandel, *The Tyranny of Merit*, 17.

29. Sandel, *The Tyranny of Merit*, 178.

30. Sandel, *The Tyranny of Merit*, 155. See also "America's New Aristocracy," *The Economist*, January 22, 2015, https://www.economist.com/leaders/2015/01/22/americas-new-aristocracy, which identifies the college degree as one of the most important indicators in the increasing hereditary wealth polarization in the United States.

31. Sandel, *The Tyranny of Merit*, 182.

32. Pope John Paul II, *Sollicitudo Rei Socialis* (December 30, 1987), 38.

33. *Compendium* 193.

34. *Compendium* 207.

35. *Compendium* 581.

36. "It should be made clear that proclamation is always more important than condemnation, and the latter cannot ignore the former, which gives it true solidity and the force of higher motivation." See *Sollicitudo Rei Socialis* 41. Martin Luther King Jr.'s "Letter from Birmingham Jail," which gives powerful and eloquent testimony to this order of priority, is rightly understood as a canonical text for conveying core principles of CST in an American context.

37. Massimo Faggioli, "Identity Crisis: We Can't Lose the 'Catholic' University," *Commonweal*, March 30, 2021, https://www.commonwealmagazine.org/identity-crisis-2.

38. *Compendium* 16.

39. *Compendium* 53.

40. St. Anselm, *Proslogion*, in *Monologion and Proslogion*, trans. Thomas Williams (Indianapolis: Hackett Publishing, 1995), 93.

41. Anselm, *Proslogion*, chap. 16, 109–10, and Eph 3:19.

42. *Compendium* 84.

43. For the recognition of the good of pluralism both within and without the visible bounds of the church, see *Lumen Gentium* (November 21, 1964), 13–16.

44. John Stuart Mill, *On Liberty* (Indianapolis: Hackett, 1978 [1859]), 42.

45. "To believe it possible to know a universally valid truth is in no way to encourage intolerance; on the contrary, it is the essential condition for sincere and authentic dialogue between persons. On this basis alone is it possible to overcome divisions and to journey together towards full truth." See Pope John Paul II, *Fides et Ratio* (September 14, 1998), 92.

46. Daniel Madigan, SJ, "Saving *Dominus Iesus*," in *Learned Ignorance*, ed. James L. Heft, SM, Reuven Firestone, and Omid Safi (Oxford: Oxford University Press, 2011), 270.

47. Simone Weil, *Waiting for God*, trans. Emma Craufurd (New York: HarperCollins, 2009 [1950]), 69.

48. *Compendium* 43. Pope Francis emphasizes this problem in his social encyclical *Fratelli Tutti*.

49. *Compendium* 47.

50. *Compendium* 49.

51. Faggioli, "Identity Crisis."

52. Pope Francis, *Laudato Si'* (May 24, 2015), 106.

53. *Compendium* 16.

54. *Compendium* 462–63.

55. Pope John Paul II, *Sollicitudo Rei Socialis* 28.

56. W. E. B. Du Bois, *The Souls of Black Folk* (New York: Dover Publications, 2016 [1903]), 51.

57. Du Bois, *The Souls of Black Folk*, 51.

58. See Mark Shiffman, "Majoring in Fear," *First Things*, November 2014, 19–21.

59. Zygmunt Bauman, *Liquid Modernity* (Cambridge: Polity Press, 2000), 139.

60. Tim Clydesdale, *The Purposeful Graduate: Why Colleges Must Talk to Students about Vocation* (Chicago: University of Chicago Press, 2015), 20–21.

61. Clydesdale, *Purposeful Graduate*, 97.

62. Dorothy L. Sayers, *Why Work? Discovering Real Purpose, Peace, and Fulfillment at Work. A Christian Perspective* (n.p.: CreateSpace Independent Publishing Platform, 2014 [1942]), 3.

5

HIGHER EDUCATION AND THE ECOLOGICAL CRISIS

Integral Ecology as a Catalyst for Critical and Creative Transdisciplinary Engagement

Vincent Miller

The unfolding ecological and climate crises pose a profound challenge to Catholic higher education. Indeed, they pose a profound challenge to all contemporary institutions. The issue is frequently imagined in primarily normative, moral terms. What are an institution's practices regarding its investment portfolio, energy use, and physical plant? Those are important questions indeed, and Catholic colleges and universities have exercised leadership and responsibility in taking proactive measures. Responding to the ecological and climate crises is often considered as essential for mission. But mission, in its common use, has multiple overlapping meanings that can be in tension with one another. Mission-driven investment and energy policies can be ascribed to the religious character of the institution—cast as sacrifices that must made for the institution to remain true to its identity. There is much that is helpful in this portrayal of mission, but it can relegate these actions and practices to a realm outside of the central educational component of a college or university's mission. Mission in this sense can be subtly reduced to a value-added dimension of an institution that distinguishes it from other institutions, but that relates to the central educational mission merely as an optional enhancement.

Catholic social thought (CST) is, likewise, frequently understood in primarily normative and moral terms. For example, Pope Francis's encyclical *Laudato Si'* was widely greeted by climate experts and advocates as bringing the moral force of the Catholic Church both to guide its believers and to contribute to global civil society debate on responding to climate change. CST, however, addresses much more than ethics. As the *Compendium of the Social Doctrine of the Church* explains, CST includes extended reflections on the nature of reality (ontology), the human person (anthropology), and society. Indeed, *Laudato Si'* expands CST into matters of epistemology and forms of inquiry. It argues that the crises we face are not simply the result of moral failure, but a failure of the dominant forms of thinking to properly understand the nature of reality and the human person.

Thus, both CST and its relevance to the ecological crises are much more than matters of moral evaluation and motivation that can be relegated to operations, finance, and an ethics requirement within the curriculum. They concern matters that cut to the heart of colleges and universities' educational mission and affect every department and major. Accordingly, this chapter aims to show how *Laudato Si'* can serve as a catalyst for substantial critical and creative dialogue among the disciplines. Moving beyond an exclusively moral approach to these questions is important for two reasons. First, the current crisis in the moral authority of Roman Catholicism makes many skeptical of its ability to offer moral wisdom. Second, the enormous scope of the demands posed by the unfolding environmental crises will require both a critical evaluation and creative synthesis of the insights of all the disciplines.

I begin by considering *Laudato Si'*'s diagnosis of the source of our environmental crisis in terms of its concept of "the technocratic paradigm"; I use that concept as a lens to evaluate contemporary Catholic higher education. The discussion then turns to "integral ecology," which is *Laudato Si'*'s proposal for an alternative thoughtform; I pay particular attention to the encyclical's ontological and epistemological dimensions in addition to its ethical teaching. Finally, I outline how integral ecology can provide a guiding vision for summoning a fuller response to the ecological crises by Catholic colleges and universities. My aim is to show that *Laudato Si'* fits well into long-standing debates about the nature of Catholic higher education and gives new urgency to our desires for truly critical interdisciplinary conversation and education. Broadening the debate beyond ethics to include worldview and epistemology promises to provide a way to engage pressing questions of epistemic pluralism and the decolonization of education.

The Technocratic Paradigm

In *Laudato Si'*, Pope Francis offers an analysis of the "Human Roots of the Ecological Crisis," a key aspect of which is his discussion of the "technocratic paradigm"—a term that extends the encyclical's moral critique into dominant forms of thought and their epistemologies.[1]

The technocratic paradigm is not a problem with technology itself, but with its modern forms. Francis describes it as a distorted imagination of the human relationship to the rest of creation. It "exalts the concept of a subject who, using logical and rational procedures, progressively approaches and gains control over an external object." The encyclical contrasts this attitude with earlier human "interventions in nature," which involved "being in tune with and respecting the possibilities offered by the things themselves" (106).

The encyclical does not present the technocratic paradigm as a foreign or secular imposition upon Christianity, but as arising from an "inadequate presentation of Christian anthropology" that "gave rise to a wrong understanding of the relationship between human beings and the world." This wrong understanding interprets the biblical notion of dominion in "Promethean" terms (116). By contrast, *Laudato Si'* claims that the biblical passages referring to dominion express human responsibility, not capricious power (67).[2]

Although it is rooted in an anthropological error, the technocratic paradigm is not simply an idea or doctrine. It is mediated materially in the practices of science and engineering and in technological products themselves, which "are not neutral." Indeed, technological devices condition "lifestyles and social possibilities" and threaten to "dominate" users with "their internal logic" (107–8). For example, studies show that, even as smartphones make many tasks more convenient, they are likely a significant culprit in increasing rates of depression and anxiety among young people.[3]

Laudato Si' finds this technocratic paradigm manifest in economics as well as in the dominance of economics over other forms of thought. The idea "of infinite or unlimited growth" rests upon the paradigm's objectifying view of nature, "the lie that there is an infinite supply of the earth's goods" and that "the negative effects of the exploitation of the natural order can be easily absorbed." The paradigm is manifest, what's more, in the narrowing of politics into economic policy, dominated by finance. The dominant neoliberal policy approach of prescribing economic growth as the solution to all problems is cited here (106, 109).

The aspect of the technocratic paradigm most relevant to education is Francis's description of it as an epistemology and a way of thinking. It functions as well as an "epistemological paradigm" that generalizes the "method and aims of science and technology" in a way that shapes "the lives of individuals and the workings of society" (107). That is, it tends to view human moral and cultural problems as adequately understood by the methods of the natural sciences (what is often called "scientism") and best addressed through technical solutions. The specialization and fragmentation of technical knowledge are the source of its great practical power. This specialization "makes it difficult to see the larger picture" and can lead to a "a loss of appreciation for the whole" and "for the relationships between things." Such an approach is particularly inadequate for complex problems such as those "regarding the environment and the poor," which are "problems [that] cannot be dealt with from a single perspective or from a single set of interests" (110).

The encyclical calls for a different, "more integral" vision. In order to address the ecological crisis, we need "a distinctive way of looking at things, a way of thinking, policies, an educational program, a lifestyle and a spirituality which together generate resistance to the assault of the technocratic paradigm." Such a form of knowledge would "take into account the data generated by other fields of knowledge, including philosophy and social ethics" (110–12).

Francis's account of the technocratic paradigm as a form of thinking resembles many contemporary concerns in higher education concerning the fragmentation and instrumentalization of knowledge and the reduction of higher education's mission to offering technical training and professional credentialling.[4] The account also raises important curricular questions: How to form students to have a critical awareness of the particularity and limits of disciplinary methods? How to cultivate critical and synthetic relationships between disciplines? How to foster robust interdisciplinary and transdisciplinary integration in an age where education is permeated with consumer choice and professional training models?

For all its value, the encyclical's account of the technocratic paradigm is frustratingly ahistorical. It makes no mention of specific strands of either scientific or technical thought that could be used to distinguish good from bad forms of technology. For that reason, the account is difficult to engage in an academic setting, especially in dialogue with scientific and technical disciplines. It is also silent on the broader issue of the colonial roots of the objectification it decries. European colonialism, in which the Church was and remains profoundly complicit, exterminated, subordinated, and enslaved Indigenous peoples. Viewing the rest of the world as *terra nullius*—"land of no one"—colonizers set up a system of plunder that treated the geological and biological goods of the earth as resources that could be extracted without concern for local communities or ecologies.[5] This was the genesis of contemporary environmental destruction. No critique of contemporary technical objectification is adequate without facing this history.

Integral Ecology as an Understanding of Reality: Each Creature Is a "Caress of God"

That said, *Laudato Si'* offers a constructive alternative to the corrosive and fragmenting force of the technocratic paradigm: "integral ecology." Like the analysis of the technocratic paradigm, integral ecology is a multidimensional concept. It encompasses an ontological understanding of the nature of reality as relationship, an epistemology that cultivates attentiveness to interrelationship, and, finally and consequently, a normative, moral valuation of creation and its manifold relationships.[6] When considered from this multidimensional perspective, the breadth of its relevance to the curricular and institutional dimensions of Catholic higher education becomes apparent.

As a vision, integral ecology is an understanding of the interconnections among all things. In philosophical terms, it is an ontology describing the relational nature of reality. This understanding is based upon specific doctrines, beliefs, and scriptural themes that teach these interconnections. Francis traces this understanding to the Hebrew Scriptures: "human life is grounded in three fundamental and closely intertwined relationships: with God, with our neighbor, and with the earth itself" (66).

Francis notes that the "laws found in the Bible dwell on relationships, not only among individuals but also with other living beings," such as the obligation to help fallen beasts of burden; the prohibition on simultaneously hunting mothers and their young, even eggs; and Sabbath requirements that even donkeys and oxen be given rest (68).

This vision is rooted in the doctrine of creation: that is, belief both in God as the Creator of all things and that all created things thus have a role in the harmony of creation. Francis cites St. Thomas Aquinas's argument that the diversity of creatures expresses the infinite goodness of God, "which could not be represented fittingly by any one creature." The diversity of creatures in their "multiple relationships" together conveys the goodness of the Creator (86, citing *Summa theologiae* I, q. 47, a. 1). Thus,

> Each creature has its own purpose. None is superfluous. The entire material universe speaks of God's love, his boundless affection for us. Soil, water, mountains: everything is, as it were, a caress of God. (84)

The ultimate foundation of this vision of the interrelatedness of all things is the triune God, who creates all things. In a passage that can be read as the spiritual core of the encyclical, Francis connects the three levels of integral ecology (ontological, epistemological, and normative/moral) with the relational character of the triune God:

> The divine Persons are subsistent relations, and the world, created according to the divine model, is a web of relationships. Creatures tend towards God, and in turn it is proper to every living being to tend towards other things, so that

> throughout the universe we can find any number of constant and secretly interwoven relationships. (240)

This understanding that all of creation reflects God's relationality gives rise to a way of perceiving the world that is attentive to interconnection:

> This leads us not only to marvel at the manifold connections existing among creatures, but also to discover a key to our own fulfilment. (240)

We humans do not simply notice these interrelations in the world around us; we participate in them socially and ecologically. We learn from the triune God, and the created world that reflects that God, that our fulfillment and indeed our "sanctification" are found not in isolation, but in embracing and deepening relationship through human solidarity and care for creation.

> The human person grows more, matures more, and is sanctified more to the extent that he or she enters into relationships, going out from themselves to live in communion with God, with others and with all creatures. In this way, they make their own that trinitarian dynamism which God imprinted in them when they were created. Everything is interconnected, and this invites us to develop a spirituality of that global solidarity which flows from the mystery of the Trinity. (240)

All of this resonates deeply with what Monika Hellwig called the Catholic intellectual tradition's "attention to the community dimension of all human behavior,"[7] or, to use the words of the *Compendium of the Social Doctrine of the Church*, "the constitutive social nature of human beings."[8] In contrast to liberal anthropologies that conceive of the human person as essentially an individual who subsequently enters into relationships (think of Thomas Hobbes's work, or John Locke's), the Catholic imagination sees the human person as constituted in relationships. Literary scholars and historians such as Paul Giles and Una Cadegan have argued that Catholic literature departs from the solitary heroes of modernism and focuses instead on the individual's entanglement within community and history.[9]

Although Pope Francis's understanding of interconnection is rooted in the Trinity and trusts in the power of the Holy Spirit to bring all things into communion, he understands this vision to be accessible and available to people of any faith or none at all. Following in the footsteps of Pope John XXIII, who addressed his 1963 encyclical *Pacem in Terris* on war and peace to "all men of good will," Francis presents *Laudato Si'* as a "dialogue with all people about our common home" (3). Catholicism does not separate faith and reason. Both describe the same universe. Honest openness to the world will find interconnection regardless of faith commitment or lack thereof.

Laudato Si' clearly engages the other Abrahamic faiths—Judaism and Islam—in developing this understanding of reality. As we have seen, Francis roots integral ecology in the text of the Book of Genesis. It is noteworthy that the papal encyclical quotes a Sufi Muslim mystical writer, Ali al-Khawas, as a teacher who calls us to recognize the mystical encounter with the divine that can be found in listening "to what is being said when the wind blows, the trees sway, water flows, flies buzz, doors creak, birds sing, or in the sound of strings or flutes, the sighs of the sick, the groans of the afflicted" (233n159). While *Laudato Si'* engages Indigenous traditions in terms of their concern for the land and future generations (179), it does not, however, consider what they have to teach about the ontology of relationship. This receives more attention in *Querida Amazonia*, Francis's response to the Synod for the Amazon. There he writes,

> We should esteem the indigenous mysticism that sees the interconnection and interdependence of the whole of creation, the mysticism of gratuitousness that loves life as a gift, the mysticism of a sacred wonder before nature and all its forms of life.[10]

Surprisingly, similar teachings can be found in other faith traditions as well. Key among these is the Buddhist notion of *Pratītyasamutpāda*, or "interdependence." These are striking parallels with Pope Francis's notion of integral ecology, providing an opening for interreligious dialogue. Moreover, a similar view of the world as deeply interconnected is found in many scientific disciplines.

Integral Ecology as a Way of Seeing

These beliefs about God and the nature of creation inspire a way of seeing, a certain kind of gaze that serves as an epistemological alternative to the technocratic paradigm by seeking to perceive the interconnections in creation. In Francis's understanding, this epistemological alternative is of a piece with his spiritual and theological commitments. He speaks of "an attitude of heart...which approaches life with serene attentiveness, which is capable of being fully present to someone." Jesus is the supreme example of this loving gaze:

> Jesus taught us this attitude when he invited us to contemplate the lilies of the field and the birds of the air, or when seeing the rich young man and knowing his restlessness, "he looked at him with love" (Mk 10:21). He was completely present to everyone and to everything, and in this way he showed us the way to overcome that unhealthy anxiety which makes us superficial, aggressive, and compulsive consumers. (226)

This gaze of Jesus is very important to Pope Francis. The scene of Jesus's encounter with another rich young man—the calling of Matthew the tax collector—is the basis for the motto on his papal coat of arms: *miserando atque eligendo*. The phrase can be roughly translated as "by having mercy and choosing him." Francis likes that the Latin word *miserando* has no easy modern translation. It means "by having mercy," or as he prefers to say "mercying."[11] Jesus's gaze is "mercying"; he looks upon people and things with a love that sees the fullness of what they are and might be.

There is always more to someone or something than meets the eye. In Matthew's case, the something more is that a wealthy tax collector for the Roman occupiers—at that time, a position closer to an extortionist than a bureaucrat—might become a great apostle. In the case of integral ecology, it is the patient openness to imagine and to understand the many interconnections among the other creatures with whom we share the world. All things around us—soil, trees, bees—are so much more than the simple objects that meet our eyes. They are interconnected in ways that have profound importance for our lives.

Consider soil. We know that it is more than dirt, of course. It is where plants grow. But it is teeming with microscopic life—bacteria, fungi, microscopic animals—all essential for supporting plant life. In ecologist Aldo Leopold's analysis, soil is the foundation of "a fountain of energy" that flows from the sun through plants and animals, gives us life, and nourishes a community to which we give back through care as well as our own death and decay.[12] No soil, no humans. Curiously, the Hebrew name of the first human in the Bible, *Adama*, literally means "being of the soil." Integral ecology inspires us to gaze with the patient openness required to learn these connections. This attentiveness to connection has value beyond ecological relationships. All disciplines can be enhanced by such attentiveness to relationship.

Pope Francis's model for integral ecology is St. Francis of Assisi, whose great prayer-poem the "Canticle of the Sun" provides the title for the encyclical. According to Pope Francis, St. "Francis helps us to see that an integral ecology calls for openness to categories which transcend the language of mathematics and biology, and take us to the heart of what it is to be human." St. Francis was open to all of creation. He responded to it, not with mere "intellectual appreciation or economic calculus," but with love. "Just as happens when we fall in love with someone, whenever he would gaze at the sun, the moon or the smallest of animals, he burst into song, drawing all other creatures into his praise." For St. Francis, "each and every creature was a sister united to him by bonds of affection. That is why he felt called to care for all that exists" (11).

Pope Francis argues that there is more here than "naïve romanticism." Our attitudes of love and attentiveness affect what we see and, thus, what we are able to value. For Francis, awareness of our relationships is a path to moral transformation. Seeing can precipitate moral conversion. It is not simply a matter of our priorities following what we love; rather, it is that love enables us to see more of reality. If "we feel intimately united with all that exists, then sobriety and care will well up spontaneously." On the other hand,

> If we approach nature and the environment without this openness to awe and wonder, if we no longer speak the language of fraternity and beauty in our relationship with

> the world, our attitude will be that of masters, consumers, ruthless exploiters, unable to set limits on their immediate needs. (11)

Integral ecology is a way of seeing that opens our eyes to the myriad creatures with whom we are interrelated. It helps us to understand our interdependence and thus to value the rest of creation.

Laudato Si' argues that such attentiveness comes naturally to us, much the way the naturalist E. O. Wilson argues that humans have evolved an intrinsic interest in other creatures and life processes, which he terms "biophilia."[13] Openness to the rest of creation is a value shared beyond the Church. Despite its frequent critiques of the narrowness of scientific, technological, and economic perspectives, *Laudato Si'* repeatedly stresses the positive relationship between religion and science. Francis proposes that integral ecology and science are mutually enriching ways of seeing the world. He opens the chapter on integral ecology with a discussion of the science of ecology. Ecology studies the relationships between organisms and their environment. Similarly, Francis notes that the existence of human society is as much a matter of relationship with other species as it is a matter of economic development (137).

Francis in fact believes that integral ecology can contribute to science as well. He argues repeatedly that our current crises can only be solved if the full range of human wisdom is brought to bear. Faith has much to contribute to the scientific task, not least in the loving and attentive gaze of integral ecology that seeks to know and love the depths of things in their complex relationships. Whereas religious fundamentalists too often provoke a conflict between faith and science, Catholicism seeks their mutually enriching harmony. Pope Francis views faith and science as mutually enriching ways of seeking the truth. In that regard, he quotes at length from *Lumen Fidei*, the encyclical he wrote with his predecessor, Pope Benedict XVI:

> The gaze of science thus benefits from faith: faith encourages the scientist to remain constantly open to reality in all its inexhaustible richness. Faith awakens the critical sense by preventing research from being satisfied with its own formulae and helps it to realize that nature is always greater. By stimulating wonder before the profound mystery

> of creation, faith broadens the horizons of reason to shed greater light on the world which discloses itself to scientific investigation. (199n41)[14]

There is, here, a vision for a truly transdisciplinary engagement between the sciences and humanities, and between secular and theological forms of knowledge.

Integral Ecology as a Moral Principle

We can now turn to the more familiar moral dimension of the encyclical's teaching. It is particularly important in a higher education context to appreciate how these ontological and epistemological moves form the foundation for *Laudato Si*'s moral teaching.

Laudato Si' views the myriad creatures and their manifold interrelationships as good. Humans should thus work to preserve, restore, and cultivate the interrelationships among our fellow creatures. But the straightforward moral dimension of this teaching does not itself do much to motivate and transform people to act. We do not live in a world where magisterial moral exhortations have significant social force. The moral teaching has much more transformative power in the context of the encyclical's vision of the nature of the world and epistemological vision.

Integral ecology can be understood as an expansion of well-established aspects of CST. It expands solidarity from social interdependence with other human beings, to human interdependence with the rest of creation. Just as an infant grows into an adult and learns to contribute to the society in which he or she matured, so humankind must now develop a vision that allows it to perceive, appreciate, and cultivate its interconnections with the rest of creation.

Laudato Si' discusses other sorts of moral interconnection. It addresses questions of environmental justice in terms of the interconnection of the "the cry of the earth and the cry of the poor" and the environmental debt owed by "developed countries" (25, 52, 56) because of wealthy countries' disproportionate use of limited natural resources and contributions to environmental devastation. Francis concludes the chapter on integral ecology with a discussion of its relationship with the common good, expanding this concept beyond the current human community to include future generations and all creation (156–60).

Integral ecology thus offers a transformative way of seeing that opens us up to the interconnections with the rest of creation that sustain us. By opening ourselves to the world and attending to it deeply, we can be moved to respond to these connections with respect, love, and care. The path of transformation begins by opening our eyes and attending to the world around us.

Integral Ecology and Catholic Higher Education

This analysis of the multidimensional nature of *Laudato Si*'s critique and constructive proposal illuminates the broad possibilities of a response to the ecological crisis in Catholic higher education. Because its moral dimensions are founded upon substantial ontological and epistemological components, it cannot be adequately addressed with a few ethics or moral theology requirements. Integral ecology calls for, and can provide the basis for, a broad and inclusive interdisciplinary dialogue to understand and address the ecological crisis. This speaks to the central educational and research work of higher education.

Integral ecology's understanding of the relational character of reality provides the possibility for engagement with just about every discipline, beginning with a critical conversation about the principles and methods of the disciplines. While many disciplines may not provide much basis for participating in moral debates about the environmental crisis (e.g., mathematics), all presume an implicit or explicit construction of reality. Certainly mathematics, along with disciplines from anthropology and finance to mechanical engineering and history, has distinct postulates concerning the nature of reality and understanding of its complexity. Ethical discussions can leave these fundamental interpretations of reality both unengaged and unchallenged. All disciplines' assumptions are open to question, and each discipline has resources to contribute toward imagining the complexity of the world.

Admittedly, *Laudato Si*'s critique of the technocratic paradigm and proposal for integral ecology are not fully developed conceptual frameworks on the scale of most academic disciplines. They can, however, serve to catalyze a critical conversation across the disciplines about their respective constructions of reality and their complicity in or critical value for addressing the climate and environmental crises.

The same holds for the epistemological aspect of integral ecology. Each discipline has its own methods for what counts as data or evidence and its methods for interpreting, analyzing, and employing them. A large part of both undergraduate and graduate education is training students to work within such epistemological frameworks: consider the historian's concern for proper use of sources and hesitance to narrate beyond what they warrant, the mathematician's concern for conceptual and logical clarity, and the specific skills necessary for acquiring and interpreting data in the various natural sciences. Each discipline cultivates attentiveness consistent with its understanding of reality.[15] Transdisciplinary conversation about these forms of attentiveness could contribute much to developing the ethos of attentiveness called for by integral ecology.[16]

Interdisciplinary dialogue does not mean only agreement and synthesis; it also involves critique and challenge. The Catholic intellectual tradition (CIT) is, perhaps, too frequently conceived in terms of theologies of creation and incarnation. Discussions of CIT tend to emphasize unity, coherence, and consensus. Disciplines can be conceived as multiple ways of knowing the one reality created by God, which will ultimately converge in the truth. But academic disciplines are the work of fallen humankind. Their insights are born of the desire for domination as much as selfless understanding and wonder. Indeed, they are a leading component of civilization's current destruction of the living world. We are on the wrong path and need to question our assumptions. Thus, any interdisciplinary dialogue must also make room for profound and fundamental critique. *Laudato Si'* offers integral ecology as a correction for the distortions of the technocratic paradigm. In theological terms, critique can be understood in terms of the cross. Henri de Lubac spoke of how every humanism must submit to conversion. The gospel maxim "to find ourselves, we must lose ourselves" is "as imperative in all its severity for humanity as the individual."[17] Paradoxically, the theology of the cross can serve as the principle upon which

Catholic colleges and universities can host the most critical disciplines and debates.

These two levels of dialogue, ontological and epistemological, contribute not only to *Laudato Si'*s project of responding to the ecological crisis, but also to the central educational project of higher education. Interdisciplinary conversations of the sort I have proposed would greatly enhance students' understandings of their own majors and of the other disciplines that they encounter.

Discussions of the nature of colleges and universities, especially Catholic ones, often describe them as places of sustained debate and dialogue. But day-to-day practice often falls far short of this ideal. Faculty do the bulk of their work within their own disciplinary communities; students focus on their majors. Students may encounter other disciplines through their general education or core requirements, but they often have little or no guidance in, or experience of, mutual critique and synthesis. (See further Anna Moreland and Mark Shiffman's chapter in this volume.) The project of integral ecology highlights the need for structures and practices at colleges and universities to enable such dialogue and debate. While many institutions foster transdisciplinary research, these often are very focused, project-oriented undertakings. Those are quite valuable. But there is need for a much broader interdisciplinary project addressed at understanding the origins of the environmental and climate crisis and developing means to address it.

An advantage of this broadened dialogue is that it might enable us to face the colonialism implicit within the disciplinary presumptions of Western colleges and universities. As we saw above, *Laudato Si'* does not adequately treat the colonial roots of environmental destruction. That said, the conversations, suggested above, regarding the ontological and epistemological presumptions of the disciplines provide a possible practice for grappling with the colonialism of Western education. Like the questions raised by integral ecology regarding the environment, decolonization is not simply a moral stance in support of the cultures destroyed and marginalized by colonialism. Decolonization, too, must grapple with the ontologies, anthropologies, and epistemologies presumed within the disciplines. Ramón Grosfoguel describes the Western university as a machine of "epistemicide" that "inferiorizes and destroys the epistemic potential of non-Western epistemologies." He calls instead for a "*pluri*-versity" in which diverse cosmologies and epistemologies can be brought into dialogue and debate.[18]

Integral ecology can also provide a focus for campus interreligious and intercultural dialogue. Questions of tolerance and inclusion can be rendered concrete by focusing on each tradition's ontological and epistemological understanding of nature, natural relationships, and the role of humankind in them. Religious traditions also have their own ritual and contemplative resources that can be engaged to foster epistemological attentiveness.

Further, integral ecology illuminates how college and university policies and practices concerning investments, energy use, and the campus plant have formative and educational import. If imagined as more than simple (or not so simple) moral questions, but as complex negotiations of the ecological consequences of our collective and institutional actions, they can serve as formation in the imagination of connection.[19] Divestment policies can illuminate the external costs (to people and ecologies) generally left unexamined in matters of finance. Carbon neutrality pledges and the difficult logistical work of achieving them are profound pedagogical opportunities that should involve, as much as possible, the campus community. The operation of the campus physical plant likewise has an important and generally overlooked formative power. For example, automatically watered lawns that remain green even during seasonal droughts subtly but powerfully form us in environmental disconnection. Programs such as on-campus composting can form the community in a deeper awareness of the resource and nutrient cycles in which we participate.

There is a final reason broadening the conversation about sustainability beyond ethics to include ontology, anthropology, and epistemology is valuable: the volatility of climate disruption. Ethics is often conceived as providing guidance for well-established practices. Indeed, it often appears in our curricula in specific courses for practical and professional programs (e.g., business, engineering, or healthcare ethics). These are needed and valuable. The future currently unfolding, however, will be marked by profound discontinuities and disruptions. The geophysical nonlinearities of climate change will have profound nonlinear effects upon human economic, political, legal, and social systems. Indeed, the relatively minor crisis (in light of what is to come) of the COVID-19 pandemic profoundly eroded the stability of healthcare and higher education institutions within months. What sorts of preparation will students need to face an unstable future in which the systems presumed by the professions for which they are training may unwind in radical and unanticipated ways? Traditional training in the disciplines and professions will certainly remain valuable. Responding to what David Korten has called "the great unraveling" will require profound creativity and analytic and political skills.[20] In this context, awareness of the presuppositions and constructions of disciplines, in addition to their current consensus forms, will have profound practical value for refiguring them to navigate a changed world.

Laudato Si', like the tradition of CST to which it belongs, offers much to Catholic higher education. The relevance of both is enhanced by attending not just to their normative moral teachings, but also to their ontological, anthropological, and epistemological dimensions. These provide substantive concepts for a critical and creative dialogue among multiple disciplines. Such an approach is particularly valuable in two ways for the current moment. First, we live in a time when the moral authority of Roman Catholicism is in significant crisis. For that reason, presenting the tradition as a catalyst for dialogue is likely to be more productive than presenting it simply as a font of moral wisdom. Second, as human civilization presses ever further into climate and ecological disruption and crisis, no extant system of thought is adequate to the demands we face. Radically new ways of thinking and proceeding are needed. Critical and creative dialogue is a promising way of bringing all available resources to bear on these most pressing needs.

Questions for Consideration and Discussion

1. Miller claims that, because the ecological crisis has "substantial ontological and epistemological" dimensions—that is, it is rooted in ways of conceiving and regarding the world—"it cannot be adequately addressed with a few ethics or moral theology requirements." Instead, scholars and educators need to engage in interdisciplinary or even transdisciplinary discussion. He also claims that "college and university policies and practices concerning investments, energy use, and the campus plant have formative and educational import." What are your institution's goals regarding environmental sustainability and climate change? How do your curriculum and cocurriculum deliver on those goals? Do your

institution's own policies and practices figure in your students' education? Do they support, or work against, your institution's goals? What could be improved?

2. Miller contrasts the "technocratic paradigm" with the vision of "integral ecology" presented in Pope Francis's 2015 encyclical *Laudato Si'*. How do these two paradigms influence your institution's operations, curriculum, and cocurriculum? In other words, how are these paradigms manifest on your campus? Further, which is the dominant paradigm? Or are different paradigms evident in different departments and divisions?
3. Miller proposes that "broadening the [climate] debate beyond ethics to include worldview and epistemology promises to provide a way to engage pressing questions of epistemic pluralism and the decolonization of education." To what extent does your institution facilitate such an education, and how could it be developed within current disciplinary structures? What are the obstacles? Where are opportunities? How do you or could you develop students' capacities for awe, wonder, and patient awareness as preconditions for responding adequately to the climate crisis? How can you develop students' capacities for critique?
4. Among other resources that CST provides for educating in the context of the climate and environmental crises, Miller points to CST's understanding of the human person in relation to God, neighbor, and the rest of creation. What elements of CST (e.g., symbols, stories from your institution's founding, lives of holy women and men in your tradition, principles, biblical stories) do you or could you draw upon to articulate a compelling response to the climate and environmental crises?
5. To close his chapter, Miller underscores "the volatility of climate disruption" and the increased likelihood of "profound discontinuities and disruptions" such as we experienced with the COVID-19 pandemic. Is your institution preparing students for such a future? As you conclude your discussion of this chapter, what are three to five ways you can strengthen current initiatives and enact positive change on your campus with respect to educating students for "climate and ecological disruption and crisis"?

Notes

1. Pope Francis, *Laudato Si'* (May 24, 2015), 3. This and other Church documents are available at https://www.vatican.va/. Subsequent references will be given in the body of the text.

2. For an explanation of how the notion of dominion has been commonly misinterpreted, as well as a more adequate interpretation, see Randall Smith, "Creation and the Environment in the Hebrew Scriptures: A Transvaluation of Values," in *Green Discipleship: Catholic Theological Ethics and the Environment*, ed. Tobias Winright (Winona, MN: Anselm Academic, 2011), 74–92.

3. Jonathan Haidt and Jean M. Twenge, "This Is Our Chance to Pull Teenagers Out of the Smartphone Trap," *New York Times*, July 31, 2021, https://www.nytimes.com/2021/07/31/opinion/smartphone-iphone-social-media-isolation.html.

4. For an example of work to counter these trends, see Association of American Colleges and Universities, "What Liberal Education Looks Like: What It Is, Who It's For, and Where it Happens" (Washington, DC: Association of American Colleges and Universities, 2020), https://portal.criticalimpact.com/user/25043/image/whatlibedlookslike.pdf.

5. See Daniel Castillo, *An Ecological Theology of Liberation: Salvation and Political Ecology* (Maryknoll, NY: Orbis, 2019) and Vincent Miller, "Resource Extraction and the Call for Solidarity: The Networks We Have and the Synodal Network the Church Is Called to Be," in *Catholic Peacebuilding and Mining: Integral Peace, Development, and Ecology*, ed. Gerard Powers and Caesar A. Montevecchio (London: Routledge, 2022).

6. This section is adapted from Vincent Miller, "Integral Ecology: Francis's Moral and Ecological Vision of Interconnectedness," in *The Theological and Ecological Vision of* Laudato Si': *Everything Is Connected*, ed. Vincent Miller (London: Bloomsbury, 2017), 11–28. Used with permission.

7. Monika Hellwig, "The Catholic Intellectual Tradition in the Catholic University," in *Examining the Catholic Intellectual Tradition*, ed. Anthony J. Cernera and Oliver J. Morgan (Fairfield, CT: Sacred Heart University Press, 2000), 7.

8. *The Compendium of the Social Doctrine of the Church* (2004), 37.

9. See Paul Giles, *American Catholic Arts and Fictions: Culture, Ideology, Aesthetics* (Cambridge: Cambridge University Press, 1992) and Una Cadegan, *All Good Books Are Catholic Books: Print Culture, Censorship, and Modernity in Twentieth-Century America* (Ithaca, NY: Cornell University Press, 2013).

10. Pope Francis, *Querida Amazonia* (February 2, 2020), 73.

11. Pope Francis, "A Big Heart Open to God," interview with Antonio Spadaro, SJ, *America*, September 30, 2013, at https://www.americamagazine.org/faith/2013/09/30/big-heart-open-god-interview-pope-francis.

12. Aldo Leopold, *A Sand County Almanac and Sketches Here and There* (Oxford: Oxford University Press, 1968), 216.

13. Edward O. Wilson, *Biophilia* (Cambridge, MA: Harvard University Press, 1984).

14. See Pope Francis, *Lumen Fidei* (June 29, 2013), 34.

15. For a project akin to the one proposed here, see the contributions from multiple disciplines in *Becoming Beholders: Cultivating Sacramental Imagination and Actions in College Classrooms*, ed. Karen E. Eifler and Thomas M. Landy (Collegeville, MN: Liturgical Press, 2014).

16. For a theological engagement with ecology that attempts to develop such an ethos of attentiveness, see Vincent Miller, "A Cathedral Not Made by Hands: *Laudato si'* in an Old-Growth Forest," *Commonweal*, December 30, 2019, 20–25, https://www.commonwealmagazine.org/cathedral-not-made-hands.

17. Henri de Lubac, *Catholicism: Christ and the Common Destiny of Man*, trans. Lancelot C. Sheppard and Elizabeth Englund, OCD (San Francisco: Ignatius Press, 1988), 368.

18. Ramón Grosfoguel, "The Dilemmas of Ethnic Studies in the United States: Between Liberal Multiculturalism, Identity Politics, Disciplinary Colonization, and Decolonial Epistemologies," *Human Architecture: Journal of the Sociology of Self-Knowledge* 10, no. 1 (2012): article 9, http://scholarworks.umb.edu/humanarchitecture/vol10/iss1/9.

19. See Gerald J. Beyer, *Just Universities: Catholic Social Teaching Confronts Corporatized Higher Education* (Washington, DC: Georgetown University Press, 2021), chap. 4, "Socially Responsible Investment, the Stewardship of Resources, and Integral Ecology," 135–68.

20. David Korten, *The Great Turning: From Empire to Earth Community* (Sterling, VA: Kumarian Press, 2006), 251, cited in Joanna Macy and Chris Johnstone, *Active Hope: How to Face the Mess We're in without Going Crazy* (Novato, CA: New World Library, 2012), 239–40.

6

HELP WANTED

Labor Problems, Labor Policies, and the Challenge of Solidarity

Joseph A. McCartin[1]

For more than a half-century, a tension has been developing at the heart of U.S. Catholic higher education between its evolving labor practices and Catholicism's own prophetic social teaching about the rights and dignity of workers. This tension has been deepened over time by both changes in the U.S. economy and the transformation of higher education as a whole. While longstanding, this tension has also been heightened by a range of recent developments in labor law, managerial practices, and the likely long-range impacts of the COVID-19 pandemic on our institutions. We must understand the growth of this tension and seek to alleviate it if Catholic colleges and universities are to survive and thrive in the decades ahead. If we do not, these institutions seem destined to become increasingly corporatized brick-and-mortar negations of the foundational values of human dignity and solidarity that they seek to propagate.

To begin, it is important that we remind ourselves of the central role that the dignity of work and the rights of workers have played in Catholic social teaching from *Rerum Novarum* through *Laudato Si'*. From Pope Leo XIII to Pope Francis, popes and bishops have repeatedly emphasized these themes. It is equally important that we remember that the Church has never exempted its own institutions, including colleges and universities, from the application of its labor teachings. As Pope John Paul II wrote in *Ex Corde Ecclesiae*, "A Catholic university, as Catholic, informs and carries out its research, teaching, and other activities with Catholic ideals, principles, and attitudes."[2] In the 1986 pastoral letter *Economic Justice for All*, the U.S. bishops explicitly asserted the applicability of the Church's labor teachings to its own practices, declaring that "all the moral principles that govern the just operation of any economic endeavor apply to the Church and its agencies and institutions; indeed the Church should be exemplary."[3]

An Unresolved and Long-Running Tension

There has nonetheless been a long history of tension regarding the application of labor teachings on Catholic campuses. That tension was present, if unacknowledged, at the dawn of modern Catholic higher education. Whether celebrated or decried, the 1967 Land O'Lakes Statement drafted by leaders of a number of (male) Catholic universities is widely seen as a foundational document that "changed the trajectory of Catholic higher education."[4] Although it offered a bold vision for Catholic higher education, that document was ambiguous at best regarding how Catholic institutions should approach their labor relations. It declared the need for "appropriate participation by all members of the community of learners in university decisions" and encouraged "greater internal cooperation and participation," but it was vague as to how this ought to happen.[5]

The lack of clarity is telling, because the issue of faculty unionization had already burst into view before Land O'Lakes. The drafters of the statement were doubtless aware of a highly publicized labor conflict that had erupted at St. John's University in New York more than a year beforehand. That fight began when a chapter of the American Association of University Professors (AAUP) formed on the St. John's campus and its members began advocating for a greater voice in university governance. The St. John's administration pushed back hard, abruptly laying off twenty-one of the active AAUP members in December 1965.

The national AAUP and New York's robust union movement swiftly condemned the action, and, in January 1966, a strike began that lasted until June 1967. By then, thirteen of the dismissed had accepted the university's offer of binding arbitration, and others had found positions elsewhere.[6] Rather than deal with the implications of the St. John's fight and the question of unions, the Land O'Lakes Statement opted for generalities, suggesting that "experimentation" would "be necessary" as Catholic institutions adapted to the new era.

In the 1970s, such experimentation did lead several Catholic institutions to accept faculty unions, including St. John's, which began collectively bargaining with faculty in 1970. Over time, a number of other institutions followed suit, including the University of San Francisco, the University of Scranton (PA), Fairfield University (CT), and St. Leo University (FL). The spread of faculty unionization was arrested in 1980, however, with the U.S. Supreme Court's *Yeshiva* decision, which ruled 5–4 that full-time professors in private universities were excluded from collective bargaining rights because they exercised managerial discretion in academic matters.[7]

The unionization of noninstructors was unaffected by the *Yeshiva* decision, and in some settings they succeeded in unionizing. But by the time the U.S. bishops issued *Economic Justice for All*, which proclaimed that "all church institutions must...fully recognize the rights of employees to organize and bargain collectively with the institution," the labor question had receded in importance at Catholic colleges and universities (CCUs). Instead, cultural and religious controversies roiled campuses. As neoconservatives such as Allan Bloom launched a fight against liberal secular universities that no longer paid "attention to natural rights or the historical origins of our regime, which are now thought to have been essentially flawed and regressive,"[8] a parallel battle played out within CCUs on questions of Catholic identity. In *Ex Corde Ecclesiae*, Pope John Paul II stressed that "Catholic teachers are to be faithful to, and all other teachers are to respect, Catholic doctrine and morals in their research and teaching," but he said nothing about those teachers' (or other workers') rights as employees. Indeed, the words *worker* or *employee* did not appear in English translations of the papal document.[9] Even those who took issue with aspects of John Paul II's efforts to ensure professors' fidelity tended to frame their views in terms of academic freedom, not workers' rights.[10]

Helping to keep the labor question on the margins into the 1990s was the fact that Catholic higher education was still coasting on the economic forces that had contributed to its rapid growth after World War II. While 92,000 students were enrolled in CCUs in 1945, by 1970, the number had soared to 430,000 and continued to grow through the 1970s. That growth was fueled by the larger context within which Catholic institutions operated. They benefited from government's investment in higher education through the GI Bill, federally guaranteed student loans, and federally funded research. They also benefited from the low levels of income inequality and household indebtedness that characterized the thirty years of postwar expansion—what the French call *Les Trentes Glorieuses*[11]—a phenomenon that economists Claudia Goldin and Robert A. Margo have labelled the "Great Compression."[12] During these years, a highly unionized (28 percent of workers in 1970) and relatively well-paid working-class was determined to send its sons and daughters to college, the surest portal into a growing professional middle class. Yet the economic context within which both these families and the CCUs to which they sent their children operated was already beginning to change radically.

A Changing Context

If the labor question lay dormant in most CCUs as the 1980s drew to a close, larger economic transformations were emerging that would irresistibly force that question to the surface over time in ways that could no longer be ignored. Several changes played a role in decisively transforming the economic context within which Catholic institutions operated.

One of the most profound changes was the financialization of the economy. The 1970s proved a turning point. Over the course of that decade, runaway inflation, growing pools of capital (some created by the pension funds workers had achieved in the postwar era) seeking to maximize returns on investment, and a newly aggressive attitude of "maximizing shareholder value" took hold on Wall Street. All this led to a sea change in the behavior of investors and corporations. The emergence of hedge funds and private equity partnerships, returns-conscious institutional investors, and the rise of leveraged buyouts, hostile takeovers, and the securitization of a rising array of assets began transforming the expectations of investors and the behavior of corporations. The so-called FIRE sector of the economy (finance, insurance, and real estate) saw its profits grow faster than any other. Financialization accelerated the erosion of postwar "stakeholder capitalism"—in which leading firms generally sought to balance the interests of stakeholders like workers with those of investors—in favor of "shareholder capitalism," which elevated the pursuit of shareholder value above all else. As historian Judith Stein reminds us, the rise of financialized capitalism did not occur naturally or spontaneously, but rather was the product of neoliberal thinking and policies that became ascendant in the 1970s and dominated the political economy of the Reagan era. The influence of such thinking and policies persists into this century.[13]

Financialization in turn helped to drive a transformation in the employer-employee relationship, as investors sought to realize gains by making corporations "lean and mean." In response, corporate executives, whose compensation became increasingly tied to stock price, downsized, contracted out, and extended their supply chains across the Pacific in search of cheaper labor.[14] Within the United States, meanwhile, corporations moved increasingly away from models of full-time/life-time employment toward part-time and temporary work, a shift often incentivized by the rising costs of healthcare benefits.[15] The largest private sector employer of the immediate postwar years, when America's institutions of Catholic higher education began expanding, was General Motors, which paid its employees union wages, sought to employ them for all of their working lives, and delivered them defined benefit pensions when they retired. By the early twenty-first century, the nation's largest private sector employer was Walmart, which operated on a very different model, resisting unionization and relying on a low-wage part-time, high-turnover workforce, many of whose members were forced to rely on public benefits such as food stamps to supplement their meager earnings.[16]

As the economy changed, income and wealth inequality—long held in check by the Great Depression, the New Deal, and the postwar expansion of unions, regulation, and the welfare state—began surging. The story has become all too familiar. At the top end, the richest claimed an increasing share of income growth and wealth accumulation. The share of aggregate income that went to upper income families shot up from 29 percent in 1970 to 48 percent in 2018, while the share going to middle income families dropped from 62 percent down to 43 percent. Wealth redistribution was even more pronounced. The wealthy saw their share of aggregate wealth increase from 60 percent in 1983 to 79 percent by 2016, while the share held by middle income families dropped from 32 percent to 17 percent.[17]

The loss of workers' power to push back against these trends, economists Anna Stansbury and Larry H. Summers argue, was "the major structural change responsible" for increasing inequality.[18] Workers' diminished power stemmed from the decline of unionization (from 28 percent of workers organized in 1970 to only 10.8 percent by 2020), expanding globalization, technological displacement, deregulation, corporate reorganization and job "fissuring," and a string of judicial decisions that weakened their ability to collectively contest their employers' power. During the years between World War II and 1980, wages grew at the same pace as productivity, as workers were able to claim their fair share of a growing economy. But the decline of worker power had a devastating impact on that pattern: while productivity grew 69.6 percent between 1979 and 2018, average hourly compensation grew only 11.6 percent. Hardest hit were people of color and those lacking a postsecondary education. In 2000, median Black wages were 79.2 percent of white wages; by 2019, that number had dipped to 75.6 percent. Meanwhile, the "college premium"—the comparatively higher incomes of those with college degrees—doubled, from 40 percent more in 1979 to 80 percent more in the 2000s.[19]

As this divergence grew, colleges and universities, including CCUs, began to preside over what Michael Sandel calls the "system by which modern societies allocate opportunity" in a competitive capitalist economy: namely, a putative meritocracy, in which colleges and universities figure as "the animating heart."[20] While Catholic higher education flowered in the context of a comparatively egalitarian postwar economy that offered broad-based upward mobility, over the past forty years it has been gradually reshaped by the changed context within which it operates. That context, Sandel argues, has bred hubris among the winners, who believe their achievements have come through dint of their hard work and college educations, and humiliation among the losers, who absorb the toxic message that they lacked the necessary talent or dedication to "succeed."[21] As this reshaping has proceeded, a growing breach between Catholic social teaching on labor and the praxis of CCUs has become more visible. (See further Laura Nichols's chapter in this volume, on the growing breach between mission and the demographics of students whom many CCUs seek to enroll.)

A Growing Divergence between Praxis and Teaching

One of the most visible ways in which the changing economy has impacted Catholic higher education is in the composition of its leaders. While the Land O'Lakes Statement marked the transition to an era of CCUs with independent boards of directors, in the early years the boards still retained a strong clerical influence, and institutions were still usually led by members of the religious order that founded them. By 2013, however, two-thirds of CCUs were led by lay presidents.[22] Boards of directors, meanwhile, increasingly drew from the business leaders who had helped to implement the broader economic changes described above.[23] Overall patterns in higher education suggest that the percentage of board seats held by finance industry professionals doubled between 1990 and 2015, to the point that 56 percent of research university board positions came from the financial sector.[24] Evidence suggests that leading CCUs are not far behind. In 2021, Georgetown, Boston College, and Notre Dame all boasted boards with at least a third of members from the financial sector.[25]

The transition to lay leadership and boards increasingly under the sway of businesspeople, especially those with backgrounds in finance, accompanied a shift in CCUs toward what Gerald Beyer aptly calls "corporatized higher education."[26] The problem was not only that CCUs could have done a better job educating their leadership on Catholic social teaching, as Alice Gallin among others argued, but that the environment within which CCUs operated was naturally entangling them in the patterns and thinking produced by the larger economy from which business leaders emerged.[27] Catholic ethicist James Keenan argues that the corporatization of higher education has risked commodifying students to the point that "they become simply objects that keep the university afloat with cash."[28] Yet, if students risked becoming mere customers, the employees—instructors, educational support, clerical, janitorial, security, and food service workers—risked being evaluated by CCU administrators according to the same cost-benefit rubric that applied in service industries in general.

Several tendencies and practices emerged as the values and practices of the broader economy seeped into the functioning of Catholic institutions of higher education. One was subcontracting. In the 1970s, most CCUs ran their own bookstores and food service operations and directly employed the janitorial and security workforces that staffed campuses. By the early twenty-first century, most of these institutions had contracted out some or all of these services. While subcontracting provided economies of scale to save institutions money in the provision of key services, it also injected the business models that were beginning to predominate in the private sector economy into CCU campuses and insulated campus administrators from the claims and concerns of subcontracted workers.

Food service provides a case in point. In that sector, three multinational companies—Aramark, Sodexo, and Compass—have emerged as the dominant players in food provision on campuses. Unfortunately, such companies have been repeatedly cited for violations of labor, workplace safety, wage and hour, and employment discrimination laws. Aramark (which has contracts at Georgetown University and Loyola University of Chicago [LUC], among many others) was fined seventy-six times for violations between 2010 and 2020, accruing fines totaling over $9.5 million (a remarkable figure given the generally lax enforcement by overstressed agencies such as the Department of Labor's Wage and Hour division).[29] Like Aramark, many other profit-seeking service providers lavish their CEOs with bloated incomes, employ frontline workers with wages and benefits often inadequate to their needs, and squeeze students as well. Thus, while food prices rose on average 26 percent between 2007 and 2017, college meal prices rose almost twice as fast. Rising labor costs were not to blame, for the average pay of food preparation workers rose by only 21 percent over that period.[30] Managerial compensation, meanwhile, ballooned. For example, the salary of Aramark's CEO rose by 70 percent over this period (not even including stock, stock options, and bonuses).[31]

The compensation patterns characteristic of companies like Aramark, in which those at the top see their incomes increase much faster than others, have increasingly been replicated by colleges and universities. One 2015 study found that the ratio of pay of college and university presidents to their lowest paid instructors could range as high as 357:1.[32] CCUs have not been immune to skewed income growth, although the disparities tend not to be so glaring. According to data gathered by the *Chronicle of Higher Education*, salaries for associate professors at Jesuit colleges and universities rose on average by 15 percent between 2008 and 2018.[33] Analysis of the data from IRS Form 990 (which all nonprofit organizations file annually with the IRS) shows that the pay of the top five nonofficer salary earners at these institutions rose on average by 50 percent.[34]

A contributing factor to the increasingly unequal distribution of income within individual campuses is the growing reliance of CCUs—like other institutions of higher education—on part-time adjuncts and non–tenure track instructors. The AAUP reports that the proportion of instructors in higher education who hold full-time tenured or tenure-track positions dropped 26 percent between 1975 and 2015.[35] That same period saw a 70 percent increase in adjunct instructors.[36] "Reliance on adjuncts varies at Catholic colleges and universities," Beyer notes, "but these institutions generally reflect the larger national trends."[37] Existing evidence backs up his contention. According to data gleaned from the U.S. Department of Education's Integrated Postsecondary Education Data System (IPEDS), by 2013 more than half (53 percent) of instructional faculty at Jesuit colleges and universities were nontenured and not on a tenure track line, and 43 percent were part time.[38] AAUP data indicate that religious institutions tend to pay adjuncts even more poorly than secular institutions do.[39] The cost savings of relying on adjunct faculty are clear: the union-sponsored advocacy group Faculty Forward calculated that Jesuit institutions saved an average of $42,109 from each class taught by an adjunct professor in 2013.[40] But those savings exact a human cost. As adjunct theologian and organizer Kerry Danner observes, adjunct work at most Catholic institutions "burdens physical and psychological health and inhibits spiritual flourishing by exclusion and inequality, killing literally and spiritually persons and the full vision of Catholic higher education."[41]

That institutions have felt driven toward greater reliance on adjuncts is understandable. Debra Erickson describes the situation faced by Siena College, where she taught from 2012 to 2014. As a tuition-driven liberal arts institution in upstate New York, Siena faced a shrinking revenue base and found that its excellent regional reputation was no longer helping it compete for a shrinking pool of students from higher income families. Whereas it had once employed a stable group of decently paid nontenured faculty in three-quarter time positions without benefits, when faced with having to provide health benefits for those instructors under the Affordable Care Act, it converted them to course-by-course adjuncts.[42]

If it is understandable why so many schools have relied increasingly on adjuncts, it is equally clear why adjuncts, in turn, would be drawn to unionization. According to data gathered by the Coalition on the Academic Workforce, by 2012 unionized adjuncts earned 25 percent more per course than their nonunion peers on average.[43] Adjuncts were unaffected by the *Yeshiva* decision because, unlike tenured faculty, they lack a say over curricula and hiring and thus cannot be classified as managerial employees. Most legal experts also believe that the majority of adjuncts at Catholic institutions were unaffected by the Supreme Court's 1979 decision in *NLRB v. Catholic Bishop of Chicago*, which blocked instructors directly involved in religious instruction from using federal labor law to claim the right to organize.[44] But adjuncts did not need legal opinions to perceive their cause was just. They could point to the words of the U.S. bishops' 1986 pastoral letter: "All church institutions must...fully recognize the rights of employees to organize and bargain collectively with the institution through whatever association or organization they freely choose."[45]

As they launched a host of organizing campaigns after the Great Recession, adjuncts found that the bishops' words from 1986 had no impact on most CCU leaders. Beset by financial pressures and influenced by an approach now commonplace in the private sector from which so many of these institutions' board members hailed, one Catholic campus after another dug in to resist adjunct unionization. The battle was joined in fights on the campuses of Manhattan College (NY), Duquesne University (PA), Seattle University, and St. Xavier University (IL), among others. In these cases, administrators predicated their opposition to unionizing adjuncts on the grounds of religious freedom. They contended that labor law should not apply to *any* instructors on Catholic campuses—a far more expansive position than that formulated in *Catholic Bishop*.

The degree to which CCU leaders began justifying union opposition as a defense of religious freedom was illustrated by Rev. Dennis H. Holtschneider, CM, who, as president of DePaul University (IL), took a prominent stand against union rights in 2016. Holtschneider's argument was somewhat surprising given his background. As a faculty member at St. John's University early in his career, he joined a faculty union himself; later, as an administrator at Niagara University (NY), he led amicable negotiations with a faculty union. Yet, indicative of the shifting attitudes of CCU leaders nationally, as president of DePaul, Holtschneider claimed that it was his duty "to oppose organizing efforts of part-time faculty" and to protect his institution from the encroachments of federal labor law. "The freedom to determine what is or what is not religious activity inside our church is at stake," he warned. If federal labor law continued to uphold the rights of adjuncts to organize on Catholic campuses, he predicted, "the consequences will be grave—not only for Catholics but also for all Americans."[46]

Rev. Holtschneider's views reflected a broad consensus among CCU leaders. Both the Association of Catholic Colleges and Universities (ACCU) and the Association of Jesuit Colleges and Universities joined amicus briefs that used the same reasoning to challenge the jurisdiction of the National Labor Relations Board (NLRB) over adjuncts' union rights.[47]

Yet the argument underlying this consensus holds up poorly under scrutiny. CCU leaders contend that in fighting unionization they are merely defending their religious freedom against government encroachment, but their actions suggest that it is unions—not government—that they really fear. Although unions have repeatedly indicated their willingness to accept alternative methods of recognition that do not involve the government, CCUs have repeatedly refused such offers. Nor has the ACCU, whose presidency Holtschneider assumed in 2019, offered to create an independent Catholic labor board to guarantee adjuncts' union rights in lieu of the NLRB. Instead, "brandishing the First Amendment," CCUs have waged a legal fight over the union rights of adjuncts. That fight has become bound up with partisan politics. Republican judges and appointees to the NLRB have generally sided with CCU administrators in opposing NLRB jurisdiction, while Democrats have sided with adjunct unions. At this writing, the CCUs are winning in the courts. In a January 2020 decision regarding Duquesne University, the U.S. Court of Appeals for the District of Columbia ruled 2–1 that the question of adjuncts' union rights on religiously affiliated campuses is "no business of the state." The ACCU said it was "gratified" by this decision, which left the power to decide whether adjuncts can unionize entirely in the hands of their employers.[48]

Stirrings of Reform

Even as Catholic institutions' labor practices became increasingly entangled in what Pope Francis has called "an economy that kills," stirrings of reform have emerged in numerous settings. Among the first was the antisweatshop movement that swept many college campuses in the late 1990s. That movement saw college students challenge campus administrations to sever ties with brands that made apparel under exploitative conditions overseas. That agitation spread to many Catholic campuses, led to the formation of United Students Against Sweatshops (USAS) in 1998, and gave birth to the Worker Rights Consortium (WRC) in 2001. The WRC was created to investigate alleged abuses in the factories where college- and university-licensed brands manufacture their goods. It is funded by more than 150 affiliated universities, twenty of which are CCUs. Georgetown was a founding member of the organization and has held a seat on its governing board ever since. WRC investigations and pressure from USAS have repeatedly won labor reforms from large-scale brands such as Nike.[49]

Following the WRC's creation, students' concern for workers' rights abroad was soon expanded to the needs of workers on their own campuses. Inspired by the campaign of activist students at Harvard University to win a living wage for all university employees, students at Georgetown launched a similar campaign in 2002.[50] After two years of organizing and pressure, the university created a committee to study the living wage issue and recommend a solution. When that solution fell short of the students' demands, they staged a hunger strike in March 2005, which pushed Georgetown to finalize a more ambitious Just Employment Policy. That policy guaranteed a living wage and the right to organize for both directly hired and subcontracted workers. Under its protection, subcontracted janitorial and food service workers soon won unions on the campus. Student activism demanding adoption of living wage and just employment policies began to spread just prior to the Great Recession. Although no other Catholic college or university has yet matched Georgetown's policy, several have adopted measures that raised pay for the directly employed and enforced some standards for subcontracted employees.[51]

The next reform push emerged when the wave of austerity created by the Great Recession contributed to a renewed push for adjunct unionization on many Catholic campuses. As resistance to adjunct unionism began to coalesce among many CCUs, as described above, some prominent institutions broke ranks. Among the first was Georgetown. When its adjuncts turned to Local 500 of the Service Employees International Union (SEIU) in 2012, the university cited its Just Employment Policy and declared neutrality, leaving the decision to unionize entirely up to the adjuncts, who voted to unionize in overwhelming numbers.[52]

Although union resistance continued at most CCUs, Saint Louis University and St. Mary's College (CA) recognized adjunct unions in 2016, issuing statements supporting employees' right to make their own informed choice about unionization.[53] Fordham University initially fought to prevent its adjuncts from unionizing, but in May 2017 President Joseph M. McShane, SJ, whose own scholarship explores the history of Catholic social teaching in the United States, reversed his position, explaining that he had become "convinced of the rightness" of the workers' desire to unionize.[54] Adjunct unions were also recognized at Loyola University Chicago, Notre Dame de Namur University (CA), Trinity Washington University (DC), St. Francis University (PA), Le Moyne College (NY), and St. Michael's College (VT).[55]

President Barack Obama's appointees to the NLRB opened a new front in the union fight on CCU campuses by ruling in 2016 that graduate assistants enjoyed union rights under the National Labor Relations Act (NLRA). Graduate assistant unions were not a new phenomenon. In 1970, the Teaching Assistants' Association of the University of Wisconsin was the first to negotiate a contract.[56] By the 1980s, teaching assistants were organizing at many other state universities. Yet graduate assistant unions were stalled in private universities by an ongoing controversy over whether the assistants were workers or students. If categorized as the latter, they had no union rights. NLRB rulings had waffled on that question for years. The Obama board ended the waffling, ruled that they were both and that as workers they had rights to negotiate over their work. Graduate assistants at multiple private universities soon unionized. In February 2017, LUC's graduate employees were the first at a CCU to vote for a union. In September 2017, their counterparts at Boston College followed suit. But as President Donald J. Trump began reconstituting the NLRB with his appointees, both these institutions declared that graduate assistants were actually students, not employees, anticipating that the Trump board would back their view. Even Georgetown took this tack. In December 2017, when graduate assistants asked the university to recognize the Georgetown Association of Graduate Employees (GAGE), the university demurred, saying that they were "not employees."[57]

Georgetown's stand elicited an eruption of protest that forced the university to reconsider. Desiring to extend its positive record on labor issues, Georgetown opened negotiations with GAGE. Both sides recognized that the state of legal opinion on assistants' union rights was in flux. The Trump board was almost certain to reverse the Obama board's decision. Georgetown could have followed the example of LUC and Boston College and simply walked away from GAGE, knowing that the union, like its sister organizations, would not seek relief from a hostile Trump board. Instead, Georgetown and the union made a groundbreaking agreement to bring in a nongovernmental election monitor, the American Arbitration Association, and let it conduct a union election no matter what the NLRB ruled regarding graduate assistants' union rights. GAGE won that election by a landslide, 555–108, and, after a year of negotiation, GAGE and Georgetown signed their first contract in April 2018.[58]

Pandemic and the Limits of Reform

The Georgetown-GAGE election agreement was perhaps the high-water mark of labor reform at CCUs prior to the arrival of the COVID-19 pandemic. The agreement highlighted an option that had always been on the table for Catholic institutions sincerely concerned about the NLRB's potential infringement on religious freedom: negotiating private election agreements that do not involve the government. That no Catholic institutions other than Georgetown have exercised that option suggests that, as noted above, it is unionization (with its expectation of increased wages) rather than infringement upon their religious liberties that they actually fear.

Any effort to expand the beachhead of the labor reform initiatives of recent years will face daunting obstacles, thanks to a series of governmental actions and COVID-19. After Donald Trump's election, Republican-appointed judges and NLRB members dealt several blows to the cause of union rights among workers at CCUs. One blow, noted above, was the DC federal appeals court's 2–1 ruling on January 28, 2020 that Duquesne University's status as a Roman Catholic institution bars its adjuncts from claiming the protections of the NLRA, thus undermining a union that Duquesne's adjuncts had supported by a 50–9 margin in 2012 but which the university had adamantly refused to recognize.[59] That court ruling was followed on June 10, 2020, by a decision of the NLRB that adjuncts at religious institutions possessed no union rights.[60] What's more, in September 2019, the NLRB initiated a rule-making effort to establish that graduate assistants are exclusively students and not also university employees, and therefore have no recourse to the NLRA. Although that effort was blocked following the election of the nation's second Catholic president, Joseph R. Biden, in 2020, the union rights of graduate employees remain tenuous.[61]

The profound impact of the pandemic on CCUs has further clouded the picture for labor reform. Although the pandemic hit all of U.S. higher education hard, tuition-driven private residential colleges and universities were hardest hit since they lost not only enrollments, but valuable income earned from housing and food service, among other revenue streams. Across Catholic higher education, the pandemic brought a sudden wave of austerity. Funding for higher education included in the Coronavirus Aid, Relief, and Economic Security (CARES) Act was not enough to prevent salaries, contributions to retirement, and hiring from being frozen at most institutions.[62]

But freezes were not enough at many: draconian cutbacks ensued at some. Canisius College (NY) discontinued nine academic programs and terminated twenty-two faculty members (most of whom had tenure) and laid off seventy-one other employees.[63] D'Youville College (NY) laid off sixty employees, prompting the faculty senate to vote no confidence in the college's president, who had failed to consult them in advance.[64] Fairfield University (CT) asked faculty to take a 3 percent salary cut and a 5.5 percent reduction in retirement payments.[65] John

Carroll University (OH) eliminated its art history department, fired two faculty members, sought changes in the faculty handbook that would make it easier to fire others, and terminated an unknown number of noninstructional staff, refusing to disclose how many.[66] Loyola University New Orleans cut administrative salaries by 10 percent, furloughed fifty-nine staff, and dropped its contributions to employees' dental coverage.[67] Such measures proliferated.

In many cases, faculty and staff pushed back against such cuts. When Edgewood College (WI) laid off targeted faculty who refused to accept voluntary buyouts, it triggered a conflict with faculty and the AAUP, which resulted in the reinstatement of most of those laid off.[68] The AAUP chapter at Loyola Marymount University (CA) demanded an "equity budget" that would distribute the costs of budget cuts more fairly based on income.[69] At several institutions, ad hoc coalitions sprang up to resist the cuts and protest the lack of consultation over the cutbacks. At John Carroll, the group was called Save JCU.[70] At Marquette University (WI), it was Our Marquette.[71] But such groups faced stiff headwinds. Where unions existed, administrations generally steamrolled them. The University of San Francisco forced its faculty union back to the bargaining table in June 2020 by threatening to terminate the jobs of sixty-eight union members if an agreement was not reached.[72] St. Xavier simply announced that it was withdrawing recognition of its faculty union after forty-one years in order to be "nimble and responsive" in response to the COVID crisis.[73]

It seemed at the outset that institutions with healthy endowments would be better able to weather the crisis without draconian measures. For example, Gonzaga University (WA) drew on its endowment and reserves and made no layoffs.[74] Notre Dame froze salaries and hires but continued to contribute to faculty retirement accounts.[75] LUC managed to nearly double its graduate assistants' stipends by April 2021 (even as it still refused to recognize their union).[76] Although Georgetown suspended retirement account payments and sought voluntary pay reductions from its faculty, it committed itself to a no-layoffs policy and instituted a program called Redeploy Georgetown, intended to reassign workers whose normal work assignment was not possible to perform in a socially distanced way to new tasks such as contact tracing.[77] Even so, problems emerged at Georgetown—and other institutions—over the failure of administrators to consult in meaningful ways with faculty, staff, and students prior to devising a policy response. GAGE and other Georgetown constituencies urged a suspension of Redeploy Georgetown pending such consultations.[78]

Yet the impact of the crisis was not directly proportional to the size of an institution's endowment. Some smaller tuition-dependent institutions with high percentages of Pell Grant–eligible students received supplemental funds from the federal government that helped cushion the economic impact of the pandemic in academic year 2020–2021. Thus the College of Saint Mary (NE), a small university with an endowment of only $26 million, cut no positions, offered cost of living raises, and even provided on-campus support for the children of faculty, staff, and students.[79] As that case indicates, the impact of the pandemic on labor relations at CCUs, although profound, varied considerably from institution to institution.

In general, though, CCUs were hard hit by the pandemic. Where do we stand now? While the long-term impacts of COVID-19 austerity for Catholic higher education are impossible to accurately assess at this writing, three things seem clear. First, campus labor relations have suffered as CCUs overall have become financially more precarious. Conservative estimates suggest that higher education overall lost $120 billion to COVID-related impacts between March 2020 and March 2021. Some $76.5 billion in federal relief was channeled to colleges and universities, and Catholic institutions that feared that federal interference with their labor relations would undermine their religious freedom did not hesitate to accept government help. But half of allocated funds were reserved for students' needs. The resulting shortfall hit tuition-dependent institutions especially hard.[80] CCUs had already seen their total enrollments drop by 6 percent between 2010 and 2018. From 2019 to 2020, Catholic elementary and secondary schools—a key feeder for CCUs—saw their largest enrollment drop in fifty years. Unfortunately, the increased financial precarity many institutions now face might only incentivize them to further entrench tendencies, such as reliance on adjuncts, that have exacerbated labor conflict on so many campuses.[81]

At the same time, the crisis triggered an unprecedented level of organizing and mobilizing among faculty, staff, and students. Perhaps the most striking example was the effort to build a multicampus, worker-driven antiausterity effort on Jesuit campuses: the Coalition of Jesuit Higher Ed Workers and Students. Formed in the fall of 2020, the group circulated a petition protesting the "rash of austerity-driven layoffs, firings and program eliminations" that were "decided without meaningful input from faculty and staff." It called for a range of reforms, including budget transparency and "fair and democratic process for unionization for all academic workers and staff who wish to pursue it." According to one organizer, the coalition represented "the first time that workers are coming together to advocate for the…uniqueness of Jesuit higher education."[82]

Whether the Jesuit campus coalition can succeed in pressuring institutions to bring their labor policies in line with Catholic social teaching is unclear. There is no gainsaying how daunting that challenge is, for there is little evident appetite among cabinet-level leaders of Catholic higher education to address labor issues squarely. In June 2021, Jesuit colleges and universities gathered virtually to commemorate the twentieth anniversary of Superior General Peter-Hans Kolvenbach's challenge to North Americans in 2000 that they make "the promotion of justice…the characteristic Jesuit university way of proceeding and of serving socially."[83] That commemoration included plenaries on spirituality, racial justice, immigration, women's leadership, and environmental justice, but none addressed labor rights, let alone working conditions on Jesuit campuses.[84] Jesuit institutions are not unique in this regard. Unfortunately, it remains much easier for most CCUs to support social justice beyond campus gates than within them.

Finally, the pandemic made clear that the fate of CCUs cannot be disentangled from that of the overall U.S. economy and higher education in general. Catholic institutions must navigate a world in which both the economy and higher education in general are changing in ways that challenge them at their core—and in ways that COVID-19 only exacerbated. Many of these institutions are financially precarious. Yet, as the institutional repository of Catholic social teaching on the dignity of labor, CCUs possess a rich resource that can help heal what is broken in our economy and society. Rather than continuing to be swept along by the larger economic forces that have steadily separated their praxis from their teaching, these institutions should rediscover Catholic teaching on the rights and dignity of workers and implement it on their campuses, modeling a solidarity that counteracts the inequality-generating features of twenty-first century capitalism. They should also advocate for national economic and educational policies that make such solidarity sustainable.

Questions for Consideration and Discussion

1. McCartin observes that the Land O'Lakes Statement and *Ex Corde Ecclesiae* say next to nothing about just employment policies and practices at CCUs. Consult §10 of the Land O'Lakes Statement (available online, cited by McCartin in n5). Drawing from CST, what should be added to correct its vagueness? If the "total organization" is to reflect the "Christian spirit," as the Statement affirms, what principles need to guide a CCU's labor policies and practices? In other words, what would you add to §10?
2. According to McCartin, the transition over the last several decades to lay leadership and independent boards increasingly composed of businesspeople with backgrounds in finance has led CCUs to adopt the "patterns and thinking produced by the larger economy from which business leaders emerged." Do you see evidence of this shift at your institution? Has it become "corporatized": as Gerald Beyer uses this term, "characterized by processes, decisional criteria, expectations, organizational culture, and operating practices that are taken from, and have their origins in, the modern business corporation" (*Just Universities*, 14–15)? If so, how, and what have the net effects been? Have any been positive? Also, what is the alternative? Is resistance futile, or are there constructive ways that your institution can reverse what McCartin calls "the growing divergence between praxis and teaching"?
3. McCartin comments that "it remains much easier for most CCUs to support social justice beyond campus gates than within them." Is that true at your institution, or is attention accorded not only to issues off campus, but to labor policies and practices on campus (e.g., with respect to wages and benefits for adjuncts and staff and the outsourcing of services)? How much information is available regarding labor issues on campus? What efforts are there to help right any wrongs? What are the constraints that your institution is operating under? Finally, what are the possibilities for progress, postpandemic?
4. As you conclude your discussion of this chapter, what are three to five initiatives you might affirm or undertake on your campus in support of worker justice? Who might lead those initiatives? What voices need to be amplified?

Notes

1. Thanks to Bernard Prusak, Jennifer Reed-Bouley, and Daniel Rhodes for suggestions, to Ethan Greer for extraordinary research help, and to Gerald J. Beyer, from whose work I have learned so much. None of them bears any responsibility for the arguments I advance here.

2. Pope John Paul II, *Ex Corde Ecclesiae* (August 15, 1990), Article 2, 2. This and other church documents are available online at https://www.vatican.va/.

3. National Conference of Catholic Bishops (now United States Conference of Catholic Bishops), *Economic Justice for All: Pastoral Letter on Catholic Social Teaching and the U.S. Economy* (1986) 347, https://www.usccb.org/upload/economic_justice_for_all.pdf.

4. Patrick Reilly, "The Land O'Lakes Statement Has Caused Devastation for Fifty Years," *The Cardinal Newman Society*, July 20, 2017, https://newmansociety.org/land-o-lakes-statement-caused-devastation-50-years/.

5. "Land O'Lakes Statement: The Idea of a Catholic University," 10, https://cushwa.nd.edu/assets/245340/landolakesstatement.pdf.

6. Gene Currivan, "Inquiry Censures St. John's Layoffs," *New York Times*, April 1, 1966; Martin Arnold, "Picketing Marks St. John's Opening," *New York Times*, September 20, 1966; and "Our Chapter's History," on the home page of the St. John's University AAUP chapter, https://stjaaup.wildapricot.org/.

7. *National Labor Relations Board v. Yeshiva University*, 444 U.S. 672 (1980).

8. Allan Bloom, *The Closing of the American Mind: How Higher Education Has Failed Democracy and Impoverished the Souls of Today's Students*, 25th anniversary ed. (New York: Simon & Shuster, 2012 [1987]), 27.

9. Pope John Paul II, *Ex Corde Ecclesiae* 50.

10. For one example, see David J. O'Brien's *From the Heart of the American Church: Catholic Higher Education and American Culture* (Maryknoll, NY: Orbis, 1994), 78–79.

11. Jean Fourastié, *Les Trentes Glorieuses, ou la révolution invisible de 1946 à 1975* (Paris: Fayard, 1979).

12. Claudia Goldin and Robert A. Margo, "The Great Compression: The U.S. Wage Structure at Mid-Century," *Quarterly Journal of Economics* 107, no. 1 (February 1992): 1–34.

13. See Sanford Jacoby, *Labor in the Age of Finance: Pensions, Politics, and Corporations, from Deindustrialization to Dodd-Frank* (Princeton, NJ: Princeton University Press, 2021); Eileen Appelbaum and Rosemary Batt, *Private Equity at Work: When Wall Street Manages Main Street* (New York: Russell Sage, 2014); Gerald F. Davis, *Managed by the Markets: How Finance*

Re-shaped America (New York: Oxford, 2011); Greta R. Krippner, *Capitalizing on Crisis: The Political Origins of the Rise of Finance* (Cambridge, MA: Harvard University Press, 2011); William Lazonick, "The Fragility of the US Economy: The Financialized Corporation and the Disappearing Middle Class," in *The Third Globalization: Can Wealthy Nations Stay Rich in the Twenty-First Century?*, ed. Dan Breznitz and John Zysman (New York: Oxford University Press, 2013), 232–76; Judith Stein, *Pivotal Decade: How the United States Traded Factories for Finance in the Seventies* (New Haven, CT: Yale University Press, 2019).

14. David M. Gordon, *Fat and Mean: The Corporate Squeeze of Working Americans and the Myth of Corporate Downsizing* (New York: The Free Press, 1996); David Weil, *The Fissured Workplace: Why Work Became So Bad for So Many and What We Can Do about It* (Cambridge, MA: Harvard University Press, 2014); Marc Levinson, *The Box: How the Shipping Container Made the World Smaller and the World Economy Bigger* (Princeton NJ: Princeton University Press, 2006).

15. Erin Hatton, *The Temp Economy: From Kelly Girls to Permatemps in Postwar America* (Philadelphia: Temple University Press, 2011); Louis Hyman, *Temp: How American Work, American Business, and the American Dream Became Temporary* (New York: Viking, 2018).

16. Nelson Lichtenstein, *The Retail Revolution: How Wal-Mart Created a Brave New World of Business* (New York: Metropolitan Books, 2019).

17. Juliana Menasce Horowitz, Ruth Igielnik, and Rakesh Kochhar, "Trends in Income and Wealth Inequality," Pew Research Center, January 9, 2020, https://www.pewresearch.org/social-trends/2020/01/09/trends-in-income-and-wealth-inequality/.

18. Anna Stansbury and Lawrence H. Summers, "The Declining Worker Power Hypothesis: An Explanation for the Recent Evolution of the American Economy," National Bureau of Economic Research Working Paper (2020), 1, http://dx.doi.org/10.3386/w27193.

19. See for these data Elise Gould, "The State of Working America, 2019," Economic Policy Institute, February 20, 2020, https://www.epi.org/publication/swa-wages-2019/.

20. Michael Sandel, *The Tyranny of Merit: What's Become of the Common Good?* (New York: Farrar, Straus and Giroux, 2020), 155–56.

21. Sandel, *The Tyranny of Merit*, 183.

22. Association of Catholic Colleges and Universities, "The Catholic College and University Presidents" (Washington, DC: ACCU, 2013); Christine Pharr, "Changing Catholic College and University Leadership: Retaining Catholic Identity," *Integritas* 9, no. 2 (Spring 2017): 1–14.

23. Melanie M. Morey and John J. Piderit, *Catholic Higher Education: A Culture in Crisis* (New York: Oxford University Press, 2006), 275–306.

24. Gary W. Jenkins, "The Wall Street Takeover of Nonprofit Boards," *Stanford Social Innovation Review* (Summer 2015): 46–52.

25. Percentage of board members from finance, insurance, and real estate (FIRE) in 2021: Georgetown 38 percent; Notre Dame 35 percent, Boston College 35 percent. These calculations are based on an examination of information available on university websites regarding board membership supplemented by information available on their IRS Form 990s.

26. Gerald J. Beyer, *Just Universities: Catholic Social Teaching Confronts Corporatized Higher Education* (New York: Fordham University Press, 2021). See 14–15 for his definition of "corporatization."

27. Alice Gallin, *Negotiating Identity: Catholic Higher Education since 1960* (Notre Dame, IN: University of Notre Dame Press, 2000), 119–20.

28. James F. Keenan, *University Ethics: How Colleges Can Build and Benefit from a Culture of Ethics* (Lanham, MD: Rowman & Littlefield, 2015), 133.

29. Data from the Good Jobs First Violation Tracker, http://violationtracker.goodjobsfirst.org/prog.php?parent=aramark.

30. See Tara García Mathewson, "Here's Why Food Is So Insanely Expensive at College," *Money*, January 18, 2017, https://money.com/why-food-college-expensive/. The Bureau of Labor Statistics indicates that the mean wage of a food preparation worker rose from $18,480 in 2006 to $22,920 in 2016. See Bureau of Labor Statistics, *Occupational Employment and Wages, 2006*, https://www.bls.gov/news.release/archives/ocwage_05172007.pdf; Bureau of Labor Statistics, *Occupational Employment and Wages, May 2016*, https://www.bls.gov/news.release/archives/ocwage_03312017.pdf.

31. Aramark CEO Joseph Neubauer earned $1 million in 2006; his successor Eric J. Foss earned $1.7 million in 2016. See Joseph A. McCartin, "Confronting the Labor Problem in Catholic Higher Education," *Journal of Catholic Higher Education* 37, no. 1 (2018): 71–88, at 78–79.

32. Laura McKenna, "The College-President-to-Adjunct Pay Ratio," *The Atlantic*, September 2015, https://www.theatlantic.com/education/archive/2015/09/income-inequality-in-higher-education-the-college-president-to-adjunct-pay-ratio/407029/.

33. Faculty salary data gathered from the *Chronicle of Higher Education* survey, Chronicle Data, https://data.chronicle.com/category/sector/2/faculty-salaries/.

34. This analysis is based on data collected from the IRS Form 990s filed by member institutions of the Association of Jesuit Colleges and Universities. Form 990 data is available at ProPublica Non-Profit Explorer, https://projects.propublica.org/nonprofits/.

35. American Association of University Professors, "Visualizing Change: The Annual Report on the Economic Status of the Profession, 2016-2017," *Academe* 103, no. 2 (March–April 2017): 1–64, at 7.

36. John B. Lee, "Faculty Salaries, 2002–2013," *The NEA 2014 Almanac of Higher Education*, ed. Harold Wexler (Washington, DC: National Education Association, 2014), 13. See also Liang Zhang, Ronald Ehrenberg, and Xiangmin Liu, *Changing Faculty Employment at Four-Year Colleges and Universities in the United States* (Bonn, Germany: Institute for the Study of Labor, 2015), http://ftp.iza.org/dp9595.pdf.

37. Beyer, *Just Universities*, 52.

38. These calculations are based on IPEDS final data release for fall 2013. These figures include all institutional faculty employees at these institutions, excluding medical schools. See IPEDS Data Center, http://nces.ed.gov/ipeds/datacenter/.

39. American Association of University Professors, "Visualizing Change: The Annual Report on the Economic Status of the Profession, 2016-2017," 23, as cited in Beyer, *Just Universities*, 304.

40. "Faculty Working Conditions at Jesuit Colleges and Universities" (April 2015), http://seiufacultyforward.org/wp-content/uploads/2015/03/Jesuit-Factsheet.pdf.

41. Kerry Danner, "Saying No to an Economy That Kills: Undermining Mission and Exploiting Vocation in Catholic Higher Education," *Journal of Moral Theology* 8, no. 1 (2019): 26–50, at 50.

42. Debra Erickson, "Adjunct Unionization on College Campuses: Solidarity, Theology, and Mission," *Journal of Moral Theology* 8, no. 1 (2019): 51–75, at 55.

43. Coalition on the Academic Workforce, *A Portrait of Part-Time Faculty Members* (2012), www.academicworkforce.org/CAW_portrait_2012.pdf.

44. See Gerald J. Beyer, "Labor Unions, Adjuncts, and the Mission and Identity of Catholic Universities," *Horizons* 42, no. 1 (2015): 1–37.

45. National Conference of Catholic Bishops, *Economic Justice for All* 353.

46. Rev. Dennis H. Holtschneider, CM, "Refereeing Religion?" *Inside Higher Ed*, January 28, 2016, https://www.insidehighered.com/views/2016/01/28/new-nlrb-standard-could-have-major-consequences-catholic-colleges-essay.

47. See, e.g., the "Brief for Amici Curiae Association of Catholic Colleges and Universities, Lasallian Association of College and University Presidents, and Association of Jesuit Colleges and Universities on Behalf of Employer," filed in Manhattan College's long-running NLRB case, NLRB Case No. 02-RC-2354, April 25, 2011, https://content.manhattan.edu/hr/4.25.11_ACCU-LACUP-and-AJCU-Amicus-Brief.pdf.

48. Carol Zimmerman, "Court Says Catholic Universities Not under Labor Board's Authority," *National Catholic Reporter*, January 30, 2020, https://www.ncronline.org/news/justice/court-says-catholic-universities-not-under-labor-boards-authority; ACCU, "Statement Following Today's Decision from the U.S. Court of Appeals," January 28, 2020, https://www.accunet.org/Portals/70/Docs/Program%20Files%20%26%20Statements/Duquesne-decision-1-28-20.pdf. On the ways conservatives have used the First Amendment to attack unions and regulation in general, see Tamara R. Piety, *Brandishing the First Amendment: Commercial Expression in America* (Ann Arbor: University of Michigan Press, 2012).

49. See Liza Featherstone, *Students against Sweatshops: The Making of a Movement* (New York: Verso, 2002). The CCUs affiliated with the WRC are Boston College, College of the Holy Cross, Creighton University, DePaul University, Fairfield University, Fordham University, Georgetown University, Gonzaga University, Loyola Marymount University, Marquette University, Providence College, St. John's University, St. Joseph's University, St. Louis University, Santa Clara University, Seattle University, University of Dayton, University of Notre Dame, Villanova University, and Xavier University. See Worker Rights Consortium, https://www.workersrights.org/affiliates/affiliate-institutions/.

50. Amy Offner, "The Harvard Living Wage Campaign: Origins and Strategy," *Employee Responsibilities and Rights Journal* 25 (2013): 135–42.

51. See Nicholas M. Wertsch and Joseph A. McCartin, "A Just Employment Approach to Adjunct Unionization: The Georgetown Model," in *Professors in the Gig Economy*, ed. Kim Tolley (Baltimore: Johns Hopkins University Press, 2018), 87–103, at 89–94.

52. Wertsch and McCartin, "A Just Employment Approach," 96–97.

53. See St. Mary's Messages and Updates, May 23, 2016, https://www.stmarys-ca.edu/president/contingent-faculty-union-effort/messages-and-updates.

54. See Joseph M. McShane, SJ, *Sufficiently Radical: Catholicism, Progressivism, and the Bishops' Program of 1919* (Washington, DC: Catholic University Press, 1986). See McShane's letter at http://www.justemploymentpolicy.org/fordham-cites-catholic-teaching-in-accepting-faculty-unionization/.

55. See the Catholic Labor Network Catholic Employer Project, July 8, 2021, online at https://catholiclabor.org/catholic-employer-project/catholic-higher-education/.

56. See TAA's "History," https://taa-madison.org/history/.

57. Menachem Wecker, "Georgetown Denies Unionizing Effort of Graduate Student Group," *National Catholic Reporter*, December 12, 2017, https://www.ncronline.org/news/justice/georgetown-denies-unionizing-effort-graduate-student-group.

58. Joseph A. McCartin, "Georgetown's Game-Changing Agreement," *Commonweal*, April 30, 2018, https://www.commonwealmagazine.org/georgetown%E2%80%99s-game-changing-agreement; "GAGE: Our History," https://www.wearegage.org/our-history.

59. Scott Jaschik, "Appeals Court Blocks Adjunct Union," *Inside Higher Ed*, January 29, 2020, https://www.insidehighered.com/news/2020/01/29/federal-appeals-court-blocks-adjunct-union-duquesne.

60. Colleen Flaherty, "No NLRB Jurisdiction at Religious Colleges," *Inside Higher Ed*, June 11, 2020, https://www.insidehighered.com/news/2020/06/11/no-nlrb-jurisdiction-religious-colleges.

61. Colleen Flaherty, "Green Light for Graduate Student Employee Unions," *Inside Higher Ed*, March 15, 2021, https://www.insidehighered.com/news/2021/03/15/labor-board-withdraws-planned-rule-against-student-employee-unions.

62. See Marshall Anthony Jr. and Marissa Alayna Navarro, "The State of Higher Education Spending from the CARES Act," Center for American Progress, January 29, 2021, https://www.americanprogress.org/issues/education-postsecondary/news/2021/01/29/495178/state-higher-education-spending-cares-act/.

63. See on Canisius the AAUP's "Special Report: COVID-19 and Academic Governance," May 2021, 4–9, https://www.aaup.org/file/Special-Report_COVID-19-and-Academic-Governance.pdf.

64. Jay Tokasz, "President's Moves at D'Youville College Lead to Lawsuits, Unprecedented Staff Turnover," *Buffalo News*, August 2, 2020, https://buffalonews.com/news/local/education/presidents-moves-at-dyouville-college-lead-to-lawsuits-unprecedented-staff-turnover/article_9ba59f64-d332-11ea-a433-a7650de4f345.html.

65. Dave Crawford, "On Restoration," May 24, 2021, http://www.faculty.fairfield.edu/fwc/newsletters/2020-2021/8_From%20the%20President_On%20Restoration%205_25_2021.pdf.

66. Alexander Thompson, "Deep Cuts at Catholic Colleges Draw Backlash," *National Catholic Reporter*, November 30, 2020, https://www.ncronline.org/news/coronavirus/deep-cuts-catholic-colleges-draw-backlash; Members of the John Carroll University Chapter of the American Association of University Professors, "Letter to the Editor," *The Carroll News*, October 1, 2020, https://carrollnews.org/4110/letters-to-the-editor-opinion/letter-to-the-editor-16/.

67. Khayla Gaston, "Loyola Faces a Budget Deficit, Staff Furloughs Due to COVID-19," *Loyola Maroon*, June 14, 2020, https://loyolamaroon.com/10028379/news/loyola-faces-a-budget-deficit-staff-furloughs-due-to-covid-19/; Brandon Tate, "Loyola Increases Employee Health Insurance

Premiums," *Loyola Maroon*, February 3, 2021, https://loyolamaroon.com/10030649/news/loyola-increases-employee-health-insurance-premiums/#.

68. Kelly Meyerhoffer, "Facing Scrutiny, Edgewood College Board Reinstates 6 Laid-Off Professors," *Wisconsin State Journal*, July 25, 2020, https://madison.com/wsj/news/local/education/university/facing-scrutiny-edgewood-college-board-reinstates-6-laid-off-professors/article_0a07a609-9cc2-501b-92b0-63ffdf69bcd2.html.

69. Loyola Marymount Chapter, AAUP, "A Call to Justice," https://www.lmuaaup.org/wp-content/uploads/2021/02/LMU-AAUP-Equity-Budget-Open-Letter-For-Publishing.pdf.

70. Save JCU, https://savejcu.org/.

71. Our Marquette, https://ourmarquette.net/Our-Vision.html.

72. Ethan Tan, "Full-time Union, Administration Clash over Budget Solutions," *San Francisco Foghorn*, May 28, 2020, http://sffoghorn.com/full-time-union-administration-clash-over-budget-solutions-68-faculty-librarians-in-limbo/.

73. Emma Whitford, "St. Xavier No Longer Recognizes Faculty Union," *Inside Higher Ed*, June 22, 2020, https://www.insidehighered.com/news/2020/06/22/citing-pandemic-related-pressures-st-xavier-university-cuts-ties-faculty-union.

74. Dawson Neely, "Gonzaga Weathers a Budget Storm during the COVID-19 Pandemic," *The Gonzaga Bulletin*, February 24, 2021, https://www.gonzagabulletin.com/news/gonzaga-weathers-a-budget-storm-during-the-covid-19-pandemic/article_f3451e2a-7544-11eb-b25d-af5d7bc25f9c.html.

75. Allie Kirkman, "University of Notre Dame Braces for Estimated $100 Million Loss Because of Coronavirus Pandemic," *South Bend Tribune*, September 26, 2020, https://www.southbendtribune.com/story/news/education/2020/09/26/university-of-notre-dame-braces-for-estimated-100-million-loss-because-of-coronavirus-pandemic/116060774/.

76. Elyssa Cherny, "Should Grad Students Be Considered Employees? Loyola University Nearly Doubles Stipends for Ph.D. Candidates but Doesn't Recognize Graduate Workers' Union," *Chicago Tribune*, April 27, 2021, https://www.chicagotribune.com/news/ct-loyola-grad-student-stipend-tt-20210427-d5hbcjy2bnf2hd4a5mfsrw6neu-story.html.

77. Redeploy Georgetown, https://hr.georgetown.edu/redeploy-georgetown/#.

78. Lauren Lumkin, "Georgetown University Staff Resist after Being Asked to Take New Public Health Roles or Unpaid Leave," *Washington Post*, January 29, 2021, https://www.washingtonpost.com/local/education/georgetown-workers-pandemic-work/2021/01/29/57f484b8-619b-11eb-9430-e7c77b5b0297_story.html.

79. "College of Saint Mary Creates Innovative 'Kids Club' to Support CSM," August 26, 2020, https://www.csm.edu/news/college-saint-mary-creates-innovative-%E2%80%98kids-club%E2%80%99-support-csm-families.

80. Jenny Smulson, "Government Relations," Association of Jesuit Colleges and Universities, March 24, 2021, https://www.ajcunet.edu/march-2021-connections/2021/3/23/government-relations.

81. Rick Seltzer, "Narrowing Enrollment Pipeline Pressures Roman Catholic Colleges," *Inside Higher Ed*, March 5, 2021, https://www.insidehighered.com/quicktakes/2021/03/05/narrowing-enrollment-pipeline-pressures-roman-catholic-colleges.

82. Elizabeth Redden, "Jesuit College Workers Unite," *Inside Higher Ed*, December 1, 2020, https://www.insidehighered.com/news/2020/12/01/workers-and-student-groups-across-jesuit-colleges-form-alliance-protest-cuts-people. The quotation is from Marquette graduate student Sarah Kizuk.

83. Peter-Hans Kolvenbach, SJ, "The Service of Faith and the Promotion of Justice in American Jesuit Higher Education," Santa Clara University, October 6, 2000, part III, C, https://www.scu.edu/ic/programs/ignatian-worldview/kolvenbach/.

84. See the Virtual Conference Schedule, https://csj.georgetown.edu/justice2020/schedule/#.

7

HEDGE FUNDS RUNNING CATHOLIC SCHOOLS ON THE SIDE?

Socially Responsible Investing and the Economic Ethics of Financing Catholic Higher Education

Matt Mazewski[1]

In 2016, a slate of candidates calling itself "Free Harvard, Fair Harvard" launched a campaign for the university's Board of Overseers, a body whose members are elected by Harvard alumni, on a platform that included a call for the complete elimination of tuition. The defunct website of the slate declared that "Harvard is now one of the world's largest hedge-funds, with its $38 BILLION portfolio tax-exempt because of the college it runs as a charity off to one side....Paying tuition to a giant hedge-fund is unconscionable."[2]

The quip that Harvard is a hedge fund running a school on the side may sound like hyperbole, but the stock of wealth held by the endowments of the richest private universities in the country has indeed ballooned over the last decade. And while there is no Catholic school that controls as large an investment portfolio as Harvard's, the combined endowment assets of all U.S. Catholic colleges and universities (CCUs) nevertheless constitute an enormous pool of capital and source of economic power. Debates in recent years at both secular and religious institutions over divestment from fossil fuel producers show that this power is widely recognized as deserving of serious moral scrutiny. But it should be scrutinized all the more carefully at CCUs, which are ostensibly conducted in accordance with the doctrines of the Catholic Church and the principles of Catholic social thought (CST). In his 1990 apostolic constitution on Catholic universities, *Ex Corde Ecclesiae*, Pope John Paul II writes that "a Catholic University, as Catholic, informs and carries out its research, teaching, and *all other activities* [emphasis added] with Catholic ideals, principles and attitudes."[3] This surely includes revenue-generating activities such as investing endowment funds, negotiating licensing agreements, soliciting bequests and donations, and operating hospitals or university presses.

In this chapter, I focus on CST and investment, not because this topic presents moral challenges that are not faced in other areas, but because relatively little scholarly attention has been devoted to the limitations of approaching it from the perspective of individual CCUs rather than that of CCUs seen as a network of actors with a common faith tradition and a shared set of values and educational goals. The collective assets of CCUs can be deployed to bring about more humane and sustainable economic arrangements, as well as to level extreme inequalities among CCUs themselves and thereby assist CCUs serving underresourced populations. To avoid ending up as the side businesses of hedge funds, CCUs can and should find ways to put their capital to work that not only steer clear of "cooperation with evil," but that actually expand the space of economic possibilities.

Admittedly, my basic proposal cuts against the long-standing, deeply rooted tendency of CCUs to fend for themselves and only themselves, competing both for dollars and for students. (And I recognize that, for the great majority of CCUs that are highly tuition dependent, competing for students is part of competing for dollars.) Part of the relevant background here is the incorporation of most CCUs as separate entities from their founding religious congregations in the late 1960s and early 1970s.[4] Whatever the full explanation, the contemporary project of Catholic higher education in the United States would be better served by breaking away—or even just edging away—from dog-eat-dog capitalism. Consider, too, the message that flatly rejecting new and creative ways of doing business that are consonant with CST would communicate to students at CCUs: namely, that the institutions do not in fact believe what they preach. By contrast, well-publicized creativity would bring CCUs immense credibility, which all Catholic institutions could use more of nowadays.

Endowments at Catholic and Non-Catholic Private Universities

Using Harvard as the starting point for a conversation about endowments can be both illuminating and unhelpful. Even though a handful of elite institutions have in fact amassed mind-boggling piles of lucre, most private colleges and universities come nowhere close to being "hedge funds running a school on the side." The extent of inequality of endowments can be obscured by focusing only on what is happening at the very top.

To get a clearer picture of the magnitude and distribution of private university wealth in the United States at both Catholic and non-Catholic colleges and universities, we can turn to the Integrated Postsecondary Education Data System (IPEDS), a dataset compiled and made freely available by the U.S. Department of Education's National Center for Education Statistics (NCES).[5] Detailed information on endowments was first included in IPEDS in 2008, and as of the time of writing the most recent year for which data were available was 2019. My list of CCUs comes from the website of the United States Conference of Catholic Bishops (USCCB) Committee on Education, which identifies 246 such institutions.[6] Of these, however, only 218 appear in the IPEDS data.[7]

To form a reasonable comparison group of non-Catholic colleges and universities (NCCUs), I constructed a sample consisting of only two- or four-year private schools. While some other types of institutions do report endowment assets, including for-profit and public universities, I excluded these on the grounds that no CCUs fall into those categories. The size of my comparison sample fluctuates over time, ranging from 1,286 institutions in 2008 to 1,498 in 2019.[8]

Adding up the figures for each category, we find that the total endowment wealth of private universities was $447 billion in 2019—on the order of 2 percent of U.S. GDP.[9] Of that total, $409 billion, or just over 90 percent, was held by NCCUs, with the remaining $38 billion held by CCUs. Figure 1 illustrates the growth of endowment wealth over time, which is striking: endowment assets in 2019 nearly doubled in less than a decade, increasing from a post–Great Recession trough of $246 billion in 2010. CCU endowments have been growing slightly faster on average than those of NCCUs: the mean annual growth rate of the former was 4.2 percent over the sample period, while for the latter it was 3.1 percent.[10] (An inquiry into the reasons for that divergence is beyond the scope of this chapter.)

Figure 1. Aggregate Endowment Assets at CCUs and NCCUs, 2008-2019

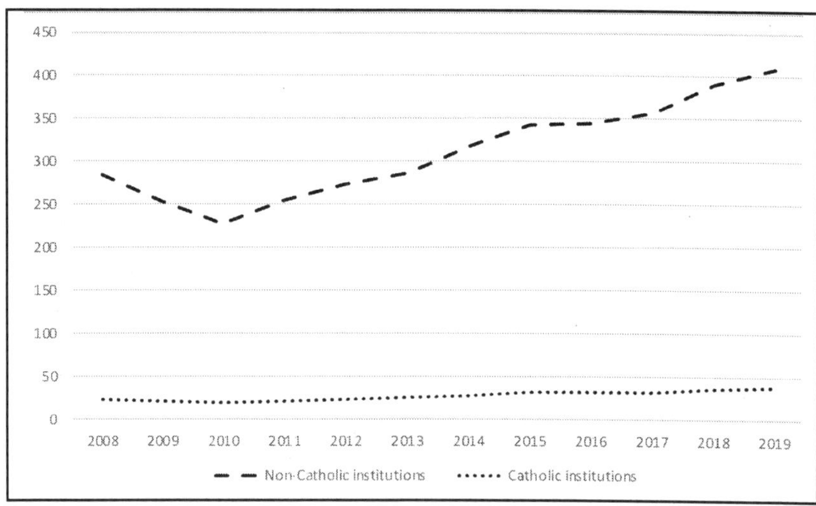

The endowment wealth of both CCUs and NCCUs is extremely concentrated. Tables 1 and 2 give the holdings of the top ten CCUs and NCCUs, respectively, and the stark inequality is apparent even from looking at these small subsets. The $11.3 billion endowment of the wealthiest CCU, the University of Notre Dame, by itself accounts for about 30 percent of total CCU endowment wealth in 2019, while the $2.5 billion endowment of the second wealthiest, Boston College, accounts for less than 7 percent. Meanwhile, the $40.1 billion endowment of Harvard University, the richest NCCU, constitutes about 10 percent of aggregate NCCU holdings. That said, CCU wealth is not necessarily more concentrated by every measure: an alternative measure of inequality, the Gini coefficient, was 0.80 for CCUs in 2019, while for NCCUs it was 0.89.[11]

Table 1. Top Ten CCUs by 2019 Endowment Assets

Rank	Institution	2019 Endowment (in billions of dollars)
1	University of Notre Dame	11.32
2	Boston College	2.47
3	Georgetown University	1.80
4	Saint Louis University	1.24
5	Santa Clara University	1.00
6	College of the Holy Cross	0.79
7	St. John's University (New York)	0.75
8	Fordham University	0.73
9	Villanova University	0.73
10	Marquette University	0.68

Table 2. Top Ten NCCUs by 2019 Endowment Assets

Rank	Institution	2019 Endowment (in billions of dollars)
1	Harvard University	40.08
2	Yale University	29.87
3	Stanford University	27.08
4	Princeton University	25.53
5	Massachusetts Institute of Technology	16.92
6	University of Pennsylvania	14.21
7	Columbia University	10.90
8	Duke University	8.57
9	Northwestern University	8.32
10	Emory University	8.31

Average endowment wealth per full-time student is also substantially higher at NCCUs: $107,576 in 2019, compared to $43,849 for CCUs. However, this is a consequence of the fact that the richest NCCUs are *much* wealthier than even the richest CCUs, as shown in figure 2. Except at the very top, the two distributions look quite similar: the median endowment wealth of NCCUs in 2019 was approximately $35 million, and even the 90th percentile was "only" about $418 million, or around one percent of Harvard's $40 billion hoard. For CCUs, the median was $39 million and the 90th percentile was $307 million.

Figure 2. Distribution of Endowment Assets at CCUs and NCCUs, 2019

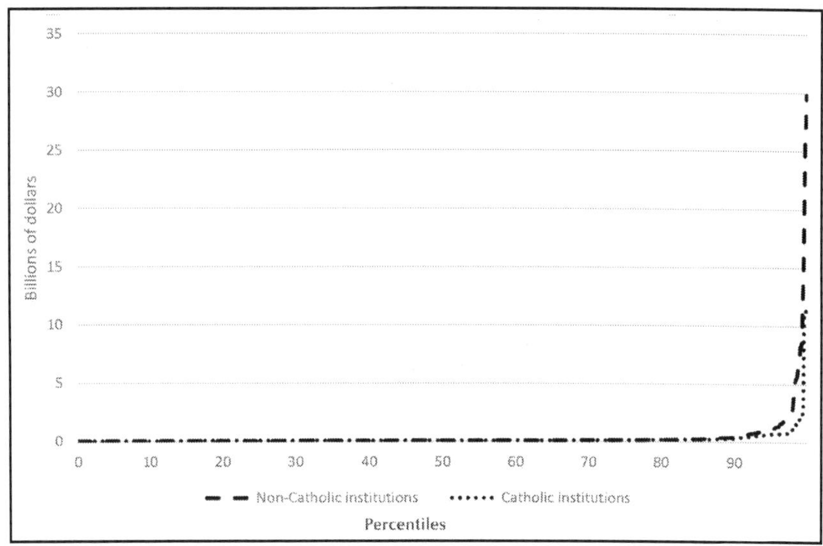

Because endowment wealth is highly unequally distributed, it logically follows that income generated from investments is unequally distributed as well. Though most private colleges and universities have nowhere near enough investment income to contemplate abolishing tuition, such supplemental revenues may help to limit the growth rate of tuition or to fund financial aid grants that reduce the cost of attendance for lower-income students.[12] Using the IPEDS data, we can assess the relative extent to which CCUs rely on investment returns compared to other sources of revenue. As expected, we find that tuition is much more important for the *average* CCU than it is for the wealthiest. In 2019, the mean share of revenue coming from tuition and fees for all CCUs was 60.4 percent, while the mean share coming from investment returns was only 4.6 percent. By contrast, for the top ten CCUs by endowment assets, these figures were 51.0 percent and 8.9 percent, respectively.

What these data show is that wealthier institutions not only have higher *levels* of investment income, but that such income accounts for a larger *proportion* of their total revenues as well. Both findings are potentially alarming from the perspective of CST, since they suggest a substantial degree of inequality in the resources that CCUs have available to provide for their students. Though it might be countered that this is not necessarily cause for concern, since wealthier institutions also tend to have larger student bodies, the distribution of endowment wealth *per student* at CCUs is also very skewed: the median for 2019 was $22,055, while the 90th percentile was $94,192.[13]

The U.S. bishops, in their 1986 pastoral letter *Economic Justice for All*, assert that

> unequal distribution should be evaluated in terms of… the priority of meeting the basic needs of the poor and the importance of increasing the level of participation by all members of society in the economic life of the nation. These norms…suggest that extreme inequalities are detrimental to the development of social solidarity and community.[14]

The same document also insists that the Church should always set an example by applying its moral principles consistently to its own "agencies and institutions."[15] This injunction suggests that any criticism of wealth inequality in society writ large applies with equal if not greater force to CCUs themselves inasmuch as they are Catholic institutions, and that taking steps to redress extreme inequalities, for instance by pooling endowment assets in a common investment fund, is an imperative of CST. Before considering how such a proposal might work in practice, however, it is first worth examining what the Catholic tradition has had to say on the subject of ethical investing, as well as how that tradition might be developed going forward.

Moral Reasoning about Investment

Discussions of CST and investing, especially as they relate to the management of college and university endowments, typically rely heavily on the traditional concepts of cooperation with evil and the principle of double effect (PDE). A representative example can be found in the comprehensive study of "market complicity" from a Christian perspective by the economist and theologian Albino Barrera, OP, who observes that "for Christian ethicists, the scholastic notion of 'cooperation with evil' (also known as the principle of legitimate material cooperation) is the logical starting point in evaluating our moral responsibility for inadvertently facilitating others' wrongdoing."[16] As opposed to "formal cooperation," which involves *intentionally* facilitating or collaborating in such wrongdoing, "material cooperation" refers to situations in which one makes a causal contribution to the bad actions of others without sharing their malicious intent.

Under this framework, formal cooperation with evil is always immoral (after all, the cooperator is intentionally facilitating a principal's wrongdoing), but material cooperation may be permissible according to the circumstances. The PDE is invoked to attempt to delineate precisely when such circumstances obtain. Barrera offers the "general and concise" formulation of the PDE laid out by the philosopher Thomas Cavanaugh. According to this formulation, an act that has two effects, one good and one bad, is permissible when it meets the following conditions:

1. The act considered independently of its evil effect is not in itself wrong;
2. The agent intends the good and does not intend the evil either as an end or as a means; and
3. The agent has proportionately grave reasons for acting, addressing his relevant obligations, comparing the consequences, and, considering the necessity of the evil, exercising due care to eliminate or mitigate it.[17]

Barrera applies double-effect reasoning to the issue of socially responsible investing (SRI) by laying out the following considerations that should guide investment decisions:

> At the very least, three factors must be considered in weighing whether or not one should invest in a particular firm with its collateral harms. First, we have to consider the nature of the harms: their toxicity, their scope, whether or not they are avertible, and the firm's causal contribution and functional role in facilitating or sustaining such ills. Second, we have to evaluate the firm's capacity to avoid or to attenuate such direct or indirect harms. Third, if such damage is unavoidable, we must weigh it relative to the benefits produced using double-effect reasoning. We have to consider the remoteness of the injury, the causal contribution, and the gravity of the wrongdoing.[18]

Barrera's analysis of how these considerations should affect actual investment practice focuses on the concept of "negative screens," whereby fund managers "screen and exclude particularly problematic industries from their portfolios," such as "alcohol, tobacco, defense, gambling, pornography, and those with poor environmental and human rights records." He goes on to caution that this is easier said than done, given that modern corporations tend to be "bound by a complicated web of interconnected ownership and formal or informal alliances," necessitating judgment calls about how to define companies that are "'significantly' or 'primarily' engaged in these excluded products or services."[19]

Faced with this "complicated web" of entanglements, it can be tempting to throw up our hands in defeat. If the entire economy is a morass of morally problematic behavior, then why not just withdraw from it entirely? The economist Teresa Ghilarducci recounts how the pension plan of the Amalgamated Clothing Workers of America "for many years would invest only in government securities in order to remain aloof from the capitalist system it criticized."[20] Stowing your money under a mattress also might seem like an appealing option, but Barrera warns that it is no solution either: "Besides being impractical, it is not morally right to do so because of the societal opportunity cost of such conduct....Hoarding such funds raises the cost of capital for everyone."[21]

A drawback of examining the problem of ethical investment through the lens of cooperation with evil is that it can lead to an undue focus on negative screening and can reinforce a mindset that morality only demands avoiding "bad" investments rather than actively seeking out "good" ones.[22] Gerald Beyer shines a spotlight on this very problem with the example of the Ave Maria Mutual Funds, an investment firm established in 2001 with Catholic investors in mind. As Beyer explains, quoting cofounder George P. Schwartz, Ave Maria's funds are "designed to help investors 'get good returns' without investing in corporations that violate certain core teachings of the Catholic Church." Schwartz "touts the fact that all of these funds 'screen out...companies that support abortion or pornography.'"[23]

Ave Maria's website calls its approach "Morally Responsible Investing (MRI)," described as a

> subset of socially responsible investing, which often screens out companies engaged in environmental issues, tobacco products, alcohol, nuclear power, defense, oil, and "unfair" labor practices. MRI is different in that it screens out companies engaged in activities that are not pro-life or pro-family.[24]

The website goes on to explain that "we employ four main moral screens," namely, abortion, embryonic stem cell research, Planned Parenthood, and pornography.

As Beyer writes, "It is certainly appropriate for Catholic investors to screen out such companies, whose products contradict important Church teachings." But he goes on:

> While it is encouraging that Catholic institutions have developed screens to eliminate investments in companies that produce abortifacients or pornography, CST on workers' rights and other issues such as weapons of mass destruction, the environment, racial and gender discrimination, and access to pharmaceuticals should also inform what Catholic institutions do with their money, as the USCCB maintains.[25]

Indeed, it is disconcerting that Ave Maria *contrasts* "morally responsible investing" with other concerns associated with "socially responsible investing," as if such concerns were not also shared by the Catholic Church or central to CST. Confusingly, Ave Maria also describes MRI as "different" from SRI immediately after characterizing the former as a "subset" of the latter. And even worse, the fund appears to minimize or dismiss the other concerns, as when it uses quotation marks in the phrase "'unfair' labor practices." Not only does Ave Maria seem to flatten the problem of ethical investment to one of implementing negative screens, but it also adopts a blinkered view of what negative screening should entail.

The papal encyclical tradition has never explicitly dealt with SRI,[26] but the American bishops have offered a much more nuanced and holistic perspective on SRI than Ave Maria's. The USCCB maintains a set of "Socially Responsible Investment Guidelines" (henceforth, the Guidelines), which are technically written as a statement of the USCCB's philosophy on managing its own investments, but which nevertheless offer a template for individual or institutional investors seeking to align their financial activities with CST.[27] The Guidelines decisively reject the view that negative screens alone are sufficient. Rather, they maintain that the principles of CST "are carried out through strategies that seek: 1) to avoid participation in harmful activities, 2) to use the Conference's role as stockholder for social stewardship, and 3) to promote the common good."[28] These three approaches are encapsulated as the following:

1. Do No Harm (avoid evil);
2. Active Corporate Participation; and
3. Positive Strategies ("Promote the Common Good").[29]

The Guidelines further explain that the first class of strategies consists both of "refus[ing] to invest in companies whose products and/or policies are counter to the values of Catholic moral teaching" and of "divesting from such companies" if investment has already taken place.[30]

The second set of strategies, which the Guidelines call "active corporate participation," but which may also be termed activist investing or shareholder activism, encompasses efforts to "use one's position as shareholder to work actively to influence or redirect the activities or policies of the corporation toward [those] which are socially beneficial and serve the common good."[31] Concretely, this may take the form of introducing shareholder resolutions, voting company proxies, or working to replace members of a corporate board of directors.[32]

Selecting companies as targets for active corporate participation requires careful discernment. The quotation above from Barrera, on considerations that should guide investment decisions, suggests that double-effect reasoning may weigh in favor of shareholder activism rather than divestment or negative screening if one judges that a firm's "capacity to avoid or attenuate" a certain harm is especially high. The Guidelines note that "mixed investments," or those in which "socially beneficial activities and socially undesirable or even immoral activities are...inextricably linked," "may be tolerated, after careful application of the principle of cooperation and the duty to avoid scandal, so long as the Conference engages in active participation and there is a reasonable hope of success for corporate change."[33]

In a 2015 interview with the *National Catholic Reporter* on "Catholic investing in changing times," Daniel Nielsen of Christian Brothers Investment Services (CBIS) discussed the difficulty in discerning when "active participation" is justified. Using the example of fossil fuel producers, he stated that, while "there's no ethical way to produce coal, as it's the dirtiest fossil fuel," CBIS nevertheless "want[s] to work with fossil fuel companies in order to reduce the negative impact on the environment." He pointed to firms engaged in hydraulic fracturing or "fracking" as potential partners to that end, and he claimed that although "some view fracking as negative to the environment...it's a better alternative than coal and it can be a chance to improve society."[34]

As Nielsen himself acknowledged, however, some "will make prudential judgments and come to different conclusions." Beyer, for his part, insists that pursuing active participation is futile in the case of fossil fuel producers, since "the scientific evidence demands an almost complete abandonment of harvesting fossil fuels from the earth in order to adequately address climate change." From his point of view, Catholic investors are "morally required to call for the abandonment of the raison d'être of these companies. It is naïve to assume that shareholder advocacy might get them to relinquish their primary practices."[35] The University of Dayton became the first U.S. Catholic university to effectively endorse this view by committing, in 2014, to complete divestment from fossil fuels.[36]

The third and final category of approaches outlined by the USCCB comprises "positive strategies" to "promote the common good." The Guidelines explain that such strategies

> involve at least two possible courses of action: 1) supporting policies and initiatives in companies…that promote the values of Catholic moral and social teaching…while earning a reasonable rate of return; 2) investments that promote community development, which, in some cases, may result in a lower rate of return, but which nevertheless are chosen because they give expression to the Church's preferential option for the poor or produce some truly significant social good.[37]

Though the first point reads like another reference to shareholder activism, the second point and subsequent text make clear that positive screening is what the USCCB has in mind here: more fully, "support[ing] companies and financial institutions which, in addition to their fiscal merits and investment advantages, have strong records in such areas as labor relations, affirmative action, [and] affordable housing."[38]

The USCCB Guidelines are obviously far more sophisticated in their application of CST to SRI than is the methodology of the Ave Maria Funds. But even sophisticated applications of CST to the problem of ethical investing tend to suffer from a further limitation: namely, they treat the set of available investments as static and exogenously given. Whether the question is framed as one of which companies or investment vehicles to *avoid*, which ones to *seek out*, or which ones to try to *nudge in better directions*, the task facing the would-be ethical investor is to figure out how to relate to or engage with (or not engage with) those companies or investment vehicles that are to be found already existing in the world. The distribution of investment opportunities is taken as given; there are assumed to be "good companies" and "bad companies" (or at least better and worse companies), and the best that one can often hope for is to make some of them slightly less bad through active participation. Aside from that, the distribution is thought to be mostly unchangeable.

Granted, over a long enough time horizon, the decisions of investors to favor or disfavor certain investments may have an effect on what types of companies remain economically viable. But the individual investor who practices screening-based SRI ordinarily has no expectation of being able to effect change at that scale. Active participation represents a move in a more transformative direction, since those who engage in it are assumed to have at least some capacity to shape a company's policies and behavior. Community investing goes even further still, by deliberately channeling capital to places that have traditionally been neglected and underserved by the current financial system.

Of course, a key factor in determining how much power investors have to shape the opportunities available to them is the amount of capital they have at their disposal. The power of active participation, for instance, comes from being able to leverage a stake that is large relative to the value of a given company. The more wealth that individual investors control, the less constrained those investors are to settle for the set of investments currently open to them.

As we have already seen, the aggregate endowment assets of CCUs represent a sizable pool of financial capital. If deployed collectively, these resources could help to promote more humane economic arrangements that otherwise face significant obstacles to emerging and thriving under our current economic system. By banding together in this way, small and mid-sized CCUs in particular not only could find new sources of revenue, but also could do more good with their investments than would be possible for most of them acting on their own.

Leveraging the Collective Economic Power of CCU Endowments

Discussions of SRI both within and beyond Catholic circles rarely seem to address the question of why so many corporations are engaged in ethically objectionable behavior. Obviously, there is no single answer to this question, because ethically objectionable behavior comes in many different forms. In the case of "sin goods," like alcohol, tobacco, or pornography, one could say that producers are simply taking their cues from consumer demand: the problem is not only their willingness to sell such products, but the fact that so many people are willing to buy them. Any individual company operating in one of these industries could virtuously choose to cease production, but its market niche would likely be snatched up by a less scrupulous competitor. (This is not to suggest that there is not a moral problem in filling the niche, only that it likely will be filled.)

Focusing on examples such as these, however, makes it seem as if the pathologies of corporate America are the result of individual moral lapses, whether on the part of consumers or of corporate managers and executives. This tendency to "overmoralizing" goes hand in hand with an inattention to the structural forces impelling corporations toward bad behavior and may lead to the naïve position that all that is needed is more forceful moral exhortation. Against that position, Laura Nichols, another contributor to this volume, has written elsewhere that, "given the difficulty of applying the Church's full teaching on ownership in a capitalist system, it seems that our approach often focuses more on personal ethics than on structural ethics, especially when connected to ethics in business."[39]

A structural analysis is needed because the logic of modern capitalism itself creates pressures for even the most well-intentioned firms to act in socially destructive ways. Neoclassical economic theory, which is often associated with Adam Smith's "invisible hand" nudging us toward the best of all possible outcomes, in fact maintains that social welfare will be maximized only under a narrow set of conditions that almost never actually hold.[40] As a consequence, all sorts of so-called market failures are likely to be observed in the real world. Pollution, for example, is often conceptualized in economics as a "negative externality" resulting from the fact that polluters do not directly bear the costs of despoiling the environment. Instead, the cost is "externalized" to third parties.

Even in cases where standard economic theory would not technically identify a market failure, however, it is still possible to recognize *moral* failures; efficiency does not imply equity. For instance, firms may pay an "equilibrium wage" that nevertheless happens to be too meager to provide workers with a sufficient livelihood. According to the sociologist Vivek Chibber, the precarity facing modern workers does not stem from the fact that the owners and managers of firms are bad people (though some are), but rather that

> the incentive to limit [workers'] security *is built into the system*. It is the natural outcome of the profit-maximizing strategy pursued by every firm. Capitalists don't undermine their employees' wellbeing because they are mean, greedy, or callous. They do it because this is how they keep themselves afloat, and how they grow. As long as firms compete on the market, their owners and managers will be *punished* if they *don't* squeeze the most out of their labor force. So they do what they have to, and its most natural result is that their profits come at considerable cost to their employees.[41]

This logic helps to account as well for negative externalities like pollution: firms could choose to be upstanding corporate citizens and voluntarily bear the costs of cleanup and abatement, but if undertaken unilaterally such measures would likely put them at a competitive disadvantage. Thus, structural pressures militate against the decision to do what is right.

To the extent that such pressures are recognized and considered by CST, they are generally treated as issues to be dealt with through remedial state action, just as the neoclassical economic prescription for market failures is corrective government intervention. In other words, the pressures in question are treated as mostly nongermane to discussions about SRI. By way of example, Nichols observes that "the Church's teaching on just wages can leave us…at the individual mercy of the owners of the means of production to offer up just wages. In a structural reality so dominated by capitalism, such individual approaches are very difficult to realize. Thus social policy," such as the Earned Income Tax Credit (EITC), "becomes the main way to…make up for the inadequacies in the individual wages earned by many people in the U.S."[42]

Taking a system-level perspective makes it easier to understand why even active participation strategies often come up against fierce resistance. But this is where the power of scale comes in. The notion of marshalling large quantities of capital to counter the built-in tendency of market competition to undermine certain valuable social goods has a long pedigree in the literature on labor unions' pension funds. In their seminal economic study of organized labor, *What Do Unions Do?*, Richard Freeman and James Medoff credit Peter Drucker and his 1976 book *The Unseen Revolution: How Pension*

Fund Socialism Came to America with popularizing the view that "pension funds represent a growing source of capital in the United States and thus that union pension funds offer unions a potential tool to influence the economy."[43] And it did not take long for the idea to gain real traction: Freeman and Medoff note that the Executive Council of the AFL-CIO had by 1980 officially declared as one of its goals "'to exclude from union pension plan portfolios, companies whose policies are hostile to workers' rights.'"[44]

Teresa Ghilarducci has termed union pension funds "labor's capital," and in her book of that name she provides some examples of how this power has been creatively wielded.[45] The same insight that applies to union pension funds can equally well be applied to CCU endowments. The idea that CCUs could *pool* their endowments in order to enhance their power and achieve what we might call "moral economies of scale" has received comparatively little attention. Bill Purcell and Margarita Rose, however, have recognized that while "large CCUs are best equipped to influence large corporations" through the sort of active participation strategies discussed earlier, smaller CCUs can still have an impact if they commingle their financial assets.[46]

Purcell and Rose suggest three different ways in which this could be accomplished: (1) by having smaller CCUs turn over the management of their endowments to larger CCUs, "as Congregation of Holy Cross institutions King's College, Stonehill College, and the University of Portland have done in partnership with the University of Notre Dame";[47] (2) by having them turn over management to "any number of investment service companies claiming compliance with USCCB investment criteria," such as the above-mentioned Christian Brothers Investment Services or firms like Catholic Investment Strategies or Catholic Investment Services;[48] or (3) by "combining their financial resources to create their own collective investment fund. Fund managers would be accountable to their member institutions, not only on a fiduciary basis, but also on the basis of consistency with CST."[49]

Expanding on the third possibility, a pooled CCU endowment fund could leverage its capital not only to engage in active participation with existing firms, but to pursue community development investing that promotes new economic models and instantiates the vision of CST in ways that are generally difficult to sustain under our present economic order. The Federal Reserve defines community development investing as investment that is "designed to create new opportunities—primarily related to affordable housing, small businesses, and jobs—that specifically benefit lower-income neighborhoods and populations."[50] I offer three suggestions for where this kind of investment could have the greatest marginal impact, though these proposals are by no means exhaustive.

As a first suggestion, a pooled endowment fund could help to incubate the formation and growth of *worker cooperatives*, that is, firms that are owned and managed by labor. Although CST as expressed in the encyclical tradition has tended to focus on unions as a vehicle for improving the fortunes of the working class, the ability of workers to meaningfully participate in workplace decision-making in other ways has also been affirmed.[51] Indeed, one of the largest federations of cooperatives in the world, the Mondragon Corporation in the Basque region of Spain, was founded by a Catholic priest and explicitly conceived as an effort to manifest CST in the world of business.[52] Admittedly, cooperatives remain a quite rare form of corporate organization both globally and in the United States. In June 2021, the Democracy at Work Institute, an affiliate of the United States Federation of Worker Cooperatives (USFWC), estimated that there were 465 worker cooperatives in the United States employing only around seven thousand people in total.[53] Other structures that would not count as full-fledged cooperatives but that grant workers some degree of voice in their workplace or a share in profits earned, such as Employee Stock Ownership Plans (ESOPs), are more common.[54]

The reasons behind the scarcity of worker cooperatives have been debated by economists, with some pointing to purported competitive disadvantages inherent in their structure. A review of the available evidence, however, suggests that cooperatives are at least as productive as conventional firms, and in some cases possibly more so.[55] More compelling explanations focus on the fact that cooperatives are less likely to be formed in the first place. One major obstacle facing would-be worker-owners is difficulty raising capital, since cooperatives, by definition, do not issue equity to nonworker shareholders and since banks may be reluctant to lend to firms with an unfamiliar organizational structure.[56]

The Mondragon Corporation has largely overcome this problem by establishing its own credit union, the Laboral Kuxta (originally known as the Caja Laboral prior to a merger with another credit union), and by charging it with a mandate to provide financing and business services for the Mondragon cooperatives. Though there do exist financial institutions in the United States that have dedicated themselves to lending to cooperative businesses, these are fairly small. The Cooperative Fund of the Northeast (CFNE), for instance, had total assets in 2020 of around $250 million.[57] A hypothetical pooled fund created by combining the endowments of all CCUs could establish a cooperative bank an order of magnitude larger than CFNE in terms of assets under management, even if the pool allocated just 10 percent of its holdings to that purpose.

A second suggestion would be to have a pooled fund invest in the provision of low- or no-interest loans to needy borrowers, who might otherwise be compelled to turn to exploitative and unscrupulous payday lenders. Institutional investors who pursue community development investment as part of a larger commitment to SRI already frequently engage with nonprofit credit unions as a way of making relatively low-interest credit available to economically disadvantaged individuals. But while credit unions do tend to offer loans on more favorable terms than conventional banks (and certainly than payday lenders), the interest rates they charge are not necessarily "low" in an absolute sense: according to the National Credit Union Administration (NCUA), the average interest rate on a credit card issued by a credit union in the first quarter of 2021 was 10.97 percent, while for those issued by a conventional bank it was 12.55 percent.[58]

To imagine what a bolder kind of low- or no-interest lending might look like, we can consider the model of the Hebrew *gemach* or "free loan fund," which emerged as a response to the Torah's prohibition against Jews lending money at interest to other Jews.[59] Contemporary *gemachim*, many of which operate under the auspices of the International Association of Jewish Free Loans (IAJFL), facilitate interest-free loans (often but not always to fellow Jews) to help people through acute crises or financial emergencies, or to cover major life expenses like the cost of an adoption or a funeral.[60]

At first glance, an interest-free loan fund might seem like an absurd investment proposition, since, by definition, it does not generate any more revenue than it loans out. In fact, it might even seem like a guaranteed loss, since defaults will not be outweighed by profits from loans that are repaid. Real-world free loan societies, however, are actually able to grow their assets over time, mainly through donations from grateful former borrowers as well as outside donors.[61] One

IAJFL member organization, the Los Angeles-based Jewish Free Loan Association (JFLA), claims a 99.5 percent rate of repayment on funds loaned. This is likely due in large part to the fact that JFLA, like most free loan associations, requires guarantors other than the borrower to cosign the loan documents. According to its annual report, JFLA's total assets grew in 2020 by 3.2 percent on a year-over-year basis, to around $18.3 million.[62]

As of 2021, the website of the IAJFL listed forty-two member organizations in the United States. Many of these do not appear to make their financial data readily available, but, if we assume that the JFLA is an average-sized free loan fund, then we can estimate that the aggregate holdings of these funds are on the order of $750 million. As with lending to cooperatives, a pooled endowment fund that allocated even a fraction of its assets to establishing a free loan society could likely dramatically expand the size of this sector.[63]

Finally, a third suggestion would be to have a pooled investment fund establish a lending facility to provide financing for Catholic institutions, such as parishes and schools, or even other religious or secular nonprofits, to undertake environmental sustainability initiatives like installing solar panels or making buildings more energy efficient. Ideally, such financing would be made available at below-market rates, which would allow these institutions to accomplish more with fewer resources, thereby strengthening their ability to meet other critical needs. In addition, since debt service payments would be made to the pooled endowment fund rather than to external investors, these payments could help to directly support the critical missions of CCUs themselves.

There are already organizations that work with Church institutions interested in undertaking sustainability projects. A notable example is Catholic Energies, which collaborates with parishes and other Catholic organizations "to determine if solar and energy efficiency solutions are a good fit, a good value, and will achieve the sought-after end results."[64] In addition to offering advice and expertise with cost projections and economic modeling, Catholic Energies helps to connect organizations with contractors and to secure loans for project completion.

These three suggestions are but a few of the myriad possibilities that a pooled CCU endowment fund could open up. They illustrate, however, how such a fund could support the development of economic arrangements that are not only fully consonant with CST, but that otherwise face significant barriers to developing or flourishing in the contemporary economy. As Purcell and Rose remark,

> When CCUs are faced with competing claims on their resources, i.e., maximizing investment return to reduce tuition-dependence versus engaging in socially responsible investing, CST calls for creative ways of doing well while doing good. So Pope Francis writes in *Laudato Si'*: "A fragile world, entrusted by God to human care, challenges us to devise intelligent ways of directing, developing and limiting our power."[65]

Objections and Obstacles to Endowment Pooling and Alternative Investment Strategies

Any proposal to pool CCU endowments in a common, jointly managed investment fund, especially a proposal that advocates for investing those assets in nontraditional ways, is certain to invite a number of different objections. In what follows, I anticipate some of the most likely objections that would be raised against a proposal of the sort I have made here, and I offer brief responses to each.

First, even those who find the idea of endowment pooling intriguing might point to the apparent absence of existing real-world examples as a reason to be skeptical. As noted above, the endowments of several colleges and universities sponsored by the Congregation of Holy Cross are pooled with the University of Notre Dame's endowment and overseen by Notre Dame's investment managers. However, this structure relies more on smaller institutions delegating power to a larger institution rather than on true collective decision-making, which is why Purcell and Rose contrast it with their own idea for a joint investment fund.

The organization that perhaps comes closest to offering a template for how endowment pooling can be used to facilitate creative prosocial investment strategies for CCUs is Mercy Investment Services (MIS), "the asset management program for the collective investment and professional management of the endowment, operating, and other funds of the Sisters of Mercy":

> The centralization of investments, which occurred on February 1, 2010, increases the net investment returns of the participants while continuing the sisters' decades-long work for systemic change in the areas of nonviolence, racism, the environment, concern for women, and immigration through shareholder advocacy and impact investments. The program provides its participants with increased economies of scale, diversification, liquidity, and governance and oversight.[66]

It is noteworthy that MIS manages the endowments of the seventeen colleges and universities that comprise the Conference for Mercy Higher Education (CMHE).[67] My analysis of IPEDS data found that the aggregate value of these assets in 2019 was $536 million.[68]

MIS offers a detailed description of its approach to investing, which includes negative and positive screening, proxy voting and shareholder advocacy, and targeted "impact investments" pursued through dedicated funds known as the "Environmental Solutions Fund" and the "Mercy Partnership Fund."[69] According to its 2020 Accountability Report, more than 10 percent of MIS's total portfolio is dedicated to impact investing.[70]

The Environmental Solutions Fund, established in 2015, "directs capital to lower-carbon energy sources and solutions." Its "market-rate investments" are focused on "renewable energy, energy and water efficiency, materials recycling, green buildings and sustainable agriculture."[71] The Mercy Partnership Fund, which predates the establishment of MIS, "seeks to promote systemic change and support innovation across its impact objectives." MIS states that the Mercy Partnership Fund's annual returns were 2.6 percent for the year ending June 30, 2020, and 2.4 percent since its inception.[72]

The activities of both funds, and in particular the Mercy Partnership Fund, which invests in below-market-rate opportunities, closely align with my three suggestions above.[73] All in all, MIS offers a compelling model of how CCU endowment assets can be marshalled to socially impactful ends. Its financial track record ought to assuage fears about the viability of taking CST seriously in making investment decisions.

Second, it might be objected that investing endowment funds in opportunities that yield below-market returns or that are novel—and therefore excessively risky—would not constitute prudent stewardship of assets in support of the educational mission of CCUs. Worse, it could even be the case that such a strategy would run afoul of fiduciary obligations.

Both these concerns are likely to be overstated. Law professor Susan N. Gary has addressed worries that "SRI would necessarily result in lower returns and would therefore violate the duty of loyalty, a fiduciary duty that requires trustees to put the interests of the beneficiaries first." She explains that "the acceptance of below-market returns does not violate the duty of loyalty if the investment relates to the nonfinancial interests of the beneficiaries," and she cites an IRS determination that "a private foundation that engages in mission-related investing will not be considered to be making jeopardizing investments, even if the mission-related investments do not maximize financial return."[74] Assuming that experts in fiduciary law are properly consulted, there is no reason to think it would not be possible to create a structure that allows for below-market rate investments to be made in full compliance with regulatory requirements.

As for the argument that these investments, even if legal, are nevertheless unwise, evidence from entities already engaged in these sorts of activities suggests that the returns on alternative investments would not necessarily be much lower. For instance, a review of data from the Cooperative Fund of New England's investor prospectus dated April 2021 reveals that the average annual percentage increase in the fund's net assets over the period 2015–2020 was 10.4 percent, with a 4.0 percent increase reported for 2020.[75] Thus, there is no prima facie reason to believe that all such investments guarantee lower returns than could be earned elsewhere. It is also worth remembering that prudence does not require eschewing all "high-risk" investments, so long as the overall investment portfolio is adequately diversified.

Moreover, as the USCCB Guidelines observe, "although it is a moral and legal fiduciary responsibility of the trustees to ensure an adequate return on investment for the support of the work of the church, their stewardship embraces broader moral concerns."[76] CST cannot be used to justify a version of SRI that merely consists of choosing the most morally sound set of investments *from among those that maximize potential returns*. In the language of economic theory, socially responsible investors should not have "lexicographic preferences" such that ethical considerations take a backseat to investment returns.[77]

A third objection might be whether the potential for endowment pooling could be limited by donor restrictions or other stipulations that funds be earmarked for specific uses at a certain CCU. Similarly, one might worry that pooling endowments would lead to a drop in donations and bequests from alumni and alumnae, who may be motivated to donate by solicitude for their own alma mater, rather than by a desire to support Catholic higher education more generally.

One response to this objection is that it is misleading to frame the choice as being between "no pooling whatsoever" and "complete pooling of all funds." Most endowments are better understood as aggregations of funds rather than one big fund anyway,[78] and to the extent that monies have restrictions attached to their use they could be excluded from a pooled fund.

Whether pooling would have a detrimental effect on donor morale is less clear, but it does seem clear that donor motivations are often multifaceted. It should not be assumed a priori that donors could not be persuaded to see the value of a proposal that promises to reduce inequalities among students at U.S. CCUs. Moreover, any pooled endowment fund would need to establish a formula for allocating investment income among the different participating CCUs, so donors could be reassured that a portion of their contributions would directly benefit their own alma mater (or any other particular school they intend the contribution to benefit), even as the remainder benefits other schools.[79] In fact, this is a common feature of diocesan annual appeals, which are routinely structured so that a certain percentage of donations are used to support the needs of the diocese or archdiocese generally, with the rest returned to a donor's own parish. I acknowledge, however, that fundraising for the needs of a larger community may also require an appeal to parochial interests (pun intended).

Fourth, it could be objected that an effort along these lines would be unlikely to succeed because of the resistance it would encounter from institutional actors with either a vested interest in maintaining the status quo or an aversion to dramatic change. The investment managers currently responsible for administering CCU endowments, for instance, could stand to lose substantial income streams if stewardship of these endowments were taken out of their hands.

College and university trustees might also be hesitant to contemplate such a shift. As highlighted by Joseph McCartin, another contributor to this volume, seats on trustee boards—including those at CCUs—overwhelmingly tend to be occupied by individuals with backgrounds in business in general and finance in particular. "The percentage of board seats held by finance industry professionals... nearly doubled in America's colleges and universities overall in the past 25 years," and the same trend can be seen at CCUs. McCartin notes that, "in 2017, twenty-two of Boston College's forty-three lay members hailed from the finance and real estate sectors alone."[80]

Without question, board members with experience in business and finance bring valuable expertise to the complex task of running a college or university. But it is a legitimate worry that people whose background inclines them to be concerned more with traditional metrics of endowment performance than with exploring innovative ways to apply CST to the financing of Catholic higher education will likely be disinclined to support such innovations. Further, at larger and wealthier CCUs, there may be little appetite for a voluntary redistribution of wealth in which those institutions appear to "lose out."

The question of how to ensure that CCU administrators remain committed to a model of higher education that is distinctively Catholic is beyond the scope of this chapter. (See, however, the chapter in this volume by James Heft.) In any event, to reiterate a point made in response to the preceding objection, endowment pooling need not be seen as an all-or-nothing proposition, and there are certainly ways to take incremental steps toward such an arrangement in the face of status quo bias. For instance, an agreement to form such a common fund could initially involve a pledge to tithe a certain percentage of future donations or revenues in order to capitalize it. This would do less to address the massive concentration of assets in the hands of the most well-off institutions, but it might provoke less resistance since it would involve promises to give up a portion of *potential future wealth* rather than *actual current wealth*.[81] And it would be critical to highlight the potential good that could be done with returns from the common fund. Perhaps, to choose one example among many, some portion of it could be used to support diversity, equity, and inclusion efforts at less wealthy institutions, which might otherwise have great trouble recruiting and retaining women and racial minorities.

Fifth and finally, and coming from a different angle, one might acknowledge that inequality in CCU endowments is worrying for a variety of reasons, yet nevertheless see a voluntary effort of the sort I have proposed as an insufficient response to the problem. If inequality is such a serious societal ill, then why focus so much on compressing disparities only among CCUs rather than among colleges and universities generally? After all, even mainstream politicians have begun calling for increased taxes not only on high incomes, but on excess wealth as well. Private philanthropy can never fully substitute for egalitarian tax policy. Notably, the Tax Cuts and Jobs Act of 2017 contained provisions that for the first time ever imposed federal taxes on the endowment wealth of certain private universities.[82]

The response to this objection is that voluntary pooling of endowment assets may in some sense be a "second-best" solution to the problem at hand, but it is a step that can be taken now and that can complement advocacy for more proactive policy intervention. Realistically, bold legislative action to tax and redistribute large pools of private capital, wherever they may be found, is not likely to be forthcoming in the near future. In the meantime (and perhaps to forestall unwise legislative action), Catholic institutions should be "exemplary" in aligning their own activities with the demands of economic justice.[83] Arguably, the dramatic disparity in endowment wealth per student across CCUs should be a source of scandal among Catholics. Maybe it will be, if high numbers of smaller CCUs, educating underserved populations, start going out of business, while the rich only get richer.[84]

I do not doubt that other objections could be levied against the proposals put forward in this chapter, but those objections would likely be motivated by the same underlying concern that pooling CCU endowments and leveraging their power to bring about transformative change is "unrealistic." It is worth asking, however, whether it is realistic *not* to pursue such proposals as those I have outlined, given the increasingly dire impacts of our current economic system on our politics, our society, and the planet, as well as the damage done to the moral authority of the Catholic Church when its educational institutions reproduce and perpetuate inequalities rather than alleviate them. As the World Synod of Bishops put it in 1971, if the Church "appears to be among the rich and powerful of this world its credibility is diminished."[85]

Conclusion: Toward a More Humane Economy

The dramatic growth in the aggregate endowment assets of CCUs over the last decade and the fact that these assets are extremely concentrated in the hands of a few institutions raise ever more urgent moral questions about how this wealth should be invested. This is especially true in light of the fact that CCUs should be guided in all they do by the principles of CST.

The problem of how best to apply these principles to SRI has traditionally been framed as one of how to avoid impermissible "cooperation with evil." Just as labor activists and progressive economists have urged unions to invest their pension assets in ways that counter some of the more antisocial tendencies built into the capitalist system, however, so too can proponents of the vision of CST urge CCUs to recognize how the economic power of their endowment assets would be enhanced if they were pooled in a common fund and deployed to prosocial ends. Rather than feeling constrained to choose from among the already-existing set of investment opportunities, the vast majority of which will prove to be morally mixed, endowment pooling could be a tool for expanding the space of such opportunities by nurturing more humane economic arrangements. In addition, endowment pooling could help bring about a more equitable distribution of wealth across CCUs.

Implementing such a proposal would reinforce the principle that CCUs have some responsibility to advance not only their own particular educational missions, but also that of Catholic higher education generally. Further, it would meaningfully bolster the moral credibility of the wealthiest CCUs. While leveling inequalities in higher education is arguably a task that would be better dealt with through public policy, there are voluntary steps that CCUs can take in concert with one another now, when such bold policy action does not appear to be in the offing and might reasonably be feared if poorly structured.

SRI is just one aspect of the economic ethics of financing Catholic higher education, but it is a vitally important one. As Pope Francis has insisted, "money must serve, not rule."[86] Otherwise, CCUs, too, risk becoming the side business of a hedge fund.

Questions for Consideration and Discussion

1. Mazewski challenges CCUs to envision themselves as a potential "network of actors" with the collective means to inaugurate "new and creative ways of doing business" in service of a more humane economy, consonant with CST. At the same time, he acknowledges that status quo bias, aversion to change, and vested interests might unite in rejecting innovative ways to finance Catholic higher education as "unrealistic." Consider Mazewski's replies to the five objections he anticipates. Do the objections withstand his replies? Are there other, decisive objections that he does not anticipate? If there are not decisive objections, what stands in the way of experimenting with his proposals at your institution, and how might those obstacles be overcome?
2. Mazewski observes that structural pressures in our economy often "militate against the decision to do what is right," but that powers of scale make it possible to alter the ecology, so to speak, within which institutions live and move. What are some structural pressures limiting your institution (e.g., pressures resulting from the market in which your institution competes for students, funds, and prestige)? What are some decisions or changes that, ideally, your institution would make, if it had the means to do so? Does Mazewski's chapter suggest or inspire any ways forward?
3. According to Mazewski, the dramatic inequality of resources that CCUs have on hand for students "should be a source of scandal among Catholics." He submits that "taking steps to redress extreme inequalities, for instance by pooling endowment assets in a common investment fund, is an imperative of CST." Do you agree? Against the background of CST, what responsibilities, if any, do wealthier CCUs have toward poorer CCUs, which tend to serve students who themselves have greater need? (Consult in this regard the chapter in this volume by Laura Nichols.) To put a point on

this question, should wealthier CCUs care if poorer CCUs go out of business in great numbers?

4. Mazewski observes that both so-called negative and positive investment screens "treat the set of available investments as static and exogenously given." Drawing from literature on creative uses of "labor's capital," he sketches a third way: "a pooled CCU endowment fund could leverage its capital not only to engage in active participation with existing firms, but to pursue community development investing that promotes new economic models and instantiates the vision of CST in ways that are generally difficult to sustain under our present economic order." He offers three suggestions for this kind of investment: worker cooperatives; the provision of low- or no-interest loans; and the provision of financing for Catholic institutions to undertake environmental sustainability initiatives. What are other suggestions you can imagine? Also, what are suggestions that might make the prospect of a pooled endowment fund attractive to leadership at your institution?
5. As you conclude your discussion of this chapter, what are three to five suggestions you might present to your institution's SRI committee? If your institution does not have an SRI committee, see, as an example, the charge and structure of Georgetown's Committee on Investments and Social Responsibility (https://publicaffairs.georgetown.edu/committees/cisr/); consider how to found such a committee at your institution; and formulate three to five suggestions that you might present to it at its first meeting.

Notes

1. While writing this chapter, I benefited immensely from comments by and discussions with James Heft, SM, Gene McWilliams, Laura Nichols, Bernard G. Prusak, Jennifer Reed-Bouley, Margarita Rose, Jack Ryan, CSC, Andria Wisler, and audience participants at a virtual event hosted by the McGowan Center for Ethics and Social Responsibility at King's College in April 2021. I very much appreciate their kind and insightful feedback and suggestions. Any remaining errors or omissions are of course my own.

2. Astra Taylor, "Universities Are Becoming Billion-Dollar Hedge Funds with Schools Attached," *The Nation*, March 8, 2016, https://www.thenation.com/.

3. Pope John Paul II, *Ex Corde Ecclesiae* (August 15, 1990), part 2, article 2, 2. This and other Vatican documents cited are available at https://www.vatican.va.

4. See for this history Alice Gallin, OSU, *Independence and a New Partnership in Catholic Higher Education* (Notre Dame, IN: University of Notre Dame Press, 1996), as well as "A Brief History of Trusteeship in Catholic Colleges and Universities," in *Mission and Identity: A Handbook for Trustees of Catholic Colleges and Universities* (Washington, DC: AGB Publications, 2004), 37–43. For a more recent study, see Bernard G. Prusak, "Independent Boards of Trustees at Catholic Colleges and Universities, Fifty Years Later: Findings and Reflections from Six Holy Cross Schools," *Journal of Catholic Higher Education* 37, no. 1 (2018): 3–27.

5. National Center for Education Statistics (NCES), Integrated Postsecondary Education Data System (IPEDS), https://nces.ed.gov/ipeds/.

6. See United States Conference of Catholic Bishops (USCCB), "Catholic Colleges and Universities in the United States," https://www.usccb.org/committees/catholic-education/catholic-colleges-and-universities-united-states.

7. Most of the twenty-eight institutions named by the USCCB that do not appear in IPEDS are very small institutions or seminaries whose omission is unlikely to affect estimates of aggregate endowment assets or the distribution thereof. The full list is available upon request.

8. I use "NCCUs" to refer not to *all* "non-Catholic colleges and universities," but only those in the comparison group.

9. Bureau of Economic Analysis (BEA), "Gross Domestic Product, Fourth Quarter and Year 2019 (Advance Estimate)," https://www.bea.gov/news/2020/gross-domestic-product-fourth-quarter-and-year-2019-advance-estimate. The BEA estimated GDP in Q4 2020 at $21.48 trillion.

10. The value of an institution's endowment assets is reported in IPEDS at the start and end of each fiscal year. Since different institutions may begin and end their fiscal years at different times, I averaged these two values and used the mean for purposes of aggregation.

11. Author's calculations. A lower Gini coefficient indicates a more equal (less unequal) distribution. As a benchmark, consider that one estimate put the Gini for household wealth in the United States in 2019 at 0.85. See Credit Suisse, *Global Wealth Databook 2019*, https://www.credit-suisse.com/ch/en.html.

12. For more on the forces driving the rapid growth of tuition expenses at American colleges and universities in recent years, see Ronald G. Ehrenberg, *Tuition Rising: Why College Costs So Much* (Cambridge, MA: Harvard University Press, 2002) and Michael Mumper and Melissa L. Freeman, "The Causes and Consequences of Public College Tuition Inflation," in *Higher*

Education: Handbook of Theory and Research, vol. 20, ed. John C. Smart (Dordrecht: Springer, 2005), 307–61.

13. Author's calculations based on IPEDS data.

14. National Conference of Catholic Bishops (since renamed as the USCCB), *Economic Justice for All: Pastoral Letter on Catholic Social Teaching and the U.S. Economy* (1986), 185, https://www.usccb.org/resources/economic-justice-all-pastoral-letter-catholic-social-teaching-and-us-economy.

15. NCCB, *Economic Justice* 347.

16. Albino Barrera, *Market Complicity and Christian Ethics* (Cambridge: Cambridge University Press, 2011), 11.

17. Barrera, *Market Complicity*, 15.

18. Barrera, *Market Complicity*, 144.

19. Barrera, *Market Complicity*, 144.

20. Teresa Ghilarducci, *Labor's Capital: The Economics and Politics of Private Pensions* (Cambridge, MA: MIT Press, 1992), 46.

21. Barrera, *Market Complicity*, 143.

22. Compare, for reservations about the usefulness of the matrix of cooperation for issues of voting, Cathleen Kaveny, *Law's Virtues: Fostering Autonomy and Solidarity in American Society* (Washington, DC: Georgetown University Press, 2012), 252–53.

23. Gerald J. Beyer, *Just Universities: Catholic Social Teaching Confronts Corporatized Higher Education* (New York: Fordham University Press, 2021), 142.

24. See Ave Maria Funds, "Investment Process," https://www.avemariafunds.com/about-us/investment-process.html.

25. Beyer, *Just Universities*, 142–43.

26. See Gregory R. Beabout and Kevin E. Schmiesing, "Socially Responsible Investing: An Application of Catholic Social Thought," *Logos: A Journal of Catholic Thought and Culture* 6, no. 1 (2003): 63–99, at 84.

27. See USCCB, "Socially Responsible Investment Guidelines," "Introduction," https://www.usccb.org/resources/socially-responsible-investment-guidelines-2021-united-states-conference-catholic-bishops.

28. USCCB, "Socially Responsible Investment Guidelines," part 3, "Strategies." Other authors adopt a slightly different taxonomy of approaches to ethical investing. For example, according to Beyer, socially responsible investment "entails the tripartite strategy of community investing, 'screening' for investments that violate or promote the values of the investor, and shareholder advocacy." See Beyer, *Just Universities*, 139–40.

29. USCCB, "Socially Responsible Investment Guidelines," part 3.

30. USCCB, "Socially Responsible Investment Guidelines," part 3.1.

31. USCCB, "Socially Responsible Investment Guidelines," part 3.2.

32. See also Jesuit Committee on Investment Responsibility, "Corporate Shareholder Advocacy," https://www.jesuits.org/wp-content/uploads/2020/04/191209-JCIR-PDF-Final.pdf.

33. Jesuit Committee, "Corporate Shareholder Advocacy," part 2, "Principles of Stewardship," and part 3.2.

34. Tom Gallagher, "Catholic Investing in Changing Times," *National Catholic Reporter*, July 14, 2015, available online at ncronline.org. It should be noted that Christian Brothers Investment Services seems to have modified some of its positions in the meantime. See Brian Roewe, "Bad Day for Big Oil Is Big Win for Religious Shareholder Advocates," *National Catholic Reporter*, June 2, 2021, https://www.ncronline.org/, quoting Christian Brothers' chief investment officer, John Geissinger: "The fact is the landscape has changed....We cannot simply assume the fossil fuel sector will be as it always was. Events on climate risk are evolving rapidly. Our directors must show awareness of and responsiveness to changing circumstances and evolving risks and provide shareholders this disclosure."

35. Beyer, *Just Universities*, 159.

36. See University of Dayton, "Dayton Divests," https://udayton.edu/news/articles/2014/dayton_divests_fossil_fuels.php. For more on "integral ecology" as it relates to the mission of Catholic colleges and universities, see Vincent Miller's chapter in this volume.

37. USCCB, "Socially Responsible Investment Guidelines," part 3.3.

38. USCCB, "Socially Responsible Investment Guidelines," part 3.3.

39. Laura Nichols, "Response to Daniel K. Finn," *Integritas* 6, no. 2 (2015): 19–23, at 21–22.

40. See Hal R. Varian, *Microeconomic Analysis*, 3rd ed. (New York: W.W. Norton, 1992), 323–26.

41. Vivek Chibber, *The ABCs of Capitalism: A. Understanding Capitalism* (Brooklyn, NY: Jacobin Foundation, 2018), 36–37. See, for an account of the concrete consequences, Farah Stockman, "Becoming a Steelworker Liberated Her. Then Her Job Moved to Mexico," *New York Times*, October 14, 2017, www.nytimes.com.

42. Nichols, "Response to Daniel K. Finn," 22.

43. Richard B. Freeman and James L. Medoff, *What Do Unions Do?* (New York: Basic Books, 1984), 74–75. For another early iteration of this argument, see Jeremy Rifkin and Randy Barber, *The North Will Rise Again: Pensions, Politics, and Power in the 1980s* (Boston, MA: Beacon Press, 1978).

44. Freeman and Medoff, *What Do Unions Do?* 74–75. As it happens, Freeman and Medoff offer a classification of investment strategies according to their potential to serve the broader interests of unions that is quite similar to the classification we considered earlier:

> There is an important difference between shunning the stocks of primarily nonunion firms in the stock market ["negative screening"] and investing in projects that employ union labor ["community investment"]. Since there are millions of investors in the market, directing investment funds away from certain stocks will not permanently influence the value of those shares. Thus, the benefit to unions of excluding "hostile" companies will be largely psychic. (To influence the policies of those companies, unions would do better to direct their pension fund savings into those companies and use their ownership to pressure management to drop anti-union activity ["active participation"].) Investing in projects that employ union labor, by contrast, has direct benefit for union labor, helping to preserve the union wage differential, and thus may represent a better long-term strategy ["expanding the space of possibilities"]. (76–77)

45. Ghilarducci, *Labor's Capital*, 46. For more recent iterations of this argument about "labor's capital," see Archon Fung, Tessa Hebb, and Joel Rogers, ed., *Working Capital: The Power of Labor's Pensions* (Ithaca, NY: ILR Press, 2001) and David Webber, *The Rise of the Working-Class Shareholder: Labor's Last Best Weapon* (Cambridge, MA: Harvard University Press, 2018).

46. Bill Purcell and Margarita Rose, "Engaging Mission: Applying the Catholic Social Tradition to Investing and Licensing," *Journal of Catholic Higher Education* 37, no. 1 (2018): 53–69, at 62.

47. Purcell and Rose, "Engaging Mission," 62. A caveat here is that the smaller institutions may thereby cede all decision-making power and effectively abdicate themselves from moral responsibility for the investment decisions made by the larger, more powerful institution.

48. Purcell and Rose, "Engaging Mission," 62–63.

49. Purcell and Rose, "Engaging Mission," 63. Purcell and Rose point to the New Jersey-based Tri-state Coalition for Responsible Investing, which is now known as Investor Advocates for Social Justice (IASJ), as a model of sorts for the third type of collective action. Though IASJ is not a true pooled investment fund, it serves "investors with faith-based values who seek to leverage their investments to advance human rights, climate justice, racial equity, and the common good." See IASJ, "About Us," https://iasj.org/about-us/.

50. See Board of Governors of the Federal Reserve System, "Community Development Investments," https://www.federalreserve.gov/consumers communities/cdi.htm.

51. See for discussion Matt Mazewski, "Bringing the Workers on Board: The Catholic Roots of Codetermination," *Commonweal*, March 22, 2019, 17–21; Nathan Schneider, "'Truly, Much Can Be Done!': Cooperative

Economics from the Book of Acts to Pope Francis," in *Care for the World: Laudato Si' and Catholic Social Thought in an Era of Climate Crisis*, ed. Frank Pasquale (Cambridge: Cambridge University Press, 2019), 145–66.

52. See Fernando Molina and Antonio Míguez, "The Origins of Mondragon: Catholic Co-Operativism and Social Movement in a Basque Valley (1941–59)," *Social History* 33, no. 3 (2008): 284–98. For background on Mondragon, see William Foote Whyte and Kathleen King Whyte, *Making Mondragón: The Growth and Dynamics of the Worker Cooperative Complex* (Ithaca, NY: ILR Press, 1991). For a more critical perspective, see Sharryn Kasmir, *The Myth of Mondragon: Cooperatives, Politics, and Working Class Life in a Basque Town* (Albany, NY: SUNY Press, 1996).

53. Democracy at Work Institute, "What Is a Worker Cooperative?" https://institute.coop/what-worker-cooperative.

54. See Henry Hansmann, "When Does Worker Ownership Work? ESOPs, Law Firms, Codetermination, and Economic Democracy," *Yale Law Journal* 99, no. 8 (1990): 1749–816.

55. See Erik K. Olsen, "The Relative Survival of Worker Cooperatives and Barriers to Their Creation," in *Sharing Ownership, Profits, and Decision-Making in the 21st Century*, ed. Douglas Kruse (Bingley, UK: Emerald, 2013), 83–107.

56. Of course, there is a vicious cycle here where lenders are unfamiliar with cooperatives because they are uncommon, but the fact that they face discrimination in lending ensures that they remain so. For a comprehensive exploration of the economics of worker cooperatives, see Gregory K. Dow, *Governing the Firm: Workers' Control in Theory and Practice* (Cambridge: Cambridge University Press, 2003).

57. See Cooperative Fund of the Northeast, www.cooperativefund.org.

58. See National Credit Union Administration, "Credit Union and Bank Rates 2021 Q1," www.ncua.gov/analysis/cuso-economic-data/credit-union-bank-rates/credit-union-and-bank-rates-2021-q1.

59. See Martin Lewison, "Conflicts of Interest? The Ethics of Usury," *Journal of Business Ethics* 22 (1999): 327–39, at 335.

60. See International Association of Jewish Free Loans, https://iajfl.org.

61. Dallas Hebrew Free Loan Society, "Ways to Give," https://dhfla.org/support/.

62. See Jewish Free Loan Association, "Financials," https://www.jfla.org/about-jfla/financials. JFLA's 2020 annual report gives assets at the beginning of the year of $17,689,488, and at the end of the year of $18,251,648—an increase of $562,160, or 3.2 percent.

63. Another model of "usury-free lending" that deserves renewed attention is the *mons pietatis* or "mount of piety" of medieval Europe, which functioned as a hybrid lender-pawnbroker and offered small loans to the poor in

exchange for valuables left as security. See Leszek Niewdana, *Money and Justice: A Critique of Modern Money and Banking Systems from the Perspective of Aristotelian and Scholastic Thoughts* (Milton Park, UK: Routledge, 2015), 129.

64. Catholic Energies, "Providing Solutions with a Higher Purpose," https://www.catholicenergies.org/what-we-do.

65. Purcell and Rose, "Engaging Mission," 59.

66. Purcell and Rose, "Engaging Mission," 59.

67. These are Carlow University (Pittsburgh, PA), College of St. Mary (Omaha, NE), Georgian Court University (Lakewood, NJ), Gwynedd Mercy University (Gwynedd Valley, PA), Maria College (Albany, NY), Mercy College of Health and Sciences (Des Moines, IA), Mercy College of Ohio (Toledo, OH), Mercyhurst University (Erie, PA), Misericordia University (Dallas, PA), Mount Aloysius College (Cresson, PA), Mount Mercy University (Cedar Rapids, IA), St. Joseph's College of Maine (Standish, ME), St. Xavier University (Chicago, IL), Salve Regina University (Newport, RI), Trocaire College (Buffalo, NY), University of Detroit Mercy (Detroit, MI), and the University of St. Joseph (Pittsburgh, PA). See "The Colleges and Universities of the Conference for Mercy Higher Education," https://mercyhighered.org/mercy-colleges-and-universities-2/.

68. Author's calculations based on IPEDS data.

69. Mercy Investment Services, "Our Approach," https://www.mercyinvestmentservices.org/our-approach.aspx.

70. Mercy Investment Services, "Accountability Report 2020," https://www.mercyinvestmentservices.org/accountability-report.aspx, 2.

71. Mercy Investment Services, "Accountability Report 2020," 5.

72. Mercy Investment Services, "Accountability Report 2020," 4.

73. The 2020 Accountability Report describes how "[a] Mercy loan to Catholic Climate Covenant's Catholic Energies program," which I introduced in the previous section, "is assisting parishes and other Catholic organizations across the country to develop, install and fund renewable energy projects on its properties. The program, developed in response to Pope Francis's encyclical *Laudato Si'*, has already completed six projects, which included installing 4,186 solar panels that have generated 2.1 GWh of energy." See *Accountability Report* 2020, https://www.mercyinvestmentservices.org/accountability-report.aspx, 13.

74. Susan N. Gary, "Fiduciary Duties and ESG Investing: Corporate Governance and the Growing Importance of ESG Reporting," *Columbia Law School Blue Sky Blog*, November 11, 2015, https://clsbluesky.law.columbia.edu/2015/11/11/fiduciary-duties-and-esg-investing-corporate-governance-and-the-growing-importance-of-esg-reporting/.

75. Author calculations based on data on page 23 of the prospectus.

76. USCCB, "Socially Responsible Investment Guidelines," part 1.1, under "Background," quoting from the pastoral letter *Economic Justice for All*.

77. Ariel Rubinstein, *Lecture Notes in Microeconomic Theory: The Economic Agent*, 2nd ed. (Princeton, NJ: Princeton University Press, 2012), 15.

78. "Endowments are frequently described as if they are a single fund, when in fact, they are an aggregation of discrete funds, each with its own stipulations about the purposes for which it can be used." See American Council on Education, "Understanding College and University Endowments," 2021, https://www.acenet.edu/Documents/Understanding-College-and-University-Endowments.pdf, 2.

79. Since the goal of a pooled fund is to level inequalities and redistribute resources, the best approach to allocation, at least initially, would likely be to rely on a calculation that takes into account contribution size but also the number of students at different institutions.

80. Joseph A. McCartin, "Confronting the Labor Problem in Catholic Higher Education: Applying Catholic Social Teaching in an Age of Increasing Inequality," *Journal of Catholic Higher Education* 37, no. 1 (2018): 71–88, at 75.

81. This tendency is referred to in the literature on behavioral economics—fittingly given the present context—as the "endowment effect." See Daniel Kahneman, Jack L. Knetsch, and Richard H. Thaler, "Anomalies: The Endowment Effect, Loss Aversion, and Status Quo Bias," *Journal of Economic Perspectives* 5, no. 1 (1991): 193–206.

82. This development is intriguing given that the overall thrust of the law was to *decrease* taxes on high earners, but it makes sense when considered in the context of longstanding conservative rhetoric about the socially deleterious effects of "liberal" colleges and universities.

83. National Conference of Catholic Bishops, *Economic Justice for All* 347.

84. Compare the story of the rich man and Lazarus in Luke 16:19–31.

85. World Synod of Catholic Bishops 1971, *Justicia in Mundo* (1971) 47, available online at cctwincities.org, among other sites. Compare Matt 19:16–30, Mark 10:17–31, Luke 18:18–30.

86. Thomas Reese, "Francis to G8: 'Money Must Serve, Not Rule,'" *National Catholic Reporter*, June 16, 2013, https://www.ncronline.org/.

8

BEYOND PATRIARCHY?

Women's Leadership in Catholic Higher Education

Jennifer Reed-Bouley and Catherine Punsalan-Manlimos[1]

In orienting new faculty to Seattle University, mission officer Jennifer Tilghman-Havens juxtaposes photos of early faculty, who were white male clerics, with a recent photo of faculty of color and women faculty who worked together on an interdisciplinary project in the Yesler Terrace neighborhood.[2] Her method underscores that Jesuit education is in the hands of a different group of people today from the days of the university's founding. Similar photos displaying not only faculty, but also cabinets and boards of trustees can be found in the archives of most other Catholic colleges and universities (CCUs) in the United States today. A parallel shift can be observed by comparing yearbooks and student newspapers from the early years of most institutions with the current students on campus and those in applicant pools. Photos featuring students in the early years of these institutions show either all-male or all-female students. The earliest of these colleges, such as those founded by the Jesuits, were established to educate young men. It was with great effort, amid resistance and very limited external support, that women religious succeeded in founding similar institutions to educate women.

The demographic changes among leaders at CCUs resemble, though at a slower pace, changing student demographics. CCUs are no longer Catholic enclaves catering to Catholic students and led by women or men religious. Yet while the photographs starkly convey a present that looks different from the past, they do not tell the whole story. Not only is there still much to be done to recruit more diverse faculty and administrators, but there is even more work that must be undertaken to retain them.

This chapter describes how women have moved Catholic higher education beyond a clerical patriarchy, but it also questions whether the change has in fact overcome a white, male-dominated educational system.[3] We propose that Catholic social thought (CST) may ground the importance of attending to diversity, equity, inclusion, and justice in the recruitment, retention, and development of women who bring their gifts of leadership to Catholic higher education. Further, Pope Francis's emphasis on dialogue and a culture of encounter can serve as a guide for CCUs seeking to cultivate such leaders. Throughout the chapter, we use the term *women* to include people with diverse backgrounds and identities, including race, ethnicity, class, religion, age, sexual orientation, marriage status, and parenthood status. We recognize that these and other aspects of women's identities—as they intersect with gender identity—influence how women are perceived and treated, and we allude to the influence of race, though we keep the main focus on gender throughout the chapter.[4]

Women's Current Participation and Leadership in Catholic Higher Education

Women are well-represented among faculty and staff at Association of Catholic Colleges and Universities (ACCU) member institutions; women's representation decreases, however, among the higher, more secure professional ranks.[5] As of spring 2020, women occupied 52 percent of full-time faculty positions, and women made up 43 percent of tenured faculty and 56 percent of faculty on tenure-tracks. Women were also, however, 61 percent of faculty who were not on a tenure track, or who were employed by CCUs that do not offer a tenure system. Women represented 57 percent of full-time staff positions.[6] There are also salary disparities. Using IPEDS data from 2018 (prior to the COVID-19 pandemic), the American Association of University Professors provides a snapshot that allows us to compare salaries of women and men faculty members. These data reflect all colleges and universities, not only CCUs. "Salaries for full-time women faculty members [were] approximately 81.2 percent of men's, with women earning $79,368 and men earning $97,738, on average."[7] Among women faculty, full professors earned 85.1 percent, associate professors earned 92.7 percent, and assistant professors earned 90.7 percent of what men earned at the same ranks. The authors note that these pay disparities are often attributed to "market forces" about which little research has been undertaken, but in fact "there are many variables that contribute to the gender pay gap in academia, including biases in hiring and promotion practices, lack of institutional resources and support, and caregiving responsibilities."[8]

In addition to the challenges women have long faced in participating in higher education as faculty and staff (e.g., for some, childbearing during tenure review years[9]), the COVID-19 pandemic posed new, deleterious challenges to women's participation and leadership in higher education generally and Catholic higher education specifically. Because societal patterns are reproduced in academic institutions,[10] school closures and disruptions in eldercare and childcare disproportionately affected women. Women's workloads in colleges and universities also increased during the pandemic. As one report noted,

> Long-standing gender inequalities pervade academe in both internal and external service workloads among faculty, especially female faculty of color. Female faculty tend to bear a disproportionate share of the care labor and institutional housekeeping in academic institutions, even after controlling for rank, department and/or field. In addition, the demand for women's service and mentorship efforts often increases during times of crises and uncertainties. Early evidence suggests that the COVID-19 pandemic has been no exception.[11]

For women faculty, the pandemic caused a decrease in time available for research and an enormous increase in stress—as women faculty cared for others at home and the workplace. Unless colleges and universities shift their metrics for determining promotion and advancement in response to the pandemic (e.g., increasing the value of mentoring students, reshaping courses for online delivery, and attending to time-intensive institutional service), declines in research productivity during the pandemic, particularly for faculty employed at institutions that reward research over teaching and mentoring in tenure and advancement decisions, are expected to affect negatively women's future career trajectories and the pipeline for women faculty to become senior leaders.[12]

Regarding senior leadership, the ACCU reports that, in 2021, 33 percent of CCUs were led by women presidents (62 women and 126 men).[13] This was a decrease from 2018, when 38 percent of CCUs were led by women presidents.[14] One point to note in this regard is that, while the current trend toward growing lay leadership of CCUs reflects a move away from clericalism, it does not necessarily follow that women will continue to gain more presidential posts. With more than half of CCUs historically founded and led by women religious, the movement toward lay leadership also has led to more male presidents at these traditionally female institutions. For example, as of September 2021, there were seven women presidents (25 percent), one of whom is interim and one of whom is an acting president, of the twenty-eight Association of Jesuit Colleges and Universities (AJCU) institutions (twenty-seven in the United States and one, St. John's College, in Belize).[15] Of the male presidents, six are Jesuits and fifteen are laymen. Among the lay presidents of Jesuit colleges and universities, 32 percent were women. As of late 2021, seven of the seventeen presidents of member and affiliated Conference for Mercy Higher Education (CMHE) institutions were lay women (41 percent) and one was a member of the Religious Sisters of Mercy.[16] The upshot is that, as lay leadership rather than vowed religious leadership increases among CCU presidents, men are replacing women more quickly in traditionally women-led institutions than women are replacing men in traditionally men-led institutions.

The decline of women's leadership (in the CMHE, from 100 percent prior to Vatican II to less than half currently), and the lack of racial and ethnic diversity among CCU presidents compared to other colleges and universities, require special attention. "The majority of presidents at Catholic colleges and universities are...white (92 percent), in their 60s, and married (60 percent)."[17] The persistence of a predominantly white and increasingly male presidency runs contrary to the demographic changes among current and potential college students. Male students continue to decline in number, while the number of female students increases. According to the ACCU, as of 2018, "62 percent of students on Catholic campuses identified as female and 38 percent identified as male...compared to 56 percent of students in all of higher education identifying as female and 44 percent of students identifying as male."[18] The demographics of those graduating from elementary and high schools indicate that the pool of future college students is already majority members of minoritized communities. (For more elaboration, see Laura Nichols's chapter in this volume.) Leaders of CCUs must be prepared to recruit and retain these future students. Students themselves are making it clear that they expect to see faculty and administrators who look like them, but women of color are not represented among faculty as they are in the general population.[19] Students seek mentors who they believe will be able to understand their experiences and the culture of their communities; further, seeing people like them in the front of classrooms and occupying leadership roles enables students to imagine new possibilities for themselves.[20] Higher education remains, however, a challenging and sometimes even hostile environment for women of color.[21] According to one account,

> Existing academic structures facilitate different realities and rules of the game for members of historically underrepresented groups as compared to those of their white, heterosexual colleagues. These disparate realities create shaky ground for women of color and provide evidence that no matter how hard they work, how many degrees they possess, what titles they earn, or what levels and/or positions they acquire, they are still vulnerable to malevolent experiences as faculty members. The more -isms associated with their identities, the more personally directed is the antagonism and the more oppressive is the unchallenged, status-quo environment.[22]

How Did We Arrive Here?

Women initially entered Catholic higher education as students through one of three paths: "sister schools" to educate members of religious communities, which later welcomed laywomen; women's single-sex colleges established by women religious, most of which have either closed or been subsumed into men's institutions; and men's single-sex institutions that became coeducational and often subsumed women's institutions.[23]

The cultural context of the Catholic Church and U.S. society in the late nineteenth and early twentieth centuries created both obstacles and opportunities for the establishment of Catholic colleges for Catholic white women. Women's participation in Catholic higher education, and even more their leadership, were not givens. The cult of domesticity that characterized the understanding of the role of women in both Church and society at best saw the higher education of women as enabling them to be better prepared for marriage and being able to raise good sons.[24] Within the Catholic community, there was resistance to such education, as it was thought to encourage young women to turn away from domestic roles.[25] There also was doubt that women possessed the intellectual ability to engage in higher education.[26] Nevertheless, the rise in the socioeconomic standing of an increasing number of Catholics fueled the desire of more Catholic women to obtain higher education. At the time, these women's only option was to attend non-Catholic women's colleges. These were seen as a threat to Catholic women's faith and morals, however, so bishops who had long failed to see the value of offering higher education to women reconsidered Catholic women's colleges as a way to forestall the putative threat.[27] This opened the door for the establishment of colleges by women religious communities. Some bishops hoped that they could influence these institutions and ensure Catholic women would receive an education that would prepare them for domestic life, but many women religious were able to resist this pressure.[28]

When women religious founded Catholic women's colleges, generally in the late nineteenth and early twentieth centuries, the colleges' economic feasibility relied heavily on the labor provided by sisters and the support of their communities. While significant, these "living endowments" did not provide sufficient financial resources for hiring lay faculty, expanding facilities, or contributing to operating budgets. In fact, in the second half of the twentieth century, the strong presence and influence of members of the sponsoring communities became obstacles to accessing financial resources. Federal funding could be difficult to obtain because of the perceived sectarian nature of the institutions.[29] Efforts to build endowments were often discouraged. In the words of Archbishop Michael Curley in response to a request to support such efforts in 1944, "If young ladies want [college education], they get it and pay for it."[30] It was thought that Catholics had more important causes to support. Moreover, the sisters had already demonstrated their ability to run these institutions effectively without such assistance. The hard work and success of the sisters thus became the excuse for their not receiving diocesan support; instead, the sisters were expected to take on yet more labor as the needs of their institutions grew. There was little appreciation from bishops and the like of the pressures and possibilities for growth that came with the increasing demand for higher education on the part of women. The challenges experienced by these institutions would be exacerbated after the Second Vatican Council, which saw the start of the steep decline of women entering religious life.

In the late 1960s and early 1970s, women's colleges also had to contend suddenly with competition from newly coeducational, traditionally male institutions. When Jesuit institutions decided to enroll women at all levels, including in undergraduate programs that had been established exclusively for male students, these decisions did not necessarily emerge from a concern to improve women's role in society; rather, they emerged mainly from financial considerations. As Susan Ross observes,

> Given the increased competition for students, most of these schools realized that they would lose their most promising male students to [non-Catholic] coeducational schools. In addition, the women who were applying to and enrolling at these formerly men's schools were often academically superior to many of their male classmates.[31]

There is evidence that faculty at the time experienced women's presence (as serious students) as improving their classrooms, but there seems to have been little to no thought given to how the curriculum would need to change in order to welcome women.[32] Formation of programs in women's studies were initial attempts to address this question.

In tracing the establishment of single-sex colleges and universities as well as the movement toward coeducation, it is noteworthy that the 1967 meeting that led to the Land O'Lakes Statement on "the nature and role of the contemporary Catholic University" excluded leaders from women's institutions.[33] Describing how a college or university can both be Catholic and an institution of higher education was an issue that Catholic women's colleges had engaged as they confronted questions of their legitimacy. For example, the College of Notre Dame of Maryland (now named Notre Dame of Maryland University) faced legal challenges in the 1960s regarding its qualifications to access government grants. It was among the defendants in the Horace Mann case, which challenged the eligibility of four religiously sponsored institutions for federal funding. The college had to establish that markers of its Catholic identity did not interfere with its ability to function properly as an institution of higher learning.[34] Nonetheless, all those present at the Land O'Lakes meeting were male educators representing historically men's institutions. While the document these men produced is attentive to the diversity of traditions present at Catholic universities, it failed to be aware of missing Catholic voices, especially Catholic women educators. These challenges persist. As we saw in the first section of the chapter, women have yet to achieve parity at all levels in Catholic higher education, and most current CCUs descend from men's institutions that became coeducational.

Fostering Women's Leadership for the Future of Catholic Higher Education

Evolving understandings of the role of the laity in the Church facilitated the growth of lay leadership in Catholic higher education in the 1960s. The Second Vatican Council offered an expansive understanding of Church as "the people of God" and underscored the active role of the laity in the mission of the Church.[35] For example, *Lumen Gentium* states that "the laity are called in a special way to make the

Church present and operative in those places and circumstances where only through them can it become the salt of the earth."[36] We can also see a growing appreciation of the role of the laity in the mission of the Church by taking note of the "addressees" of magisterial Catholic social teaching. In 1891, Pope Leo XIII addressed the encyclical *Rerum Novarum* only to "patriarchs, primates, archbishops, bishops and other ordinaries of places having peace and communion with the Apostolic See."[37] Pope John XXIII extended the audience of his 1961 encyclical *Mater et Magistra* to include "the clergy and the faithful of the entire Catholic World." By his 1963 encyclical *Pacem in Terris*, he extended his call to include "all men [*sic*] of good will." When Pope Francis entered the scene and drew attention to the condition of "our common home" in *Laudato Si'* in 2015, he stated that, "in this Encyclical, I would like to enter into dialogue with all people about our common home."[38]

At the same time, scholars have provided strong evidence that Catholic social teaching, understood as official documents authored by bishops and popes, has not been receptive to women's concerns or participation.[39] Though women suffer disproportionately from social injustices regularly addressed in ecclesial teaching (e.g., related to climate change, immigration, work, and poverty), ecclesial teaching treats these issues generally rather than as they impact women's lives. Furthermore, popes and bishops have largely excluded women from consultation regarding these social issues. Kristin Heyer observes that the U.S. bishops were praised for the process of consultation that resulted in their pastoral letters *Economic Justice for All: Pastoral Letter on Catholic Teaching and the U.S. Economy* (1986) and *The Challenge of Peace: God's Promise and Our Response* (1983), but insufficient attention to women's voices and an ambivalent view of women's roles in Church and society figured among the several failures that led the bishops to abandon the letter "Partners in the Mystery of Redemption: A Response to Women's Concerns for Church and Society."[40] According to Heyer, "a tension (if not contradiction) exists between Catholic teachings on equal human dignity and affirmations of women's contributions in social and political life, on the one hand, and an emphasis on women's maternal function, familial vocation and gender complementarity, on the other."[41] It is no surprise that these contradictions can also be found in Catholic higher education. As Gerald Beyer bluntly observes, Catholic social teaching "historically…hardly helped women trying to make their way in the world of work."[42]

When Catholic social thought is considered more broadly, as it is in the introduction to this volume, it is clear that women have contributed to shaping the tradition through scholarship and action; women's contributions, however, have yet to be fully embraced, recognized, or sought.[43] Pope Francis, the first pope from the Global South, gives reason to hope for change. Francis repeatedly invites dialogue with those whose concerns are often ignored or invisible. While his predecessors emphasized the importance of attention to culture and science, he expands the possible circle of interlocutors. In *Laudato Si'*, he notes that "we need a conversation which includes everyone," for "the challenge we are undergoing, and its human roots, concern and affect us all."[44] Pope Francis's invitation to dialogue is a hopeful step. Yet Susan Ross's observation in 2012, as she reflected on the last ten years of women's experience in Jesuit higher education, remains true today: "While some things have changed for the better, some things have stubbornly remained the same."[45]

Aspects of the Catholic tradition both support and hinder CCUs' capacities to welcome women and their leadership at all levels. Because women cannot be ordained in the Roman Catholic Church, and ordained men have largely shaped the Church through their formal leadership positions, many CCUs have been influenced by clerical culture.[46] Accordingly, the summer 2021 AJCU "Justice in Jesuit Higher Education" conference included a plenary in which women leaders both celebrated Jesuit colleges' and universities' reception of women leaders and identified significant issues that require attention.[47] We focus here on three themes that emerge from the leaders' insights that could be considered and adapted at other CCUs.

First, though women hold more visible positions of leadership in Catholic higher education than they did a generation ago, they often experience barriers to the exercise of leadership related to the clerical and male cultures of many CCUs. Discomfort with women's leadership in Church and society is not just a relic of the distant past. CCU women presidents report experiences of being excluded in both higher education and ecclesial contexts.[48] In this way, contemporary gender dynamics in Catholic higher education have not changed as much as it would be hoped since Land O'Lakes. Dialogue about how to remediate the cultures of Catholic colleges and universities could prove generative. In keeping with Pope Francis's invitation to dialogue, the voices that have been excluded from the discussions would need to take center stage.[49]

Second, most colleges and universities' missions do not explicitly state that they aspire to be liberating forces for women.[50] Capitalizing on women's talents and gifts requires strategic planning and processes for developing stronger networks for women in leadership, pipelines to support women who aspire to leadership, and ongoing formation of leaders.[51] Regarding processes for women of color, "commitment to diversity should commence at the executive level (i.e., president's office) and reach every college, department, and program area."[52] As Ross remarks,

> Teaching and scholarship should not be the only areas on which we should focus; having an institutional mission and a campus climate that is fully attentive to women, gender and sexuality, as well as race and class, can help to resist the push towards the commodification of higher education, continue and expand the Jesuit tradition of *cura personalis* and make the college and university community a place dedicated to truth and the common good of all. Jesuit education can become more inclusive, more concrete and embodied and more dedicated to justice, as feminist scholars have advocated.[53]

For their part, the Jesuits have initiated a process to listen to and address contemporary concerns, which could improve Jesuit higher education's capacity to foster women's leadership. In March 2021, Arturo Sosa, SJ, in response to dialogue with women, announced the formation of an international commission on the role and responsibilities of women in the Society of Jesus. The purpose is to evaluate the extent to which General Congregation 34, "Jesuits and the Situation of Women in the Church and Civil Society," promulgated in 1995, informs current practices, and to recommend structural changes in Jesuit ministries in order to collaborate more effectively with women.[54]

The third insight is the one upon which we wish to elaborate most. As leadership of CCUs increasingly moves from members of sponsoring religious orders to lay leaders, women and men require ongoing formation in the college or university's mission and identity.

The religious formation and sense of leadership as a vocation that shaped members of religious orders cannot be replicated exactly for lay women and men. Formal faith formation in Catholic parishes typically wanes after Confirmation in the teen years rather than continuing into adulthood. Accordingly, CCUs need to develop current lay leaders of every and no faith tradition in spirituality, the Catholic intellectual tradition, Catholic social thought, and other topics that are essential for leadership in Catholic contexts.

It would be naïve to advocate for diverse lay leadership without acknowledging the challenges this entails. As suggested in the introduction to this volume, lay leadership involves hiring more leaders and educators who may have little familiarity with the heritage that animates an institution and its mission. Administrators, faculty, and staff are often brought into Catholic higher education primarily for their professional expertise; trustees increasingly hail from the financial sector. Whereas early founders shared community life—sitting together at shared meals and recreation after work and discussing their day, or praying together and celebrating liturgy—it is rare to find spaces where current faculty and administrators gather together in similar ways. Shared liturgy may occur with the Mass of the Holy Spirit at the beginning of an academic year and Baccalaureate Mass at the end. Even at these, few participate, unlike the early days of these institutions when most students and lay faculty would participate in weekly, if not daily, liturgy. Today, many faculty, staff, and administrators leave campus at the end of a workday and turn to personal responsibilities at home, possibly attending to children, parents, or spouses, and worship at their particular parishes, churches, temples, mosques, and synagogues, if they participate in organized religion at all.

Opportunities both to learn about and to experience the traditions and ways of proceeding of sponsoring communities are critical to handing on and faithfully adapting the mission and identity of an institution. Vowed religious can no longer be expected to articulate the heritage that undergirds an institution's mission. Well-prepared mission leaders at all levels—from the board of trustees and the president's cabinet to the faculty and staff—are capable of bringing the distinct gifts of the founders to the table if they are educated to do so.[55] It is exciting to imagine the richness that can be retrieved from these traditions when they are brought into dialogue with the experiences of diverse leadership, but there must be opportunities to encounter the traditions with some depth for such dialogue to be fruitful and faithful.

For example, fifteen-minute "mission moments" at the beginning of meetings, while helpful, will not suffice. It is through conversation and dialogue, through wrestling together as leaders of an institution, that what are likely chronologically distant and culturally foreign stories can be brought to bear on contemporary challenges and questions. Pilgrimages to places that shaped the founders, such as Catherine McAuley's House of Mercy on Baggot Street in Dublin for leaders of Mercy institutions, or walking in the footsteps of St. Ignatius in Spain and Rome for leaders of Jesuit colleges and universities, can be transformative.[56] Immersion into communities on the margins, coupled with reflection in light of CST and the charism of the founding order, can shed light on institutional commitment to attending to those on the margins and can have a profound impact on leaders, giving depth to their understanding of an institution's call to serve underserved populations, to engage with pressing social issues, and to support teaching and research that promote an "educated solidarity," including solidarity with women's experiences.[57] Finally, retreats and other spiritual practices are a way to experience and develop the spirituality that inspired the vision for the work of higher education of the founding communities.

This chapter has described the move beyond patriarchy in leadership of Catholic higher education in the United States: that is, the shift beyond white male clerics populating the leadership of Catholic education to include first women religious and then male and female lay leaders. It argues that, while the trend toward lay leadership away from clericalism is welcomed, attention must be given to ensuring that these leaders reflect the various dimensions of diversity, including race, present in the communities they serve and seek to educate. Pope Francis's call for dialogue affirms the importance not only of ensuring diversity at CCUs, but also of working toward equity, inclusion, and justice. The Religious Sisters of Mercy, following Catherine McAuley, affirm a pedagogy of educating by example.[58] Educating for diversity, equity, inclusion, and justice is not solely a matter of staying abreast of current trends in higher education. For Catholic institutions, these commitments express institutional identity and fidelity to CST.

Questions for Consideration and Discussion

1. How do your institution's founding and development affect how it now frames issues of gender and considerations of leadership at all levels, including the composition of the board of trustees? Whether your institution is still run by clerics or not, is the institutional culture "clericalist"? (How would you define "clericalism"?) Finally, in what ways is the Catholic Church's historic ambivalence about the roles of women visible (or present but disguised) at your institution?
2. Reed-Bouley and Punsalan-Manlimos cite national data on gender inequities in the faculty ranks and senior leadership, as well as significant compensation disparities between women and men at the same rank. What would an audit of salaries and leadership trajectories at your institution reveal? How effective is your institution's plan (if there is one) for rectifying salary disparities and fostering women's leadership? How might CST shape the ways in which your institution considers these questions?
3. National studies show that women in higher education bear a disproportionate burden of often-unrewarded "institutional caretaking," such as committee work and mentoring students, which displace time for highly rewarded work such as publishing. Is this the case at your institution? What structures and policies either facilitate or pose barriers to women's leadership and advancement at your institution?
4. Few CCUs explicitly name "fostering women's leadership" as an institutional priority or part of their mission. Is fostering women's leadership an institutional priority for your campus? If so, how would you rate your institution's success? If not, should it be? What would fostering women's leadership involve?
5. In reflecting upon your discussion of the questions above, what insights and proposals would you identify as your most pressing or promising institutional priorities?

Notes

1. The authors express their gratitude to Susan Ross for her helpful comments on a draft, as well as for her contributions to advancing women's leadership in Catholic higher education.

2. Jennifer Tilghman-Havens, "Fostering a Vibrant Jesuit Tradition," *Conversations on Jesuit Higher Education* 55 (Spring 2019): 8–9.

3. In order to limit the scope of the chapter, we do not address all obstacles to women's participation and leadership, including the well-documented, overt sexual violence that women students, faculty, and staff face on college and university campuses. The pervasiveness of sexual violence is illustrated by a recent study at Emory University, where 59 percent of female faculty reported witnessing, and 28 percent reported experiencing, sexual harassment. See Dabney P. Evans, Jessica M. Sales, Kathleen K. Krause, and Carlos del Rio, "'You Have to Be Twice as Good and Work Twice as Hard:' A Mixed-Methods Study of Perceptions of Sexual Harassment, Assault and Women's Leadership among Female Faculty at a Research University in the USA," *Global Health, Epidemiology and Genomics* 4 (2019), https://www.cambridge.org/core/journals/global-health-epidemiology-and-genomics/article/you-have-to-be-twice-as-good-and-work-twice-as-hard-a-mixedmethods-study-of-perceptions-of-sexual-harassment-assault-and-womens-leadership-among-female-faculty-at-a-research-university-in-the-usa/B5F1F9C01C6D38C1C1F1A7C02EBFB743.

4. Readers who want to think more about the relevance of these "intersections" might see Kimberlé Crenshaw's groundbreaking article "Demarginalizing the Intersection of Race and Sex: A Black Feminist Critique of Antidiscrimination Doctrine, Feminist Theory and Antiracist Politics," *University of Chicago Legal Forum* 140 (1989): 139–67.

5. The Department of Education includes seminaries and graduate schools of theology as part of Catholic higher education, but they are not the ACCU's target institutions. The ACCU estimates that there are a total of two hundred Catholic colleges and universities that offer two or four-year certificates/degrees that are not seminaries, nursing or allied medical schools, or graduate schools; most of them are ACCU members. Nadine Jalandoni, personal correspondence, September 28, 2021.

6. Information provided by Nadine Jalandoni, ACCU, from National Center for Education Statistics, Integrated Postsecondary Education System (IPEDS), 2020 collection year, https://nces.ed.gov/ipeds/datacenter/MasterVariableList.aspx?changeStep=YES&stepId=2.

7. Glenn Colby and Chelsea Fowler, *Data Snapshot: IPEDS Data on Full-Time Women Faculty and Faculty of Color; An In-depth Look at the Makeup and Salaries of Full-time Faculty Members in US Higher Education* (Washington, DC: American Association of University Professors, 2020), 5, https://www.aaup.org/sites/default/files/Dec-2020_Data_Snapshot_Women_and_Faculty_of_Color.pdf. For another discussion of gender disparities in compensation, see Gerald J. Beyer, *Just Universities: Catholic Social Teaching Confronts Corporatized Higher Education* (New York: Fordham University

Press, 2021), 209; on job and promotion disparities between faculty with and without children, and between men and women who are parents, see 211–20. On the impact of gender generally in higher education, see James F. Keenan, *University Ethics: How Colleges Can Build and Benefit from a Culture of Ethics* (Lanham, MD: Roman and Littlefield, 2015), chap. 8.

8. Glenn Colby and Chelsea Fowler, *Data Snapshot*, 12.

9. Beyer discusses a "baby penalty" for women in Catholic higher education, noting that women who become parents face promotion and wage penalties that men who become parents do not experience. See *Just Universities*, 211–18.

10. Liz McMillan, "The Pandemic Hit Female Academics Hardest: What Are Colleges Going to Do about It?" *Chronicle of Higher Education*, July 27, 2021, https://www.chronicle.com/article/the-pandemic-hit-female-academics-hardest.

11. Marwa Shalaby, Nermin Allam, and Gail Buttorff, "Gender, COVID, and Faculty Service," *Inside Higher Ed*, December 18, 2020, https://www.insidehighered.com/advice/2020/12/18/increasingly-disproportionate-service-burden-female-faculty-bear-will-have.

12. For a detailed analysis of pandemic-related declines in research productivity of women in science, as well as how colleges and universities could ensure equity in promotion postpandemic, see Molly M. King and Megan E. Frederickson, "The Pandemic Penalty: The Gendered Effects of COVID-19 on Scientific Productivity," *Socius: Sociological Research for a Dynamic World* 7 (2021): 1–24, https://journals.sagepub.com/doi/full/10.1177/23780231211006977.

13. Personal correspondence, Nadine Jalandoni, director of research, Association of Catholic Colleges and Universities, "CCU Presidential Breakdown 2021–2022." For an analysis of the situation of women presidents in higher education generally, see Elizabeth Howard and Jonathan Gagliardi, *Leading the Way to Parity: Preparation, Persistence, and the Role of Women Presidents* (Washington, DC: American Council on Education, 2018), https://www.acenet.edu/Documents/Leading-the-Way-to-Parity.pdf.

14. According to the ACCU, 27 percent of presidents at Catholic institutions are affiliated with religious orders, with approximately a third of these women. See ACCU, *Points of Distinction: The Catholic College and University President* (Washington, DC: Association of Catholic Colleges and Universities, 2018), 1. According to the Association of American Colleges and Universities (AAC&U, which includes non-Catholic colleges and universities), as of 2017, 58.1 percent of presidents were white males and 25 percent were white females, with 11.8 percent men of color and 5.1 percent women of color. See "College Students Are More Diverse Than Ever. Faculty and

Administrators Are Not," *AAC&U News: Insights and Campus Innovations in Liberal Education* (March 2019), https://acrl.libguides.com/EDI/he.

15. Personal correspondence, Sarah Dinan, executive assistant to the president of the Association of Jesuit Colleges and Universities, September 28, 2021. Seven male presidents stepped down as of summer 2021, and since summer 2021 five additional presidents (one woman and four men) announced their departures for summer 2022. For a profile of three women presidents of Jesuit institutions, see Emma Winters, "Meet the Women Leaders Who Are Transforming Jesuit Higher Education," *America*, May 14, 2019, https://www.americamagazine.org/faith/2019/05/14/meet-women-leaders-who-are-transforming-jesuit-higher-education.

16. Personal correspondence, Mary-Paula Cancienne, RSM, associate director for mission support and integration, Conference for Mercy Higher Education, September 29, 2021.

17. Association of Catholic Colleges and Universities, *Points of Distinction*, 1.

18. Association of Catholic Colleges and Universities, "Catholic Higher Education FAQs," https://www.accunet.org/Catholic-Higher-Ed-FAQs#Male/Female.

19. For example, "underrepresented minority faculty members [defined in this study as faculty who are not white or Asian] make up only 12.9 percent of full-time faculty members across the country, despite making up 32.6 percent of the U.S. population....Only 5.2 percent of full-time faculty members self-identify as Hispanic or Latino, whereas 17.5 percent of the US population self-identifies as Hispanic or Latino...[and] 6.0 percent of full-time faculty members self-identify as Black or African American, whereas 12.7 percent of the US population self-identifies as Black or African American." See Glenn Colby and Chelsea Fowler, *Data Snapshot*, 3.

20. For example, Asian and Asian-American students have expressed to one of us, Catherine Punsalan-Manlimos, both surprise and hope when seeing she is a professor at a university. Others have sought her out as a mentor, as well as to help shape research questions and discern and navigate postgraduate education. Often her office hours became spaces for students of color to unburden and reflect on their experiences in predominantly white spaces. For a discussion of these phenomena, see M. Cristina Alcalde and Mangala Subramaniam, "Women in Leadership: Challenges and Possibilities," *Inside Higher Ed*, July 17, 2020, https://www.insidehighered.com/views/2020/07/17/women-leadership-academe-still-face-challenges-structures-systems-and-mind-sets.

21. For analysis of their experiences as women faculty of color in Catholic colleges and universities, see Stephanie Y. Michem, "'What Doesn't Kill You Will Make You Strong': Black Women and Catholic Colleges," in *Women*

in Catholic Higher Education: Border Work, Living Experiences, and Social Justice, ed. Sharlene Hesse-Biber and Denise Leckenby (Lanham, MD: Lexington Books, 2003), 17–32, and Bonnie B. C. Oh, "Navigating Bi-cultural Waters," in *Women in Catholic Higher Education*, 59–72. For an anthology of personal stories and empirical research on the experiences of women faculty of color in higher education, see Gabriella Gutiérrez y Muhs, Yolanda Flores Niemann, Carmen G. Gonzalez, and Angela P. Harris, ed., *Presumed Incompetent II: The Intersections of Race and Class for Women in Academia* (Louisville, CO: University Press of Colorado, 2020). See also Jean-Marie Gaëtane and Brenda Lloyd-Jones, ed., *Women of Color in Higher Education: Turbulent Past, Promising Future* (Bingley, England: Emerald Group, 2011).

22. Yolanda Flores Niemann, "Lessons from the Experiences of Women of Color Working in Academia," in *Presumed Incompetent II*, 446–99, at 448.

23. Michael T. Rizzi, "We've Been Here Before: A Brief History of Catholic Higher Education in America," *Journal of Catholic Higher Education* 37, no. 2 (Summer 2018): 153–74.

24. See Jill Ker Conway, "Faith, Knowledge, and Gender," in *Catholic Women's Colleges in America*, ed. Tracy Shier and Cynthia Eagle Russett (Baltimore: The John Hopkins University Press, 2002), 11–16. See also Kim Tolley, "The Hallmarks of the Sisters of Notre Dame de Namur in the West: Women Religious and Education in the United States," in *Women's Higher Education in the United States: New Historical Perspectives*, Historical Studies in Education (New York: Palgrave Macmillan, 2018), 211–32.

25. See Kathleen A. Mahoney, "American Catholic Colleges for Women: A Historical Origin," in Shier and Russett, *Catholic Women's Colleges in America*, 25–54.

26. Mahoney, "American Catholic Colleges for Women," 30. While few and far between, convents proved the bias wrong by producing great women scholars.

27. Mahoney, "American Catholic Colleges for Women," 48–53. See also Kathleen Sprows Cummings, *New Women of the Old Faith: Gender and American Catholicism in the Progressive Era* (Chapel Hill: University of North Carolina Press, 2009), 6.

28. See Conway, "Faith, Knowledge, and Gender."

29. See Mary J. Oates, *Pursuing Truth: How Gender Shaped Catholic Education at the College of Notre Dame of Maryland* (Ithaca: Cornell University Press, 2021). In chapter 5, Oates argues that weakened ties between the sponsoring communities and the colleges they founded were due less to the liberalizing influence of the Second Vatican Council than to the need of these institutions to access federal and state funds. She offers the College of Notre Dame of Maryland as an example.

30. Archbishop Michael J. Curley to James Almond, December 26, 1944, quoted in Oates, *Pursuing Truth*, 126.

31. Susan Ross, "It's Been Fifty Years since Most Jesuit Colleges Went Co-Ed: But Have They Truly Embraced Their Female Students?" *America*, September 20, 2021, https://www.americamagazine.org/faith/2021/09/20/jesuit-coeducation-college-university-ross-241373.

32. Ross, "It's Been Fifty Years."

33. See "Land O'Lakes Statement," https://cushwa.nd.edu/assets/245340/landolakesstatement.pdf. The Land O'Lakes Statement was crafted in preparation for a meeting hosted by the International Federation of Catholic Universities.

34. Oates, *Pursuing Truth*, 223–34.

35. *Lumen Gentium* 9ff.

36. *Lumen Gentium* 33.

37. Pope Leo XIII, *Rerum Novarum* 1.

38. Pope Francis, *Laudato Si'* 3.

39. See, e.g., Maria Riley, OP, and Nancy Sylvester, IHM, *Trouble and Beauty: Women Encounter Catholic Social Teaching* (Washington, DC: Center of Concern, Leadership Conference of Women Religious, and NETWORK, 1991).

40. Kristin Heyer, "A Feminist Appraisal of Catholic Social Thought," in *For the City and the World: Conversations in Catholic Studies and Social Thought* (San Francisco: University of San Francisco Press, 2010), 8–23. The process spanned the years from 1982 to 1992.

41. Heyer, "A Feminist Appraisal," 17.

42. Beyer, *Just Universities*, 210.

43. See Erin Brigham and Mary Johnson, SNDdeN, ed., *Solidarity toward the Common Good: Women Engaging the Catholic Social Tradition* (Mahwah, NJ: Paulist, 2022).

44. Pope Francis, *Laudato Si'* 14.

45. Susan Ross, "Women in Jesuit Higher Education: Ten Years Later," in *Jesuit and Feminist Education: Intersections in Teaching and Learning for the Twenty-First Century*, ed. Jocelyn M. Borczka and Elizabeth A. Petrino (New York: Fordham University Press, 2012), 242–54, at 243.

46. Phyllis Zagano offers a useful analysis of the ways in which clericalism pervades Church structures in "Women and the Church: Unfinished Business of Vatican II," *Horizons* 34, no. 2 (2007): 205–21.

47. Patricia Grant, Margo Heydt, Stephanie Russell, Tania Tetlow, Michele Murray, and Erika Kirby, "Women in Leadership and the Call to Justice in Jesuit Higher Education" (presentation at the Association of Jesuit Colleges and Universities' conference "Justice and Jesuit Education," June 22, 2021), https://www.youtube.com/watch?v=OZ0LYjaCCRU.

48. See Kathleen Marie Raynes Meeker, "Understanding Lay and Religious Presidents: Implications for Preparation to Sustain Catholicity in Catholic Higher Education" (PhD diss., Fordham University, 2008), 160–62.

49. For an analysis of ways in which women in the Church are routinely silenced and subjected to explanations of their own areas of professional expertise (and even their own experiences), see Natalia Imperatori-Lee, "Father Knows Best: Theological 'Mansplaining' and the Ecclesial War on Women," *Journal of Feminist Studies in Religion* 31, no. 2 (2015): 89–108.

50. For the Jesuit context, it may be significant that the Universal Apostolic Preferences for 2019–2029 do not focus on remediating women's disproportionate social suffering. See https://www.jesuits.global/uap/introduction/. For a discussion of hiring and forming faculty for mission broadly understood, see James L. Heft, SM, *The Future of Catholic Higher Education: The Open Circle* (New York: Oxford University Press, 2021), 134–47.

51. The ACCU offers a one-day "Women Executive Leaders Conference" the day before its annual meeting to "support women to meet current leadership demands and thrive in Catholic higher education executive positions." See https://www.accunet.org/Senior-Leaders. Women of color who have become senior leaders in academic institutions point to mentoring as a significant support in their ability to navigate difficult terrain. See Belinda Lee Huang, "Women of Color Advancing to Senior Leadership in U.S. Academe," in *The Changing Role of Women in Higher Education: Academic and Leadership Issues*, ed. Heather Eggins (Switzerland: Springer, 2017), 155–72.

52. Jean-Marie Gaëtane, "'Unfinished Agendas': Trends in Women of Color's Status in Higher Education," in *Women of Color in Higher Education: Turbulent Past, Promising Future*, ed. Jean-Marie Gaëtane and Brenda Lloyd-Jones (Bingley, England: Emerald Group, 2011), 3–19, at 14.

53. Ross, "It's Been Fifty Years."

54. For information on the Jesuits' process, see "8 March 2021: It's Women's Day for the Jesuits Too!," https://www.jesuits.global/2021/03/08/8-march-2021-its-womens-day-for-the-jesuits-too/. See also "Prep Educator on Commission Advancing Women in Jesuit Mission," Fairfield County Catholic, https://www.bridgeportdiocese.org/prep-educator-on-commission-advancing-women-in-jesuit-mission/. General Congregation 34, Decree 14, "Jesuits and the Situation of Women in Church and Civil Society," can be accessed at https://www.xavier.edu/jesuitresource/jesuit-a-z/terms-w/decree-14.

55. See in this regard Peter-Hans Kolvenbach, SJ, "The Service of Faith and the Promotion of Justice in American Jesuit Higher Education," Santa Clara University, October 6, 2000, part III, A, https://www.scu.edu/ic/programs/ignatian-worldview/kolvenbach/. He notes, "When the heart is touched by direct experience, the mind may be challenged to change." We

can expect that, if this is true for students, it is also true for faculty, administrators, and other leaders.

56. For testimonials regarding the impact of international immersion as part of the Association of Jesuit Colleges and University Ignatian Colleagues Program, see "International Immersion," Ignatian Colleagues Program, https://www.ignatiancolleagues.org/immersion-experience. Margo J. Heydt and Sarah J. Melcher describe their pilgrimage in "Mary, the Hidden Catalyst: Reflections from an Ignatian Pilgrimage to Spain and Rome," in Boryczka and Petrino, *Jesuit and Feminist Education*, 37–55, at 53.

57. Regarding curriculum and pedagogy, women's leadership can be affirmed by taking women's scholarship and other contributions seriously in the classroom. For examples, see chapters in *Jesuit and Feminist Education*; see also Mara Brecht, "Charismatic Circularity: Lay Faculty, Practices of Transmission, and Possibilities for Renewal," *Journal of Catholic Higher Education* 38, no. 2 (2019): 99–120, regarding how lay faculty renew and transmit the charism of the founding congregation through their teaching.

58. Mary Sullivan, "Catherine McAuley and the Characteristics of Mercy Higher Education," *MAST Journal* 16, no. 2 (2006): 18–26.

9

WHO WILL LEAD?

Shaping the Distinctive Mission of Catholic Higher Education through Catholic Social Thought

James L. Heft, SM

In the Gospel according to John, Jesus describes his followers as not belonging to the "world" though they are, of course, in it (John 15:19 and 17:14–15). If Christians are to be "in" but not "of" the world, is that also true for Catholic colleges and universities (CCUs)? What would that mean? What's more, can CCUs be not "of the world" and still attract students who wish to be gainfully employed in it? Given the financial and corporate cultures that dominate the economic environment of the United States, is it even possible for CCUs to be, in some sense, "otherworldly"? Conversely, do CCUs very much "in the world" risk losing their distinctive mission?

In this chapter, I remind readers of some of the profound changes since World War II in Catholic higher education in the United States, note the far-reaching impact of an aggressive, profit-oriented economy, and identify some of the most relevant emphases in Catholic social thought (CST) that might enable CCUs to be "in" the world but not entirely "of" it. I also stress that, since CST is based on fundamental theological teaching, leaders of Catholic institutions cannot dismiss it as discretionary, even if many Catholics imagine it to be too "idealistic" to be implemented in a fallen world.

While the sophisticated and extensive development of CST is to be applauded, it must also be acknowledged that the Church has not explained well how its social teachings should be applied to social institutions, including the Church's own. It is one thing to encourage prophetic criticism of others; it is quite another for the Church to implement that criticism within its own parishes, dioceses, and educational institutions.

Finally, I discuss the complex challenges that CCU leaders face in their efforts to implement CST, and I offer some pointers to that end. Ten years ago, I published a book about the importance and mission of Catholic high schools. I devoted two chapters to leadership, one that explored its theological foundations and the other its moral practices.[1] In preparation for writing this chapter, I reviewed those chapters. I was pleased with much of what I had written. I was quite clear that there were many different theories about leadership, not all of them helpful for Catholic educational institutions.[2] However, in retrospect, I did not pay sufficient attention to the economic environment in which our Catholic high schools existed. I am more aware now of the need to include that environment in any discussion of leadership, and thus I pay closer attention to it in this chapter.

The Current State and Diversity of CCUs

Before we consider how CST might help CCUs root themselves more deeply in their Catholic mission, a diagnosis of the current state of our institutions is needed. Accurate diagnoses can be painful and reveal some serious illness. Difficult as it is to look squarely at an institution's shortcomings and failures, it can be even more difficult to take steps to overcome them. Serious change is costly, both personally and financially. Making the diagnoses public can draw sharp criticism and sap the confidence of donors. That our educational institutions are imperfect, however, follows from a mature grasp of the inescapable consequences of sin, personal and social. Being honest about the problems CCUs have is a necessary step toward making them better. Careful diagnosis of the ills makes planning cures possible. That said, accurate diagnoses can be difficult to make, especially if a case is complex, and ill-considered prescriptions can do more harm than good.

One of the reasons that it is hard to diagnose the current state of Catholic higher education in the United States is the very complexity of institutions of higher education. In his memoir on his life in higher education and as president of Williams College, Francis Oakley writes that postsecondary educational institutions are perhaps "the most internally diverse" of all institutions:

> And if universities are indeed dauntingly complex entities, colleges, though smaller and simpler, are not altogether different in kind. If it were not quite so familiar and so very much taken for granted, the sheer multiplicity of activities characteristically pursued under their aegis would probably strike the observer as really quite odd.[3]

Consider that colleges and universities teach a wide range of subjects, run equivalents of hotels and restaurants, employ a police force, hire groundskeepers, maintain an infirmary, libraries, performance halls, laboratories, and attend to a range of audiences—students, parents, faculty. What's more, CCUs must deal with bishops and, in the United States, be sensitive to a highly divided Catholic population, in both a political and religious sense. The challenges for leaders of CCUs are daunting.

Religious orders of men and women founded over 90 percent of the current two-hundred-plus CCUs. Local bishops, and more recently laypeople dismayed over what they perceive as the loss of Catholic identity in Catholic higher education, founded the remaining 10 percent. There is no "system" of Catholic higher education in the United States. In many ways, it is "deregulated." The free enterprise nature of American capitalism has influenced how these institutions relate to each other. Catholic institutions, including those run by the same religious orders, compete for students, donors, and faculty. They rarely cooperate. CCUs founded by the same religious order do occasionally share programs for the formation of lay colleagues in their distinctive charism, but efforts at pooling resources have generally been opposed.[4] Moreover, from the beginning, CCUs have had to compete not only with other private nonprofit institutions, but also with public institutions subsidized by the government and more recently with for-profit universities and online degree programs.

Another reason that a diagnosis of the state of CCUs is difficult has to do with their geographical diversity: some institutions are located in major cities, others in small towns and suburbs, and a few even in rural areas. Many are in the Northeast and only a few in the South and Northwest. Some enroll what have typically been termed "traditional-aged" college students, others mainly working adults and part-time students. Only a few enroll only undergraduates, while most offer revenue-producing, usually part-time graduate programs, but struggle to fund full-time graduate education appropriately. Only a few members of the founding religious orders remain active in faculty and administrative positions; most of them will soon retire.[5]

Most CCUs depend solely on tuition, though a few have endowments that generate a small percentage of their annual budget. Sixty years ago, CCUs were accessible to the children of many middle-income families. Today, most CCUs depend for their financial stability on students whose families are in the top 20 percent income strata. The vast majority of CCUs remain tuition driven. With the exception of the University of Notre Dame, none of the CCUs is endowed at the level of the colleges and universities that win top spots in the annual sweepstakes competition sponsored by *U.S. News and World Report*. (See further on these points Matt Mazewski's and Laura Nichols's chapters in this volume.)

Compared to the most prestigious colleges and universities in the United States, CCUs started building endowments only recently.[6] In the 1930s, various organizations in the United States concerned about the quality of higher education required as a part of accreditation that colleges and universities demonstrate financial reserves. Catholic institutions had none. To accommodate these institutions, the accrediting agencies recognized the donated services of the founding members of the religious orders as "living endowments." This arrangement worked until the post–World War II growth in enrollments and then, in the mid-1960s, the dramatic drop in members of the founding religious communities. More lay faculty and administrators had to be hired; as a result, the cost of tuition rapidly increased, and Catholic higher education enrolled and taught fewer and fewer poor people.[7]

For years, faculty at CCUs have criticized the religious illiteracy of their students. In more recent years, it is not so much their illiteracy but their indifference that concerns Catholic educators. Much has been written about the increasing number of young adults who no longer affiliate with any religion.[8] Studies have documented that many of these unaffiliated young adults come from families in which religion was not that important. If there are more families for whom the Catholic faith is not that important, how attractive will they find CCUs in general and those, in particular, that strengthen their Catholic identity?

Both men's and women's religious orders founded CCUs. As Jennifer Reed-Bouley and Catherine Punsalan-Manlimos note in their chapter in this volume, the post–Vatican II charter for Catholic higher education, the Land O'Lakes Statement, was drawn up in 1967 by a group of men, mostly ordained, representing only the larger (male) universities. The group intended the meeting for leaders of research universities. At that time, however, none of the Catholic universities could be described as a bona fide research university. Nevertheless, they assumed that the experience of leaders of women's colleges and universities was irrelevant.

A 1965 study reported that there were 457 CCUs, 139 founded after 1950, with 216 colleges dedicated primarily to the formation of women religious.[9] It described the fragility of these 216 colleges, many of them two-year institutions that enrolled fewer than 100 students. Almost 90 percent of these 216 were not regionally accredited, only three enrolled more than 750 students, and none had endowments. In 25 percent, there were no more than two full-time faculty members; most were part-time faculty. Nearly all these colleges either closed by the late 1960s, when religious vocations dried up, or merged with nearby Catholic universities. Similarly, many men's religious orders built huge houses of formation to accommodate the unprecedented influx of vocations from the 1930s through the 1950s, only to find those buildings mostly empty by the late 1960s. Most of their colleges and universities, however, continued to survive.

Nevertheless, there were and still are examples of excellent CCUs founded by women's religious orders. Take, for example, St. Katharine Drexel, the founder of the Sisters of the Blessed Sacrament. Drawing upon a substantial inheritance from her banker-financier father, in 1925 she established in New Orleans the first and only Historically Black Catholic University, Xavier University of Louisiana. Holy Cross Sister Madeleva Wolff wanted members of her congregation to study theology at the graduate level. None of the universities run by men had graduate programs that would admit them. So, in the 1940s, she created a graduate school of theology at St. Mary's College in Indiana and welcomed not only religious sisters, but also laity of both sexes. (It was not until the late 1950s that faculty at Catholic universities began to teach theology to undergraduates, a subject that until then was reserved for seminarians. Before then, CCUs depended mainly on courses in Thomistic philosophy to equip students with arguments that would allow them to defend their faith in a country still dominated by Protestants.) As a final example, the Sisters of St. Joseph of Carondelet founded St. Catherine's College in Minneapolis in 1905. By 1917, it was accredited, and in 1937 it became the first CCU to be awarded a chapter of the Phi Beta Kappa honor society.

Despite Differences, Some Common Problems

Taken together, all these factors—difference in size, lack of collaboration, funding problems, the growth of religious indifference, and, more recently, polarizations over Catholic identity—make generalizations about Catholic higher education difficult. The results of some recent surveys of CCUs, however, have sufficiently converged to allow a few modest generalizations.[10] Despite the great diversity among CCUs, they face similar internal challenges.

In 2012, the Association of Jesuit Colleges and Universities (AJCU) examined both the distinctive characteristics of Jesuit higher education and the challenges that Jesuit institutions face.[11] In 2017, the board of trustees of Collegium, founded in 1992 and led (until June 2022) by Thomas Landy of the College of the Holy Cross (MA), gathered to discuss changes in Catholic higher education since the organization's foundation. Both organizations focused on the prospects of CCUs sustaining a robust Catholic identity. Initiatives in support of that goal include Catholic studies programs, faculty retreats, some newly created endowed chairs of Catholic thought, and the appointment of mission officers. But the list of challenges is daunting: religious illiteracy not only among students, but also among younger faculty; lay leaders who lack knowledge about the Catholic intellectual tradition; the marginalization of the liberal arts by professional education; the information revolution and scholarly specialization that make building community and integrating knowledge more difficult; and the difficulty of supporting vigorous debate on contested issues that make Church officials anxious. Jesuit schools, like all CCUs founded by religious orders, also have to contend with decreasing membership.

In addition to these two assessments, in 2013 Boston College and the Association of Catholic Colleges and Universities (ACCU) surveyed presidents of CCUs. The survey included women presidents and presidents of colleges founded by women; the researchers did not, however, distinguish among CCUs in the results. The survey found one especially troubling trend. In response to a question about the extent to which various campus constituents understood and promoted the "Catholic dimension" of their institutions, nearly all the presidents agreed that few of their faculty really helped students understand it. In fact, they thought that, among the various groups on campus (campus ministry, student development, the administration, etc.), the faculty contributed least to the "Catholic dimension," a particularly sobering thought since faculty have tenure, remain in their positions longer than most administrators, shape the curriculum, and interact daily with students. Of course, it would have been helpful had the survey been designed to ask what the presidents understood by their institutions' "Catholic dimension," and we also do not know why faculty were judged to be unsupportive. One possible explanation is that most of the presidents did not understand Catholicism as an intellectual tradition marked by debate and continuing development. Or perhaps they expected the faculty to act like campus ministers or their public relations department.

Interestingly, neither the AJCU, the Collegium board, nor the Boston College and ACCU survey directly addressed the economic environment of the United States and its impact on CCUs. Joseph McCartin's chapter in this volume outlines the profound and far-reaching financial changes in the United States that have affected how our educational institutions now operate. Along similar lines, Gerald Beyer argues that all of higher education in the United States, including Catholic higher education, has become corporatized. By "corporatization," he means a process whereby colleges and universities take on business practices modeled after those in corporate America, including forcing academic units within the institution to support themselves, referring to students as customers who must be "satisfied," downsizing nonrevenue producing academic units such as the humanities, and reducing full-time faculty positions while increasing the number of administrators.[12]

Part of the problem is the lack of leaders who know CST and, with the support of a board of trustees, have the skills to implement it creatively. In the introduction to this volume, Bernard Prusak and Jennifer Reed-Bouley cite Peter Steinfels's comment twenty years ago that new lay presidents arrived on campuses with "new questions but increasingly without old knowledge."[13] Today, some lay presidents arrive on campus with new knowledge, learned from direct experience in finance,[14] but know little about Catholicism as an intellectual tradition rooted in the humanities and dedicated to the formation of more just institutions.

Catholic Social Thought and the Catholic Intellectual Tradition

Since the pontificate of Pope Leo XIII (1878–1903), the application of the Catholic intellectual tradition to issues of society has given rise to a sophisticated and evolving set of principles that, applied prudently and vigorously, resist the neoliberal economies of the Western countries and the corporatization of Catholic higher education. Various accounts of these principles can be found. In their introduction, Prusak and Reed-Bouley direct readers to two articles (see their n33), and there are others as well.[15]

It is important to root Catholic social thought (CST) in the Catholic intellectual tradition. Detached from it, CST runs the risk of political polarization. When that happens, too many people in the United States, frequently wealthy Catholics, dismiss CST as having nothing to do with what it means to be a Catholic. American individualism and our secular culture have shaped the thinking of most Catholics, reducing the practice of the faith to personal morality, especially sexual morality.

By way of example, several years ago, I had lunch with a devout Catholic business leader a year after the publication of Pope Francis's

Laudato Si'. I was hoping to raise money for the Institute for Advanced Catholic Studies at USC. Before I said anything, he blurted out, "Why is this pope getting so involved in politics?" He was quite upset. I listened for a while. Then I asked him if he had read the encyclical. He replied that he had not. I then asked him if he would read it so that we could discuss it when we met again. I suggested that it would be best not to form a judgment about the pope's encyclical just from media reports. About three months later, we met again for lunch, and he started right in criticizing this "liberal" pope who needed to stay out of "politics." I again asked him if he had read the pope's encyclical. He said no. I then told him that I didn't want to talk about it until he did. As far as I know, he never did read it. Also, I failed to raise any money.

I further failed to help him see that the pope's encyclical was based on the theological doctrine of creation, which forms the first part of the Creed: "I believe in God, the Father almighty, the creator of heaven and earth, of all things visible and invisible." Rooting CST in Catholic doctrine and the Catholic intellectual tradition lessens the risk of its political polarization, but it does not rob CST of its political impact. Instead, when CST is theologically rooted, it can be seen more easily, for example, that creation is a gift from God to be shared by all the peoples of the earth, treated with respect, even reverence. This is not a matter of conservative or liberal politics. Vincent Miller makes clear in his chapter in this volume that *Laudato Si'* is not first a moral or political teaching. Rather, it is doctrinal and foundational. It is philosophical inasmuch as it has to do with the very nature of reality. It is epistemological in that it requires a person to see all reality in an interconnected way. The result: we come to see our place in creation in a dramatically new light.

There are reasons to be hopeful about the role of CST at CCUs. Increasingly, evidence of environmental degradation, exploitation of natural resources, and the unconscionable gap between the rich and the poor are creating a greater awareness that current economic priorities are unsustainable. At the University of Dayton, the strategic plan of the Hanley Sustainability Institute, funded by a $12.5 million gift, describes the challenge of our time in stark terms:

> The dramatic expansion of the human footprint on Earth, which has been fundamentally enabled by fossil fuels, in

> service of extractivist economies and technologies based on the ideology of domination, will soon come to an end.[16]

Environmental initiatives at the University of Dayton and at other Catholic campuses represent an important movement that has galvanized the imagination and passion of many faculty and students. These creative programs and financial priorities did not just happen. People—administrators, faculty, students, board members, and donors—have joined together to help CCUs embody CST in more visible and humane ways.

Consider one other creative response. In his chapter in this volume, Matt Mazewski offers an interesting suggestion that could overcome some of the competition among CCUs. Mazewski estimates that, taken together, CCUs have $30 billion in their endowments, which coordinated could become a considerable force of economic power. Pooled funds are not static, but could create new possibilities, he suggests, in service of building a more humane economy consonant with CST.

To reiterate, however, leaders who know CST and have the skills to implement it creatively are often lacking at our institutions. What does that leadership look like? How can it best be described? Are there special skills that characterize the leadership needed?

Leadership: Who and How?

Books on leadership fill shelves in bookstores. Most of them read like motivational talks—high on energy, "positivity," and reassurance. Most of them favor the charismatic leader. Few of them explore the complexities of leading and transforming institutions. Even those that do discuss leadership of institutions, such as James Collins and Jerry Porras's best-selling *Built to Last: Successful Habit of Visionary Companies*,[17] take for granted the rightness of our dominant neoliberal economic environment. Leadership maximizes profits, meets (and "exceeds") customer satisfaction, and outwits the competition. None of these authors writes about colleges and universities that have a theological vision that in significant ways puts them at odds with the culture and economy that surround them.

Earlier in this chapter, I stressed the many differences among CCUs, and I did so for a reason. The leadership required at a small college as opposed to a major university is likely to be quite different. Further, a university where the faculty is deeply divided or where the faculty is united in a "no confidence vote" against the administration requires different leadership from what is needed at a financially stable university that lacks a vision of CST. The leadership needed for a college that does little for the citizens of the small town in which it is located will be different from that needed by a university in a big city that risks being swallowed up by a culture indifferent or even hostile to Catholicism. My point is simple: leadership in such different institutions will not be the same. As obvious as this point is, it is often overlooked by authors who write about leadership. Major mistakes in hiring can be made. If boards of trustees searching for a new president do not do a careful diagnosis of just what their institution most needs, they will likely hire the wrong person.

If different CCUs need different types of leadership, it may appear that no generalizations can be made about the necessary skills. I do think, however, that one of the most important leadership skills for CCUs today is the ability to lead institutional change. The challenge for CCUs is that they need to be not "of the world" but nevertheless continue to exist in it. How should institutional change be understood and led?

Ronald A. Heifetz's description of "adaptive leadership" can help CCUs find ways to do a better job in realizing the key principles of CST.[18] Heifetz approaches the subject of leadership with several assumptions: (1) that leadership deals with problems and opportunities within multiple contexts; (2) that it adapts socially (institutionally) to external and internal circumstances; and (3) that dissonance is an integral part of harmony—that change is resisted and needs patient, persistent management.

Heifetz also draws several helpful distinctions. First, *authority* maintains a degree of stability within the institution while *leadership* mobilizes individuals and groups to address *their* most difficult challenges; both authority and leadership are important, but to different ends.[19] Leaders help people move from a familiar but inadequate institutional situation to a more adequate one. Heifetz also distinguishes between *technical problems* that can be fixed (as the answer to them is known and can be imposed by those competent to do so) and *adap-*

tive challenges that require new learning, because immediate answers are neither at hand nor if at hand are able to be imposed.[20] Successful adaptive changes need to involve multiple stakeholders and usually involve conflict between various people in the institution. In such situations, leaders help people see what matters most, what tradeoffs are worth making, and how to preserve a measure of continuity through the process of change. The focus is on progress, not the exercise of power; in such situations, charismatic leadership is not as valuable as leaders who can help people face their problems together. (Unchecked, charismatic leaders tend to be demagogues who discourage people from recognizing and addressing the problems that they face.) The exercise of leadership can create—and at times is designed to create—tensions and even conflict by proposing necessary changes. Power is important. Conflicts can be good, so long as they are resolved over time by moving the institution closer to the desired goal. Leaders need to disengage from the dance floor and visit the "balcony" in order to see patterns not visible from the ground. They visit, but do not remain on the balcony: what they need to learn there is how to be fully present on the floor, holding steady within a field of action and making choices of how and when to intervene at critical movements to keep the adaptive process moving forward.[21]

Heifetz's description of "holding environments" is especially relevant.[22] Sometimes leadership needs to create a "safe space" in which people can sit with, argue about, and reflect on ways to respond to change. Finally, he offers detailed examples of how leadership has been exercised both successfully and ineptly. No one form of leadership is best. Leaders can rise up from anywhere within organizations and at surprising moments, but their energy, if they are to contribute to positive change, needs prudent coordination and pacing.

With respect to Catholic higher education and CST, who are the leaders? What do they look like? At Georgetown University, students organized to secure a living wage and benefits for workers on campus. They even held a hunger strike. At other institutions, faculty and researchers, such as those who contributed to this volume, lead by their teaching and research and help form the consciences of the administrators in their institutions. The staff who make so much move smoothly day-to-day provide critical stability. Sometimes, college and university presidents lead their institutions in the gradual realization of CST, much as Patricia McGuire transformed the mission of Trinity Washington University, by reorienting it to mostly nontraditional students of color, and Michael Garanzini, SJ, established the Arrupe College at Loyola University Chicago to make it possible for economically disadvantaged students to receive a Catholic higher education. Sometimes the research agendas of faculty influence institutional decision-making. And sometimes the inspiration for change comes from outside the institution through people, like the late Congressman John Lewis, who dedicate their lives to causing "good trouble." In any event, change rarely comes easily or quickly. Significant change always evokes resistance from nearly every quarter.

Some board members from the financial industry embrace CST—but not without difficulty. A promising strategy is to assign laity who grasp CST to both the mission and budget committees of the board. Too often members of the founding religious order lead the mission committee, only to discover that board meetings are dominated by budgetary and administrative matters, often unrelated to the distinctive mission of the institution. Needless to say, without the ongoing formation of board members, leadership at the top will hamper efforts to implement CST in significant ways, beginning with budgetary matters. One strategy in this regard is to expose board members to faculty who know about CST and students who have learned about it.

CST principles pose two difficulties for those who seek to implement them in their institutions: their ideal character and their high demands. Earlier in this chapter, I alluded to the Christian teaching on original sin. In one sense, it is a very compassionate teaching. It reminds believers that no one is perfect and that we all fall short as individuals. We should not be surprised when our institutions fall short as well. Pope Francis has famously remarked that the Church is not a society for the perfect but a field hospital for the broken.[23] He could just as well have said that the Church is also a broken house in need of a hospital, a house that is filled with sinners from the top to the bottom. Working for greater justice is a never-ending process. No CCU embodies CST perfectly, or ever will.

Where does this realization of our brokenness and inevitable failures leave us? For one thing, it not only saves us from naïveté, but protects us from discouragement when our efforts do not produce immediate results. Immediate results should not be expected! Persistence, however, can bring about lasting change. For more than twenty-five years, I spent a lot of time at the University of Dayton participating in discussions about the mission of the university; I also held workshops for faculty search committees that led to the hiring of more faculty who supported Dayton's distinctive mission. I observed that, over time, faculty can design and continually improve a core curriculum rooted more clearly in the mission of the institution and see the point of hiring faculty who can teach in it. That said, a steady and persistent commitment to change is impossible if, every five years, an institution changes its major administrators who draw up a new and different strategic plan.

The high demands of CST need to be tempered by the reality of limited resources. I have already stressed how different CCUs are. Though some CCUs have more resources than others, none has enough resources to tackle all the priorities of CST, and certainly not all at once. Choices have to be made and priorities established. In their introduction, Prusak and Reed-Bouley cite the example of childcare during the pandemic. Could an institution that is already financially stretched raise money to cover childcare costs, support the unionization of adjunct faculty, offer scholarships to poor students, provide a living wage and health benefits for custodians and groundskeepers, and increase support for the humanities and service learning? The answer goes without saying. However, leaders who collaborate with various stakeholders and articulate compelling reasons for the tradeoffs inherent in difficult decisions may open the way to future adaptive change in alignment with CST, as Heifetz's model indicates.

When critics of CCUs advocate raising money in order to meet the demands of CST, I ask myself if they have ever tried to raise money for such objectives. Many years ago, I talked with Father Ted Hesburgh, CSC, about my hope to build and fund a research center that would support extended periods of research to deepen and broaden Catholic intellectual life. He smiled and said, "I always wanted to do that, but I could never raise money for it. Donors don't like to give money for open-ended faculty research." I almost collapsed. Ted Hesburgh couldn't raise the money? But I persisted, perhaps naively, and in time with the support of donors who shared the vision made modest success in building the Institute (https://dornsife.usc.edu/iacs).

Some donors prefer to name buildings, support athletics, underwrite professional education, or help build fitness centers. All these are needed. But through extended conversations, it is possible to persuade donors to support educational initiatives that increase the distinctive mission of CCUs. It is wonderful when this happens, but it requires the communication of a compelling vision that frequently lights a fire only after repeated conversations.

Fighting the Good Fight, Keeping the Faith

The more that an institution seeks to embody CST, the more it becomes not "of" the world even though it is "in" it. And in it CCUs need to be. The Church can learn from the world, as in the past the Church learned from evangelicals to oppose slavery and from Enlightenment thinkers to venerate conscience. Similarly, board members from the financial sector can offer sound advice on shepherding resources for the distinctive mission of CCUs. Finding an appropriate distance from the dominant culture without becoming across the board countercultural is *the* challenge that leadership must navigate.

The necessary balance between "in it" but not "of it" will be found only through a long and intensive formation of leadership at CCUs—among board members, presidents and provosts, deans, faculty, and students. Without careful attention to hiring, appointments, and formation, thoughtful and steady progress will be difficult to achieve. Instead, the culture, corporate and secular, will shape CCUs more than the CST does. While it is possible to formulate clear policies that spell out CST and suggest ways to implement it, these policies can easily be ignored by administrators who leave them on their office shelves.

After prudence and the ability to lead the process of change in complex institutional settings, leaders in Catholic higher education need courage and persistence. But more important than success is fidelity. Leaders can be worn down by "one damn thing after another." It might be helpful in this regard to recall all the problems that St. Paul had to address in the community he founded in Corinth. His first letter to the Corinthians listed factions created by rival leaders, incest, prostitution, divorce, lawsuits, women praying and prophesying in ways some considered "immodest," chaos in worship, people speaking in tongues, and inequality at the communal meal. If that were not enough, he also confronted idolatry and denials of the bodily resurrection of Christ and of Christians.[24] None of these problems kept Paul from continuing to work with this community, suffering much himself as he helped them learn to embody the gospel. If we read his Second Letter to the Corinthians, it is obvious that many of these problems persisted. One wonders if he would have benefited from Ronald Heifetz's recommendations for adaptive leadership! What Paul did not lack was fidelity. As the Pauline writer of the second letter to Timothy memorably states, Paul fought the good fight, finished the race, and kept the faith (2 Tim 4:7). CST is a summons to leaders of CCUs to do the same.

Questions for Consideration and Discussion

1. Heft proposes that CCUs should be "in" the world but not entirely "of" it—not "countercultural" through and through, but also not assimilated to "the dominant culture," whether economically, politically, intellectually, or religiously. He also writes that "the more that an institution seeks to embody CST, the more it becomes not 'of' the world even though it is 'in' it." How would you characterize your own institution in this regard? Is it thoroughly "worldly"—not all that different, finally, from other non-Catholic colleges or universities? Or is it distinctively Catholic (Christian) in substantive ways (e.g., in its intellectual content or temper)? Can CST help you to articulate ways in which your institution is in fact distinctive? Does CST suggest ways that your institution could or should distinguish itself?
2. Heft observes that "there is no 'system' of Catholic higher education in the United States. In many ways, it is 'deregulated.'" Accordingly, the prospects for cooperation among CCUs might seem dismal, though Heft refers approvingly to Matt Mazewski's proposal that CCUs pool some endowment funds. Are there realistic prospects that your institution might collaborate with other CCUs? If so, to what ends, and to what benefit for the institutions in question? Also, what measures can be taken now to explore these prospects?
3. Given the rapid rise of religious nonaffiliation in the United States, it is a good question whether it is wise, financially, for a CCU to

invest in strengthening its Catholic identity and to market itself as distinctively, robustly Catholic. Heft puts the question: "If there are more families for whom the Catholic faith is not that important, how attractive will they find CCUs in general and those, in particular, that strengthen their Catholic identity?" Mark Roche, formerly dean of the College of Arts and Letters at the University of Notre Dame, suggests that the challenge is to articulate a mission "that is intellectually compelling and attractive to persons who are not Catholic and, at the same time, is deeply Catholic" (*Realizing the Distinctive University: Vision and Values, Strategy and Culture* [Notre Dame, IN: University of Notre Dame Press, 2017], 77). How is your institution adjusting to the growth of religious nonaffiliation? Are you articulating your mission in ways that might resonate with students, families, and others (e.g., faculty) from varied religious backgrounds? What should the plan be? How might CST figure in it?

4. In addition to responding to growing religious nonaffiliation, what other "adaptive problems" does your institution now face—problems "that require new learning, because immediate answers are neither at hand nor if at hand are able to be imposed"? What are potential solutions to those problems? Which stakeholders' voices at your institution could be amplified in order to provide new learning and propose potential solutions?
5. What programs are in place to educate new members of the board at your institution? Are new members adequately educated in CST and the Catholic intellectual tradition? Does your institution rely on members of the sponsoring religious congregation to serve as educators of new board members? What new programs should be established, and who could contribute to those programs?
6. How are leaders recognized, formed, and advanced at your institution? Is more attention given to formation of members of the sponsoring religious congregation than to formation of lay faculty and staff? What new programs might be established, or existing programs modified? What opportunities for growth might be developed?
7. Francis Oakley, whom Heft cites, emphasizes in his account of presidential leadership "the educational and instructional side of the leader's role": the effective leader must embody and proclaim her or his institution's meaning, purpose, and values through

"myth, ritual, legend, symbol, and (perhaps above all) story" (*From the Cast-Iron Shore*, 408, 411 [see n3]). What elements of Catholic social thought (e.g., symbols, stories from your founding, lives of holy women and men, principles, biblical narratives) do you or could you draw upon to lead your institution more effectively, whatever your role might be?

8. In reflecting upon your discussion of the questions above, what insights and proposals would you identify as your most pressing institutional priorities?

Notes

1. James L. Heft, SM, *Catholic High Schools: Facing the New Realities* (Oxford: Oxford University Press, 2011), chaps. 5 and 6.

2. See Heft, *Catholic High Schools*, 96, quoting Warren Bennis about the many different theories of leadership: "As we survey the path leadership theory has taken, we spot the wreckage of 'trait theory,' the 'great man' theory, the 'situationist' critique, leadership styles, functional leadership, and finally leaderless leadership, to say nothing of bureaucratic leadership, charismatic leadership, group-centered leadership, reality-centered leadership, leadership by objective, and so on." See his *On Becoming a Leader* (Reading, MA: Addison-Wesley Publishing Company, 1989), 39.

3. Francis Oakley, *From the Cast-Iron Shore: In Lifelong Pursuit of Liberal Learning* (Notre Dame, IN: University of Notre Dame Press, 2019), 395.

4. In the 1930s, the Superior General of the Jesuits called for the consolidation of resources so that quality graduate programs could be established at St. Louis University and Fordham University. The provincials of the two provinces in which the universities were located refused to collaborate. See William Leahy, SJ, *Adapting to America: Catholics, Jesuits, and Higher Education in the Twentieth Century* (Washington, DC: Georgetown University Press, 1991), 52ff.

5. The 1947 yearbook for the College of the Holy Cross included over seventy Jesuits on the faculty; today there are only two. See also Bernard Prusak, "Independent Boards of Trustees at Catholic Colleges and Universities, Fifty Years Later: Finding and Reflections from Six Holy Cross Schools," *Journal of Catholic Higher Education* 37, no. 1 (2018): 3–27, at 14, on the plummeting numbers of Holy Cross priests and brothers at the University of Notre Dame, University of Portland, King's College (PA), and Stonehill College (MA).

6. Leahy writes that by 1900 roughly two-thirds of CCUs did not survive. From 1841–1891, Fordham averaged gifts of $2,000 a year; from 1889–1955, ten bequests given to the Catholic University of America averaged $100,000 or more, but none was larger than $1,000,000. See *Adapting to America*, 22.

7. See, for a fuller discussion, Robert B. Archibald and David H. Feldman, *Why Does College Cost So Much?* (Oxford: Oxford University Press, 2010).

8. See James L. Heft, SM, and Jan E. Stets, ed., *Empty Churches: Non-affiliation in America* (Oxford: Oxford University Press, 2021).

9. See Charles E. Ford and Edgar L. Roy Jr., eds., *The Renewal of Catholic Higher Education* (Washington, DC: National Catholic Educational Association, 1968), especially the graphs on 38, 47, and 53.

10. See for citations my book *The Future of Catholic Higher Education: The Open Circle* (Oxford: Oxford University Press, 2021), 119–21, from which I draw here.

11. See *Some Characteristics of Jesuit Colleges and Universities: A Self-Evaluation Instrument* (2012), available online at https://www.ajcunet.edu/mission-documents.

12. Gerald J. Beyer, *Just Universities: Catholic Social Teaching Confronts Corporatized Higher Education* (New York: Fordham University Press, 2021), 14–15.

13. Peter Steinfels, *A People Adrift: The Crisis of the Roman Catholic Church in America* (New York: Simon & Schuster, 2003), 11.

14. The prime example is Simon Neman, a former financial industry executive, who was president of Mount St. Mary's University (MD) from 2014 until his resignation in 2016. His presidency became national news. See, among many other stories, Susan Svrluga, "Mount St. Mary's University President Resigns," *Washington Post*, February 29, 2016, www.washingtonpost.com.

15. See John A. Coleman, "Making the Connections: Globalization and Catholic Social Thought," in *Globalization and Catholic Social Thought: Present Crisis, Future Hope*, ed. John A. Coleman and William F. Ryan, SJ (Maryknoll, NY: Orbis, 2005), 16–18. As Prusak and Reed-Bouley note, the principles of CST are all expressions of the requirements of justice, which lists of distinct principles may obscure.

16. The Hanley Sustainability Institute Strategic Plan, version 2.2, July 6, 2021, 6.

17. James C. Collins and Jerry I. Porra, *Built to Last: Successful Habits of Visionary Companies* (New York: HarperCollins, 1994). See also Collins's *Good to Great: Why Some Companies Make the Leap and Others Don't* (New York: HarperCollins, 2001).

18. See Ronald A. Heifetz, *Leadership without Easy Answers* (Cambridge, MA: Harvard University Press, 1994) and his coauthored book with Marty Linsky, *Leadership on the Line: Staying Alive through the Dangers of Leading* (Boston: Harvard Business School Press, 2002). Of particular interest for leaders at risk of becoming discouraged is chapter 11 in *Leadership on the Line*, "Sacred Heart." I am grateful to Br. Raymond L. Fitz, SM, for introducing me to the writings of Heifetz and for modeling so much of Heifetz's teaching so effectively during the twenty-three years he served as the president of the University of Dayton.

19. See Heifetz, *Leadership without Easy Answers*, 19–27.

20. Heifetz, *Leadership without Easy Answers*, 69–73.

21. See Heifetz and Linsky, *Leadership on the Line*, 65–67.

22. See Heifetz, *Leadership without Easy Answers*, 104–13.

23. Pope Francis, "A Big Heart Open to God," interview with Antonio Spadaro, SJ, *America*, September 30, 2013, www.americamagazine.org.

24. See for this list Douglas A. Campbell, "Culture Wars at Corinth," *Christian Century*, January 3, 2018, 28–31, at www.christiancentury.org under the title "Paul Wrote 1 Corinthians to a Community in the Middle of a Culture War."

10

GO OUT TO ALL THE WORLD

Catholic Higher Education and Catholic Social Thought in a Global Context

Paul Kollman, CSC[1]

Most readers of this volume likely possess an interest in Catholic higher education shaped by familiarity with its manifestations in the United States. Nearly all the chapters take as their starting point the U.S. Catholic experience in higher education, and many of the contributors have a history of analyzing U.S. Catholic colleges and universities.

This is not surprising, given that this volume is designed as a resource primarily for people who seek to help U.S. Catholic colleges and universities draw upon Catholic social teaching or thought (CST) as they pursue their missions. Not only do Catholic colleges and universities in the United States play a comparatively large role in the public life of the Catholic Church in the country, but they also occupy prominent roles in the national higher education landscape. Such schools graduate thousands each year who advance to employment or further education, while their sports teams compete successfully in popular intercollegiate athletics. Several U.S. Catholic universities and colleges offer undergraduate and graduate degree programs that are among the most distinguished in the country, and some have achieved global renown. Likely, many readers may know as well about the U.S.-based Association of Catholic Colleges and Universities (ACCU), founded in 1899, a valued contributor to national reflection on Catholic higher education.

Thus, it may in fact surprise readers that U.S.-based Catholic colleges and universities make up less than one-fifth of the world's Catholic institutions of higher education. By the count of the Vatican Congregation for Catholic Education, the United States houses 244 of the 1,358 such bodies in the world. U.S. Catholic colleges and universities educate about 850,000 students per year, while there are over 6.5 million students pursuing Catholic higher education globally. This makes Catholic higher education the largest private university network in the world by number of students. Global Catholic higher education also includes a remarkable variety of types of institutions. These range from venerable universities that emerged in the medieval period to the growing number of Catholic higher education institutions around the world founded after Vatican II.

The age of these institutions represents, of course, only one factor that distinguishes them from one another. Other differences include the precise nature of their affiliation with the Church, the scope of the education they offer (from technical education to primary and secondary school teachers' training to comprehensive research universities), the resources at their disposal, and their reputation within their national and regional settings. The oldest such universities that maintain their Catholic identity in one form or another began with official ties to the Church's hierarchy and featured a strong focus on theology and philosophy. Many remain "pontifical," with formal links to the Vatican. Some of these pontifical universities continue to focus exclusively on philosophy and theology, such as the Anselmianum in Rome, which focuses on liturgical studies. Others, like the University of Tübingen in Germany, now house a Catholic faculty of theology (often also philosophy and canon law), while the larger university is without formal Catholic affiliation. Pontifical universities also include some that are very old, like Rome's Gregorian, and others of more recent vintage, like Fu Jen University, founded in Beijing in 1925 and refounded in Taipei in 1961. And many onetime pontifical universities are now completely dissociated from the Church, like Oxford and Cambridge. By contrast, most Catholic colleges and universities in the United States began more locally. They usually were linked to founding religious congregations—or, in some cases, the dioceses in which they are located—and developed so that their formal ties with the Church were mediated by those congregations or dioceses.

This chapter considers the applicability of CST to Catholic higher education from a global perspective. It has four parts. First, I offer a brief portrayal of global Catholic higher education, highlighting the range of institutions and identifying global trends, especially the phenomenal growth of Catholic colleges and universities in the Majority World—by which I mean the so-called Global South of Africa and much of Asia, Latin America, and Oceania. This leads to the chapter's second part: three brief case studies from Catholic higher education outside the United States, each chosen to raise issues the chapter seeks to address.

Third, the chapter discusses three challenges that hinder easy application of CST in a singular way across Catholic global higher education. The first challenge derives from an unhelpful reaction to the obvious inequalities among Catholic institutions: call it a naïve solidarity. The second challenge lies in the diversity of contexts in which colleges and universities operate, with the upshot that CST principles cannot be applied everywhere in the same way. Finally, we have to reckon with the natural proclivity of institutions to focus primarily on the pressing needs of their own viability and success.

The fourth part of the chapter identifies opportunities to advance Catholic global higher education in light of CST. I make, once more, three suggestions. First, there are existing structures that might be developed to foster mutually beneficial interdependence along the lines of CST. I highlight especially the important and underutilized work of the International Federation of Catholic Universities (IFCU). Second, leaders in the United States ought to recognize that, while it is certainly the case that Catholic higher education in the United States has distinct strengths, the same is true for Catholic higher education in other places. Third, we need to discover new ways for constituent groups in global Catholic higher education to develop more lateral ties: administrators, faculty, and especially students. If a single theme emerges, it is that solidarity among Catholic higher education institutions must derive from mutual relationships forged by honest institutional self-awareness about achievements and obstacles as differently located institutions seek to advance their distinct missions.

Catholic Higher Education in a Global Perspective

There are several recent trends characterizing global Catholic higher education. One is that some traditionally Catholic colleges or universities are shedding their Catholic identity in response to contemporary processes of secularization. This occurred, in 2004, at Nijmegen in the Netherlands, now called Radboud University, as opposed to the Catholic University of Nijmegen. Similar disaffiliation occurred in the past, often in response to forms of nationalism, as anticlerical regimes took power or national governments sought to stress their independence from ecclesiastical control.[2] In the Nijmegen-Radboud case, however, the motivation was a desire for secular identity more broadly, and one imagines this trend could expand as secularization proceeds elsewhere. Clearly, religious practice and formal religious identity are becoming less common in much of Europe, as well as Latin America, and even in the United States, once considered an outlier among high-income nations due to its unusual rate of religious affiliation.[3]

A second trend has been the appearance of new Catholic colleges or universities that are organized around ideological coherence and are sponsored and generously financed by more conservative-leaning Catholics who believe that other Catholic higher education institutions are too liberal. Most of these are in the United States or elsewhere in the Global North (aka the Minority World). Sometimes these appear with tacit, sometimes with official, Catholic hierarchical approval.[4]

The third and most consequential trend in global Catholic higher education has been the explosion of the number of Catholic colleges and universities in the world, beginning after Vatican II and rapidly expanding since 1990. This growth parallels the expansion of higher education generally most everywhere.[5] Only rarely do these institutions have roots in a particular ideology, like some of the newer colleges and universities in the Global North. Instead, most Catholic colleges and universities founded since 1990 have one or some combination of three different types of origin. Some began as Catholic seminaries or other kinds of institutes of theological education with national or regional origins and have evolved toward college or university status. Others emerged with the critical support of church leaders, often the result of bishops and others working collaboratively within a country or a region.[6] Finally, a much larger group followed the common pattern in U.S. Catholic higher education: they emerged linked to the ambitions of a diocese, a religious congregation, or in some cases a particular Catholic individual or group. Some such institutions arose in concert with the national or regional Catholic leadership of the country or region in question; others arose without any coordination. These so-called independent Catholic colleges and universities—a term used simply to differentiate them from the first two types—represent the lion's share of newer Catholic institutions of higher education, in some ways repeating the U.S. pattern elsewhere.[7] And these are a very diverse group. In fact, the diversity among these institutions is likely one reason for a curious discrepancy in lists of the number of Catholic colleges and universities in the world. I noted above that the Vatican's Congregation for Catholic Education counts 1,358 such institutions. The United States Catholic Conference of Bishops, however, counts 1,861. This suggests that the criteria for defining these places as Catholic, or for that matter as colleges or universities, vary considerably. The discrepancy also points to the huge variety among the institutions.

Glimpses of Global Catholic Higher Education

Some of that variety can be elaborated through several stories, which we might consider as case studies. These stories are true, as far as I know, though simplified for present purposes and with certain details changed in order not to reveal the institutions' precise locations.

The first incident occurred in a largely non-Christian country at a Catholic university that has been in existence for only a few years. The new university has had no trouble enrolling students. The country's young people have great hunger for higher education, and the Catholic institution already enjoys a solid reputation because the international Catholic religious order that founded it has worked in the country for years and runs distinguished secondary schools that have educated the country's leading citizens, Christian and non-Christian alike.

A larger difficulty than enrollment has been leadership. The founding international Catholic religious order has provided key leaders from the university's beginning—many being religious who had worked in higher education in the West. Now the challenge lies in finding the right combination of leaders from native-born members of the religious order along with others from within the country, likely non-Christian, for key positions. At times, national laws that stipulate the required preparation for university leadership raise challenges for finding native-born religious, few of whom have the requisite experience in years of university teaching and leadership to qualify for the roles.

One telling moment occurred when the expatriate Catholic religious who had served as "chief inspector of exams"[8] sought to replace herself. She had found a native-born academic within the university who possessed an impeccable reputation for integrity and who had agreed to serve. Yet when the change was introduced, native colleagues privately told the outgoing chief exam inspector, "If your replacement isn't a [xxx]," here inserting a label mostly used to identify a European-origin outsider with slightly negative connotations (nearly every language of the once-colonized has such a term), "no one will trust the integrity of our exams and our degrees."

The second case study concerns events at another rather new Catholic university in the Global South, this one having begun as a seminary organized by several international Catholic religious congregations. The former seminary, which has trained many hundreds of men who became Catholic priests, now exists as a constituent college within the university. The university also now houses other institutes and specialized centers. All began with a focus on training members of the founding congregations and have expanded to welcome laypeople. One of these centers, founded and led by one of the original congregations that established the seminary, trains students in pastoral care and counselling. Its degrees have been conferred in the past by a university in the Global North linked to the religious order that helped establish the center. Now this budding Catholic university faces pressure from the country in which it is located to take more direct control over all its constituent colleges and other centers, if these are to remain part of the university in the future. In fact, national law aims to create institutional coherence and remove dependence on overseas ties—and the charter of the university depends on approval from national accreditors.

The problem is that the congregation that founded the pastoral training center does not want to relinquish what control it retains. In fact, the congregation threatens to take the center and its personnel—its faculty and students, labs, and library resources—to another site, to establish an independent center. This will represent a loss for this still-new Catholic university whose reputation has developed by drawing strong lay students to campus for such training.

The third story revolves around a Catholic institution, one that is not a college or university, in the Global South. In this country, soon after Vatican II, Catholic leaders decided to start an institute for theological education designed for laypeople. The country already had an established seminary system as well as Catholic teacher training institutions. In the wake of the Council, however, Catholic leaders wanted to expand access to formal training for ministry or personal enrichment beyond those preparing for ordained ministry and religious consecration.

In the years after the Council, the institute grew, eventually offering undergraduate and graduate degrees in formal subjects like theology, counseling, canon law, and Christian leadership. By the late twentieth century, there were Catholic universities in the country in question, and some amalgamated with other similar institutes. Yet this institute remained independent, guided by a board composed of laity, clergy, and religious. It continued to flourish, educating students and providing theological education to many who otherwise would have lacked such possibilities.

The difficulties emerged not with the institute's viability, but with perceptions about its Catholic identity. Beginning in the 1980s, tensions with some of the country's bishops developed, and after the millennium they only grew, so that, by the early 2010s, serious disagreements existed. Eventually, the institute's longtime director regretfully concluded that it could not maintain its identity if the bishops assumed the tighter control over it that a growing number of them demanded. That director foresaw a future in which a onetime "Catholic institute of higher education" became a "an institute of higher education run by Catholics," a choice for independence that the director had wanted to avoid, but that the director came to feel was unavoidable.

The institute's very divided board, however, rejected this change in a close vote. The institute now has bishops on its board, and the longtime director is gone.

Three Challenges in Thinking about CST and Catholic Higher Education Globally

Each case that we have just reviewed touches upon issues widely shared in higher education, Catholic or not. For example, the first case, about the plea for a foreign, thus "trustworthy," chief exam inspector, raises the common challenge of finding and preparing leaders who generate trust amid leadership transitions. The second—foregrounding the resistance of one religious order to having its pastoral training center absorbed into the larger university—engages the challenge of fostering institutional evolution in the face of previous structures that become unsustainable due to a variety of pressures. The third—about the theological institute pressed to be more linked to hierarchical control—involves tensions in the relationships between institutions of higher education and accrediting authorities.

Yet these cases also feature context-specific aspects linked to Catholic identity and other contextual factors that newer Catholic institutions often face. In the first case, these factors include postcolonial insecurity around perceptions of integrity linked to visible racialized identity, taking a particular shape in a Catholic university previously linked to a mostly expatriate Catholic leadership team. An additional factor might be the challenge that the mostly expatriate leaders experienced in establishing leadership pipelines. In the second case, a sticking point is distinctly Catholic in that it involves the roles played by religious congregations (and similar bodies) in larger institutions. The third case raises the possibility of Catholic lay leaders in higher education defying a nation's Catholic hierarchy intent on guiding it (or, perhaps, controlling it), with both sides likely arguing that they are striving to protect institutional integrity.

It is hard enough to apply CST to practices within a single institution, and the three cases suggest that it is harder still to think about the applicability of CST to Catholic higher education globally. A first challenge arises from the obvious immense gulf in resources between some Catholic universities, mostly in the Global North, and others, many of them in the Global South. This is not to say that wide gulfs do not exist among Catholic colleges and universities in the United States; of course they do (as Matt Mazewski's and Laura Nichols's chapters in this volume detail). Nor is it the case that all Catholic universities in the Global South lack resources, for some are comparatively quite well-established and supported. Examples include the many older Catholic universities in Latin America, such as the University of Central America in San Salvador (El Salvador), De LaSalle University in Manila (Philippines), Hekima University in Nairobi (Kenya), and Saint Augustine's University in Mwanza (Tanzania). Yet many of the newer Catholic universities in Africa, as well as in Latin America and parts of Asia, unfortunately lack the resources—in infrastructure, books and other media, information technology, faculty and administrative expertise, and simply money—common in secondary schools in the Global West.

In light of the principle of solidarity so central to CST, it can be easy to think that such extreme inequalities invite Catholic universities elsewhere to share their wealth. Yet without dampening that necessary and laudatory impulse to ease institutional inequalities, it is important to move beyond using CST simply as a cudgel to "share more." Development theorists often talk about "bad buys"—that is, development strategies that do not generate outcomes effectively, even when well-intentioned, and even when quite expensive. Here are some examples in the context of higher education: books sent overseas are often outdated; buildings produced without local knowledge are often expensive and ill-suited to local conditions; computers are expensive to maintain and replace; and cash transfers may be difficult to use effectively, while generally offering only short-term relief.[9]

A second challenge arises from the diversity of contexts in which colleges and universities operate. With regard to their links to the institutional church, a number of the newer Catholic universities in the Global South resemble institutions in the United States more than analogous institutions in Europe and Latin America. They derive from the efforts of religious congregations, dioceses, and even private individuals, instead of being linked to the Vatican or even to national Catholic hierarchies. That said, there are a number of distinct features of higher education in the United States. One thinks, for example, of the four-year expectation for undergraduate degree completion, the large role of private benefaction in supporting U.S. colleges and universities, broad religious freedom in the culture, a large number (if now contracting) of qualified secondary school graduates, including many from Catholic high schools, and more or less reliable economic growth creating ample career prospects for graduates. These have been typical features of the U.S. Catholic higher education landscape for generations.

Many new Catholic universities elsewhere, however, have little history of private benefaction, operate under restricted freedom of religion, must contend with uneven national secondary education, and cannot promise ample career prospects for graduates. The upshot is that many CST-inspired proposals for Catholic higher education in the United States do not translate, so to speak, to international contexts. Take, for example, the importance of the core curriculum for shaping Catholic identity in a four-year degree program, as Anna Moreland and Mark Shiffman's chapter discusses. Most colleges and universities elsewhere advance students more quickly into majors and expect core curriculum–like preparation in advanced secondary school; moreover, colleges and universities elsewhere typically provide undergraduates with a three-year course of study. Other U.S.-specific concerns include the ethics of investment and licensing practices; Catholic colleges and universities elsewhere usually lack endowments and brands to protect. We might also consider the place of engaged- and service-learning within the curriculum; elsewhere, these can appear as ill-afforded luxuries. Finally, U.S.-linked issues surrounding labor relations and employee compensation, while crucial in the U.S. context, often do not cross borders.

A last challenge to consider is that the pressing needs of every institution to advance its own resilience and well-being mean that we may need to temper our expectations with respect to what even enlightened solidarity can achieve. Institutions rightly—within limits that are difficult to ascertain—look out for themselves and the communities and countries where they are located; to expect otherwise seems misguided.

Opportunities for Greater Solidarity

That last observation, however, should not be misunderstood as a counsel of gloom. Efforts to draw together Catholic higher education across the world have been ongoing for a long time under Vatican direction, and Catholic universities have organized themselves since at least the 1920s, when the (formerly) Catholic University of Nijmegen, in the Netherlands, and Milan's Catholic University of the Sacred Heart began to confer about a federation. The first meeting of potential participants took place in 1925 in Paris, with fourteen Catholic universities represented. In 1948, a Vatican decree recognized the federation, which in 1965 became the Fédération Internationale des Universités Catholiques, or International Federation of Catholic Universities (IFCU), with its headquarters in Paris. It is a recognized body in the United Nation's registry of international nongovernmental organizations. The stated mission of the Federation is fivefold:

1. To promote collective reflection on their mission amongst Catholic higher education institutions;
2. To foster academic cooperation in the field of research, as well as the valuation and dissemination of research results toward decision-making communities;
3. To promote experience and skill exchange among Catholic higher education institutions;
4. To represent Catholic universities at international organizations and associations and to collaborate with them in line with its institutional priorities; [and]
5. To contribute to the development of Catholic higher education and to the assertion of its specific identity.[10]

Without delving too deeply into specific programs—and these are explained well on the Federation's website—I would highlight three programs as indicative of CST-linked resources the Federation provides. The first is the *Laudato Si'* Endowment Fund, which supports projects in the humanities and social sciences that address Pope Francis's emphasis on the links between the well-being of the poor and global ecological fragility. The second is the Newman Benchmarking

Framework, which invites institutions to undergo evaluations based on CST principles as a way to consider compliance with respect to environmental responsibility, labor relations, and overall mission consistency. The third is the African Institution Partnership, which seeks to move beyond a culture of support for Catholic universities in Africa rooted simply in financial aid.

There are other means besides IFCU to address the several challenges noted above. For example, the ties that bind institutions with roots in religious congregations may have untapped potential. The Jesuits have the largest international network in both the United States and internationally,[11] yet others exist, such as among the LaSallian Christian Brothers.[12] The Congregation of Holy Cross founded in recent years Notre Dame University of Bangladesh (NDUB), and relationships have developed between that institution and Notre Dame in northern Indiana. Faculty and administrators from the two schools have visited each other to build relationships of support in research and policy development, and Dhaka and environs have welcomed researchers from Notre Dame in the United States, which has supported development efforts by NDUB. Solid relationships allow the avoidance of "bad buys," because institutions have familiarity with one another and thus are less inclined to treat one another disrespectfully by, for example, sending outdated books or obsolete computers.

A second opportunity for improved global solidarity in Catholic higher education derives from the growing self-awareness within U.S. Catholic higher education of ways to inculcate CST, many of them discussed elsewhere in this volume. As noted already, some U.S.-based CST insights and practices for higher education do not translate easily to other contexts, but there are also some that cross borders. By way of example, U.S. Catholic colleges and universities can contribute to global Catholic higher education (1) professionalized management practices that seek to resist unhelpful bureaucratization at odds with Catholic personalism (James Keenan's encouragement of "horizontal accountability" in institutional structures is to the point here[13]); (2) models of campus cultures shaped by a sacramentality of daily life, where Catholic identity is fostered through architecture, liturgy, meals, and other programming; (3) the suffusing of professional programs in fields like education, business, medicine, and law with Catholic values; (4) the preparation of laypeople, especially women, for college or university leadership; and (5) high-impact practices like community-engaged learning, adapted appropriately to non-U.S. settings, so that they seem less like luxuries and more like methods to advance Catholic values in education.

We can also identity "good buys" (or at least "better buys"), as opposed to the potential "bad buys" that otherwise might tempt well-meaning institutions. These could include exchanges of personnel for brief periods of shared learning around student life, campus ministry, higher education leadership training, and advancement strategies. Further, faculty at U.S. Catholic universities and colleges could assist their colleagues elsewhere to navigate practices of peer review for academic publications in prominent academic journals and scholarly presses. This may come as second nature to U.S. academics, but in fact navigating peer review requires extensive training.

To participate in a network of global Catholic higher education also means embracing mutuality about insights from other Catholic schools. Vincent Miller's chapter in this volume discusses the need to push back against what Pope Francis calls the technocratic paradigm, and it could well be that Catholic colleges and universities elsewhere have ways to do that that could teach U.S. institutions. Many global Catholic institutions—for example, Uganda Martyrs University near Masaka, Uganda—are located in rural areas that allow easy recourse to agricultural training. This is rather uncommon in U.S. Catholic higher education, though some U.S. schools have sought to establish modest experimental farms for learning and research. In addition, many students at the newer Catholic universities around the world come from rural settings, where they live closer to the land than many U.S. students, which is an advantage in learning how to achieve environmental sustainability.

Other insights into how to integrate CST in higher education environments might emerge from the experiences in times of political turmoil faced by Catholic schools around the world. One thinks, for example, of the role of Catholic institutions in faith-based resistance to dictatorships and political violence in many places in Latin America and in the Philippines, as well as in parts of eastern Europe. The University of Central America (UCA), for instance, forged a distinctive voice in favor of a negotiated peace during the civil war in El Salvador in the 1980s. Led by Ignacio Ellacuría and other Jesuit faculty members, the UCA challenged both official Salvadoran government policies and U.S. support for the government and military.[14] More recent actions by Catholic universities elsewhere might also inspire U.S.-based institutions to envisage new ways of implementing CST. In 2015, the Catholic university in Lviv, Ukraine, was one of the few institutions in the country that could credibly criticize national corruption, due to the reputation for integrity that it enjoyed.[15] In the Philippines, the presidents of two of the leading Catholic universities in Manila, the Ateneo de Manila founded by the Jesuits and De LaSalle University founded by the LaSallian Christian Brothers, issued a statement urging a renewed commitment to remember the horrific past under the Marcos regime, especially the era of martial law that stretched from 1972 to 1986, and never again submit to martial law. Such a statement required considerable courage in the face of the Duterte regime, which has sought to suppress the memory of the violent nature of the Marcos regime and has profoundly divided Catholics in the country.[16]

Certainly, the inspiring witness of heroic figures has been felt in U.S. Catholic colleges and universities, but are there deeper lessons that might be imparted and adapted for the U.S. context? These might include, for example, the habits of truth telling within profoundly dishonest political arenas, the role of small faith-based groups in resisting oppression, and the place of liturgical action in creating shared consensus in support of collective resistance to injustice. To refer to the cases at hand, how might Ukraine's Catholic university help U.S. Catholic college and university students resist corruption in situations where it is rampant? How might the Catholic universities in the Philippines help U.S. Catholic institutions encourage responsible faith-linked remembering about past injustice, for example, historic and ongoing U.S. racism, the longstanding instrumentalization of the environment, and attempts to undermine democracy embodied in efforts to suppress voting rights?

A third opportunity for enhancing solidarity in Catholic higher education emerges in the wake of the global experience of the COVID-19 pandemic. This shared experience prompted all sorts of new connectivity, thus renewing opportunities to discover ways that constituent groups in global Catholic universities can develop more lateral ties. More concretely, how might study abroad be reenvisioned in the aftermath of the pandemic? Are there models, such as short-term programs, that should be abandoned on account of their environmental costs? More positively, what principles should guide the development of so-called satellite campuses, such as Notre Dame's multiple global gateways and centers,[17] or

Georgetown University in Qatar?[18] How *should* Catholic institutions think, in light of CST, about the development of satellite campuses? Is there coordination with existing or nascent Catholic (or not) institutions in the country in question? Is local talent tapped, not only to serve as adjunct instructors, but in the organization and administration of the institutions? What sharing of resources or expertise might be possible or appropriate? And so forth.

Conclusion

To think of CST in light of global Catholic higher education means rejecting a low-level solidarity of physical transfers of stuff and embracing instead opportunities for an appropriate interdependence. The goal is thus a solidarity that is informed by more than simple guilt stemming from the undeniable gulfs between some Catholic institutions and others. New Catholic colleges and universities globally face numerous challenges that create obstacles to their flourishing: not simply lack of resources, but also challenges particular to their national contexts, with no obvious parallels in the United States. Examples include legal requirements for minimum amounts of real estate to achieve a charter and formidable restrictions on religious practice on campus. In many countries, higher education is a very unregulated sector of the economy, with far more students eager for it than opportunities. It thus represents an easy way to make quick money, so that so-called mushroom schools spring up at every level, including higher education, even Catholic higher education. In addition, Catholic hierarchies can create burdens for Catholic colleges and universities. Many bishops are unfamiliar with higher education, with the upshot that uncertainties in national laws pertinent to higher education are matched by church uncertainties, petty rivalries among bishops, and sudden policy changes.

Despite these challenges, it is certainly in the interest of Catholics to foster educational pluralism, generally speaking—that is, a diversity of options at every educational level, including higher education. Catholic colleges and universities can be valuable in advancing educational pluralism in much of the world. And if CST, adjusted to local circumstances, guides their policies and practices, they can also be part of the advance of a more just and sustainable world, toward which all our education ought to be aspiring.

Questions for Consideration and Discussion

1. Kollman cautions that "many CST-inspired proposals for Catholic higher education in the United States do not translate…to international contexts." Casting an eye back over earlier chapters in this volume, what are some proposals that might not translate? Why not? Conversely, what are some proposals that might well translate, despite the differences in context that Kollman outlines? Consider, to begin with, Laura Nichols's and Matt Mazewski's chapters.
2. Kollman criticizes a "naïve solidarity"—and the use of CST "simply as a cudgel to 'share more'"—and remarks that, given "the pressing needs of every institution to advance its own resilience and well-being," it may be that we "need to temper our expectations with respect to what even enlightened solidarity can achieve." That said, he also asks, concretely, how study abroad might be reenvisioned in the aftermath of the pandemic, and what principles should guide the development of satellite campuses. When Catholic colleges and universities in the United States send students "out to all the world," or establish campuses elsewhere in the world, what does solidarity, among other CST principles, counsel? Further, what does CST suggest about recruiting students from other countries? Finally, what is the relevance of the climate crisis?
3. Has the explosion of online programming and instruction during the pandemic suggested to your institution new possibilities of solidarity with institutions, scholars, and students beyond the United States? What are opportunities worth pursuing in the wake of the pandemic?
4. Kollman identifies a handful of ways that U.S. Catholic colleges and universities can contribute to global Catholic higher education. What are others? Are there any that your own institution is prepared and situated to realize?
5. Does your institution have ties with any institutions in the Majority World/Global South? If not, are there mutually beneficial ties that

your institution could develop? How might your institution benefit from those ties? What could your institution offer in turn?

6. If you were to found a new Catholic college or university, whether in the United States or elsewhere in the world, what would it be for? In other words, what would its principal purpose be? Further, how would it be organized and administered? How different from your imagined institution is the institution with which you are affiliated now? Is there any hope of nudging your institution in the direction of the institution that you would found? If so, what has to be done?

Notes

1. A preliminary version of this paper was presented via Zoom through the generosity of Collegium (www.collegium.org) on February 23, 2021, with the support of its director, Thomas Landy, who also responded generously to the presentation. I am very grateful for his response, as well as other questions and contributions made in the discussion. I have sought to incorporate some of what was shared at the public presentation. I appreciate as well helpful comments made by the editors of this volume, Bernard Prusak and Jennifer Reed-Bouley, and by Anita Houck.

2. Examples include the University of Aberdeen in Scotland, the University of San Ignacio in Manila, and the Royal and Pontifical University of Mexico in Mexico City.

3. See Ronald Inglehart, *Religion's Sudden Decline: What's Causing It, and What Comes Next?* (Oxford: Oxford University Press, 2021). See also James L. Heft, SM, and Jan E. Stets, ed., *Empty Churches: Non-affiliation in America* (Oxford: Oxford University Press, 2021).

4. Schools such as Ave Maria University, Christendom College, and Thomas Aquinas College have grown in prominence in the United States, yet have been surprisingly understudied. They deserve more attention by scholars in various disciplines—history, theology, and the social sciences especially.

5. For a discussion, see Angel Calderon, "Massification of Higher Education Revisited," http://cdn02.pucp.education/academico/2018/08/23165810/na_mass_revis_230818.pdf.

6. Examples include the Catholic Institute of West Africa in Port Harcourt, Nigeria, and the Catholic University of East Africa in Nairobi, Kenya, with analogues in Francophone Africa. Such places have faced pressure recently, as individual bishops and others have responded to increasing demand to establish their own Catholic colleges and universities, at times diminishing the older schools' enrollments, capacity to attract faculty, and overall success.

7. For a partial list of Catholic colleges and universities in the world, see https://en.wikipedia.org/wiki/Catholic_higher_education. Private institutions established since the early 1990s include Our Lady of Good Counsel University in Albania (2004), Caritas University in Nigeria (2004), and Divine Word University in Papua New Guinea (1996).

8. The formal title is "invigilator" of exams—a label left over from colonial times indicating the person who testifies to the integrity of the exam processes and degree conferrals.

9. For discussion of "bad buys" and better investment, see the blog post by Keith M. Lewin, "Smart Buys, Great Sales, and Special Offers: Cost-Effective Approaches to Improve Global Learning," https://www.ukfiet.org/2020/smart-buys-great-sales-and-special-offers-cost-effective-approaches-to-improve-global-learning/.

10. See Fédération Internationale des Universités Catholiques, "Mission," http://www.fiuc.org/rubrique6_en.html.

11. See the International Association of Jesuit Universities, https://iaju.org.

12. See the website of the LaSallian Region of North American (Relan), https://lasallian.info/where-we-are/schools-ministries/colleges-universities/.

13. See James F. Keenan, SJ, *University Ethics: How Colleges Can Build and Benefit from a Culture of Ethics* (Lanham, MD: Rowman & Littlefield, 2015), 13–19, 64.

14. For an analysis, see Robert Lassalle-Klein, "The Jesuit Martyrs of the University of Central America," available on the website of the Ignatian Center for Jesuit Education at Santa Clara University, https://www.scu.edu/ic/media--publications/explore-journal/fall-2009-stories/the-jesuit-martyrs-of-the-university-of-central-america.html.

15. See Ilya Lozovsky, "The Spirit of Lviv," *Foreign Policy*, September 16, 2015, https://foreignpolicy.com/2015/09/16/the-spirit-of-lviv-ukraine-corruption/.

16. See Sofia Tomacruz, "ADMU and DSLU Presidents Tell Students: Fight Attempts to Forget Martial Law," *Rappler*, September 20, 2018, https://www.rappler.com/nation/admu-dlsu-joint-statement-never-again-to-martial-law.

17. See the website of Notre Dame International, https://international.nd.edu/about/.

18. See the website of Georgetown University in Qatar, https://www.qatar.georgetown.edu.

CONTRIBUTORS

James Lewis Heft, SM, after serving at the University of Dayton for thirty years, came to the University of Southern California in 2006 to found the Institute for Advanced Catholic Studies, of which he is now the president emeritus. He continues to serve at USC as the Alton Brooks Professor of Religion. His research interests are Catholicism, both its history and contemporary expression, and interreligious dialogue. His most recent publications are a coedited volume with Jan E. Stets, *Empty Churches: Non-Affiliation in America* (Oxford, 2021), and his *The Future of Catholic Higher Education: The Open Circle* (Oxford, 2021).

Paul Kollman, CSC, is a Holy Cross priest and associate professor of theology at the University of Notre Dame. A historian of African Christianity, with interests in mission studies and world Christianity, he is past president of both the American Society of Missiology and the International Association for Mission Studies. The author of *The Evangelization of Slaves and Catholic Origins in Eastern Africa* (Orbis, 2005) and coauthor with Cynthia Toms Smedley of *Understanding World Christianity: Eastern Africa* (Fortress, 2018), Kollman currently is preparing a study of the Catholic missionary evangelization of eastern Africa.

Michelle Gonzalez Maldonado is dean of the College of Arts and Sciences at the University of Scranton. Her research and teaching interests include Latino/a, Latin American, and feminist theologies, as well as interdisciplinary work in Afro-Caribbean Studies. She is the author of eight books, including *Afro-Cuban Theology: Religion, Race, Culture and Identity* (University Press of Florida, 2006), *Created in God's Image: An Introduction to Feminist Theological Anthropology* (Orbis, 2007), and *A Critical Introduction to Religion in the Americas: Bridging the Liberation Theology and Religious Studies Divide* (NYU, 2014).

Matt Mazewski is a contributing writer and book critic for *Commonweal*, writing regularly on economics, politics, and Catholic social thought, and a fellow at the think tank Data for Progress. He did his doctoral studies in economics at Columbia University, where he also served for nearly five years as rapporteur of the University Seminar on Catholicism, Culture, and Modernity.

Joseph A. McCartin is professor of history and executive director of the Kalmanovitz Initiative for Labor and the Working Poor at Georgetown University. He has published award-winning books and essays on U.S. labor history, politics, and policy. He is a founding convener for the Interreligious Network for Worker Solidarity and Bargaining for the Common Good, a national network that is reimagining worker bargaining to meet the challenges of the twenty-first century.

Vincent Miller is the Gudorf Chair in Catholic Theology and Culture at the University of Dayton. He is the author of *Consuming Religion: Christian Faith and Practice in a Consumer Culture* (Continuum, 2005) and editor of *The Theological and Ecological Vision of* Laudato Si'*: Everything Is Connected* (T & T Clark, 2017), and he is working on a constructive response to neoliberalism entitled *Homo Curans*. He is also a frequent contributor to *America* and *Commonweal*.

Anna Bonta Moreland is the Anne Quinn Welsh Endowed Director of the Honors Program and professor in the Department of Humanities at Villanova University. She is the author of *Known by Nature: Aquinas on Natural Knowledge of God* (Crossroad/Herder, 2010) and *Muhammad Reconsidered: A Christian Perspective on Islamic Prophecy* (University of Notre Dame Press, 2020); she also coedited *New Voices in Catholic Theology* (Crossroad/Herder, 2012). Her teaching interests include medieval theology, comparative theology with Islam, and the rise of modern atheism.

Laura Nichols is professor of sociology at Santa Clara University, where she teaches and researches in the areas of inequality and the experiences of and opportunities for aspiring first-generation college students. Her book *The Journey Before Us: First-Generation Pathways from Middle School to College* (Rutgers University Press, 2020) explores the educational trajectories of graduates from a Nativity middle school to young adulthood. She was also part of the research team that examined the resources for and experiences of students who were undocumented and attending Jesuit colleges, the results of which were published in the book she coedited with Terry-Ann Jones, *Undocumented and in College: Students and Institutions in a Climate of National Hostility* (Fordham University Press, 2017).

Maureen H. O'Connell is professor of Christian ethics in the Department of Religion and Theology at La Salle University. She is the author of *Compassion: Loving Our Neighbor in an Age of Globalization* (Orbis, 2009), *If These Walls Could Talk: Community Muralism and the Beauty of Justice*

(Liturgical Press, 2012), and *Undoing the Knots: Five Generations of American Catholic Anti-Blackness* (Beacon, 2022).

Tia Noelle Pratt is the director of mission engagement and strategic initiatives, courtesy assistant professor of sociology, and editor of the *Journal of Catholic Social Thought* at Villanova University. Her research focuses on systemic racism in the Catholic Church and how it impacts African American Catholic identity. Her work has been featured in the *Interdisciplinary Journal of Research on Religion*, multiple edited volumes, and *Faithfully*, *Commonweal*, *The Revealer*, *National Catholic Reporter*, and *America*.

Bernard G. Prusak is professor of philosophy and director of the McGowan Center for Ethics and Social Responsibility at King's College in Wilkes-Barre, Pennsylvania. His work focuses in moral and social philosophy, with recurring interests in bioethics and in theories and cases of conscience. His books include *Catholic Moral Philosophy in Practice and Theory: An Introduction* (Paulist, 2016); his criticism and other public scholarship appear often in *Commonweal*.

Catherine Punsalan-Manlimos is vice president for Mission Integration at Seattle University. She was previously assistant to the president for Mission Integration and associate professor in Religious Studies at the University of Detroit Mercy and the Malcolm & Mari Stamper Chair in Catholic Intellectual and Cultural Traditions and inaugural director of the Institute for Catholic Thought and Culture at Seattle University. She is a member of the Women Engaging Catholic Social Tradition project and most recently contributed essays to the volumes *Women Engaging the Catholic Social Tradition: Solidarity toward the Common Good* (Paulist, 2022) and *Catholicism in Migration and Diaspora: Cross-Border Filipino Perspectives* (Routledge, 2022)

Jennifer Reed-Bouley is professor and program director of theology at College of Saint Mary, where she teaches courses in Catholic social thought and environmental ethics. She is interested in anti-racist education and applying the Critical Concerns of the Sisters of Mercy to pedagogies of engagement. Her research focuses on how Catholic social thought can inform teaching across the curriculum, students' civic and political engagement, and the operations of Catholic higher education.

Mark Shiffman is associate professor in the Department of Humanities at Villanova University. A scholar of ancient philosophy who has published studies of Plato, Aristotle, and Plutarch and has translated Aristotle's *De Anima*, he is also interested in the interconnected history of philosophy, theology, and social and political thought. His publications include studies of a variety of figures from Vergil and Augustine to Wendell Berry and Pope Francis, as well as articles in *Commonweal*, *First Things*, and *Communio*.

Advance Praise for
Catholic Higher Education and Catholic Social Thought

"Leading a Catholic college or university in today's challenging circumstances requires a wide range of skills and a capacity for understanding multiple issues and heeding multiple voices. In this volume, Prusak and Reed-Bouley have assembled an impressive group of Catholic thought leaders and asked them to reflect on the critical issues we face, and the concrete circumstances in which we face them, in light of the gospel commands for justice, love, and service, which we call Catholic social thought. The result is a volume not only for educators, but for everyone—trustees, alumni, Church leaders—interested in and responsible for guiding and shaping Catholic higher education into the future."

Michael J. Garanzini, SJ, President,
Association of Jesuit Colleges and Universities

"Do not expect this book to reside exclusively in libraries at Catholic colleges and universities. To the contrary, Bernard Prusak and Jennifer Reed-Bouley's volume on Catholic social thought (CST) is an indispensable companion for *every* institution of learning where people of all faith traditions (or none) grapple with the excruciating social concerns of our time. The contributors to this essential collection are accomplished scholars known for applying the rich CST history to the thorniest problems of contemporary times."

Linda M. LeMura, President,
Le Moyne College

"This timely and useful book invites Catholic educators and administrators to change how they see Catholic social thought. It is not something to be confined to ethics classes or overarching mission statements. It is a powerful and practical tool for engaging all facets of Catholic higher education, from labor practices to admissions and budgets, to struggles for gender equity and racial justice, to the pursuit of solidarity on a local and global scale. It is a whole way of life for each campus and institution. Although the living tradition of Catholic social thought may not always provide easy or quick solutions to the complex problems we face, it helps us ask the right questions and start the right conversations. Each chapter is informative and stimulating, and, as a full collection, this volume is simply top notch."

Andrew Prevot, Associate Professor of Theology,
Boston College

"At a time when institutions of higher education are facing difficult and troubling questions about their mission, operations, and their very survival, *Catholic Higher Education and Catholic Social Thought* comes as a much-needed provocation to face these questions boldly and faithfully. Each chapter contributes solid insights from Catholic social thought applied to key issues challenging higher education today. The volume's richness comes in the breadth and depth of analysis, examining examples of successful projects at Catholic colleges and universities of the kinds of transformation needed to address challenges such as climate, racial, migrant, labor, and economic justice. But with just as much honesty, the authors analyze missed opportunities and failed attempts, and point to the road yet to travel, particularly in light of the inequities and challenges brought to light by the COVID-19 pandemic. In clear and engaging language, each chapter offers the opportunity for various decision makers and stakeholders involved in Catholic higher education to deepen their commitment to the social doctrine of the Church while tackling the hardest questions facing our institutions to date. *Catholic Higher Education and Catholic Social Thought* is a masterful example of how to apply the hermeneutical/pastoral cycle of see-judge-act to higher education with commitment, clarity, and compassion."

MT Dávila, Associate Professor and Chair,
Religious and Theological Studies, Merrimack College

"In my current role as the president of a Jesuit, Catholic liberal arts college, I know this book will become an important reference for me as I consider how I lead my institution in a way that centers its mission in the context of a vibrant, lived Catholic faith tradition, one that reckons fully with signs of the times and the realities of the world as it is. Focusing on CST, this volume tackles critical issues of economic, social, and racial justice, and reminds us that the work of Catholic education must always be centered in a faith that does justice."

Vincent D. Rougeau, President,
College of the Holy Cross

"Prusak and Reed-Bouley have produced a must-read for any leader in Catholic higher education. Each chapter challenges readers to think about their own institutions and how our shared work can be realized."

Julia Cavallo, Executive Director,
Conference for Mercy Higher Education

"This authoritative compilation from educators in the field provides Catholic higher education an important tool for grounding its work through practical engagement with the Catholic social tradition."

William Purcell, Senior Associate Director,
Center for Social Concerns, University of Notre Dame